INSIDE
ISRAEL

Books by John Miller and Aaron Kenedi

Inside Islam

God's Breath: Sacred Scriptures of the World

Muhammad Ali: Ringside

Revolution: Faces of Change

San Francisco Stories

Legends: Women Who Have Changed the World

INSIDE ISRAEL

THE FAITHS, THE PEOPLE, AND THE MODERN
CONFLICTS OF THE WORLD'S HOLIEST LAND

Edited by John Miller and Aaron Kenedi

Introduction by David K. Shipler

MARLOWE & COMPANY
NEW YORK

Compilation copyright © 2002 by John Miller and Aaron Kenedi
Introduction copyright © 2002 by David K. Shipler

Published by
Marlowe & Company
An Imprint of Avalon Publishing Group Incorporated
161 William Street, 16th Floor
New York, NY 10038

Editor's note: Changes for consistency have been made to the essays in this book.

Cover and interior design: Miller Design Partners
Cover photograph: Getty Images
Permissions research: Shawneric Hachey
Proofreading and copyediting: Mimi Kusch

Library of Congress Control Number: 2002100740

9 8 7 6 5 4 3 2 1

Printed in the United States of America
Distributed by Publishers Group West

Special thanks to
Amy Rennert
and Matthew Lore

ISRAEL

POPULATION: 9.5 MILLION

———	International boundary
– – –	Armistice boundary
·········	District boundary
⊛	National Capital
○	Town
·	Jewish Settelment
▨	Area under Palestinian Rule

0 10 20 30 40 50 60 km
0   10   20   30   40 mi

MEDITERRANEAN SEA

LEBANON   SYRIA

Tyre

Qiryat Shemona

GOLAN HEIGHTS

Israel seized Golan from Syria in 1967; it's now a mix of Syrians and Jewish settlers.

NORTHERN

Haifa   Lake Tiberias

Nazareth

HAIFA

OCCUPIED TERRITORIES

Hadera   Jenin

Netanya   Tulkarm

CENTRAL   Nabulus

TEL AVIV

Tel Aviv   **WEST BANK**

Ramla   Ram Allah

Ashdod   Jericho

No Man's Land   Jerusalem

Ashquelon   JERUSALEM

Bethlehem

Gaza   Qiryat Gat

Hebron   Dead Sea

Kahn Yunis   **GAZA**

Beersheba

Dimona

SOUTHERN

Mizpe Ramon

Jordan River

The West Bank was taken from Jordan; now split between Palestinians and Jewish settlers.

JORDAN

The Gaza Strip, once occupied by Egypt, is populated by Palestinians and Jewish settlers.

When Israel became a Jewish state in 1948, Arabs who lived in the region—then known as Palestine—were displaced. Neighboring Egypt, Syria, and Jordan vowed to return this land to the Arabs. Their retaliatory attacks culminated in the 1967 Six-Day War, a stunning success for the Israelis, which established settlements in Jerusalem, the West Bank, and the Gaza Strip. Arabs saw these attacks as aggression; Jews insisted they were for security.

EGYPT

Elat

Gulf of Aquaba

Contents

INSIDE
ISRAEL

DAVID K. SHIPLER

Introduction

I N AMONG THESE PAGES, as among the surprising labyrinths of Jerusalem, alleyways lead from one insight into another so fluidly that the traveler finally feels the familiarity of old courtyards newly seen, ancient yearnings freshly found. Israel, worn by centuries and revived each morning, still strives to exist—and to coexist alongside the Palestinian people, who still campaign for the right to be.

From Saul Bellow in 1976 to P.J. O'Rourke a quarter century later, the excerpts and essays here illuminate the sad durability of the themes of conflict. They emerge like bedrock once the surface soil of negotiable disputes is stripped away. Most of them are anchored in history, some are magnified by faith, and all draw their furious passions from the latest outrage. Every attack is revenge, every cause an effect, and no untangling is possible unless the underlying patterns are seen. That is the accomplishment of this collection of writings, which have a woeful timelessness as if little has been revised by all the years of peacemaking and war making.

Those who work in the daily press know how much they leave out of what they report—more than mere details that won't fit into limited space, more than historical digressions from accounts of today's events. "News" focuses on the "new," and so it tends to omit what is not new. At *The New York Times* before computers could be used for rapid searches, I remember editors scouring yellowed clippings to see if a statement, a position, a fact had been published before, and if so, it would probably not be published again. The criterion is an unreliable guide to understanding, especially in the Middle East, where significance lies not only in the changed but also in the unchanging.

So it has been since Israel and the Palestine Liberation Organization signed the Oslo accords in 1993. Much was altered by the famous handshake in the White House Rose Garden between Prime Minister Yitzhak Rabin and P.L.O. Chairman Yasir Arafat. But too much remained the same. For the first time, the two national movements pledged to honor each other's legitimacy. Barriers were lowered, and aversions eased. Israelis were lured to the nightlife in the Palestinian city of Ramallah and the Palestinian casino in Jericho; West Bank markets with signs in Hebrew and Russian drew Israelis to load their roof racks with cheap furniture and other bargains. Palestinian and Israeli entrepreneurs launched joint ventures; professors began joint research; teenagers went to camps with each other, made tentative friendships, and maintained e-mail contact afterwards. Arafat, Israel's arch-enemy for a generation, was permitted to enter the West Bank and Gaza Strip to establish a Palestinian Authority to govern a patchwork of territories. His security officials worked closely with their opposite numbers from Israel. And the idea of a Palestinian state went from being unthinkable to inevitable, and even desirable, in the minds of most Israelis who were polled.

Even the vocabulary evolved. Palestinian media shifted from "Zionist entity" and "colonialists" to "Israel" and "Israelis." The Israeli media dropped "terrorists" in favor of "policemen" to describe Palestinians with guns. More deeply, the gradual abandonment of historical legend on the Israeli side underwent acceleration following Oslo, most notably the myth that all Arabs who left during Israel's 1948 War of Independence did so voluntarily or under orders from their leaders. A new historiography, begun in the early 1980s by the Israeli journalist and historian Benny Morris, used declassified Israeli documents to define precisely when and where Israeli forces deliberately expelled Arab civilians. After years of resistance to these unwelcome facts, Israeli society began to accept them as part of the muddy truth of that noble war: Some Arabs had fled out of fear, some had been urged out by their leaders, some had been evicted by Israel. The mixed portrait found its way into university textbooks.

No such nuances challenged the Palestinians' myths of history, however, and here was where the unchanging bedrock could be seen. The birth of Israel remained "al-Nakba," the catastrophe, and the Palestinians' "right of return" to their grandparents' villages—now mostly destroyed—remained a centerpiece of their political rhetoric. As the Israelis negotiated away land in the West Bank and Gaza, the right of return to Israel proper grew increasingly vibrant—taught in schools, enshrined in maps, dramatized in demonstrations that used the key (to the old house) as a symbol. The Palestinians' desire gave Israelis chills of apprehension.

Nor did Israel relinquish its designs on Palestinian territory in the West Bank and Gaza Strip. While Israelis at the bargaining table were advocating the exchange of land for peace, Palestinians watched from their windows the expanding Jewish settlements, which more than doubled in population during the Oslo process, and the spreading tentacles of bypass roads connecting settlements with Israel proper. Palestinians also felt no reduction in Israel's policy of constant humiliation, a word that echoed through their complaints with stunning frequency. At Israeli checkpoints, which multiplied along the boundaries of fragmented jurisdictions, Palestinians confronted imperious delays by soldiers who were sometimes indifferent, sometimes abusive. Whenever Palestinians ventured from one town to another, they felt a humiliation that dramatized their powerlessness— as it was undoubtedly meant to do.

Another outcropping of bedrock was located in Jerusalem, whose ultimate fate kept being put aside in peace negotiations. When Prime Minister Ehud Barak offered in 2000 to share the city with the Palestinians, and give them almost all of the West Bank and Gaza for a state, Arafat did not accept. He had not weaned his people away from the right of return or the demand for exclusive Palestinian sovereignty

4

over Jerusalem. Muslim clerics had denied that any ancient Jewish temple had existed in the city, and Arafat had echoed the denials, which increased their popularity. This was a new brand of rejectionism—new to Islam, which throughout most of its history had recognized its connectivity to Judaism—and it seemed to say to Israeli Jews: You do not belong here.

The other constant was violence, although it took novel forms. An Israeli massacred twenty-nine Muslims at prayer at the Tomb of Abraham, another Israeli assassinated Rabin, Palestinians launched gruesome suicide attacks, and Israel replied with the enormous force of tanks and helicopter-fired rockets—and even jet fighters on occasion. The intifada, or Palestinian uprising, shredded most of the loosely woven strands of contact across the lines. In 2002, after a brutal spate of Palestinian suicide bombings in Israeli restaurants, markets, and a Passover Seder, Israeli forces invaded Palestinian areas of the West Bank, killing, wounding, and arresting large numbers; destroying whole quarters of Nablus and Jenin; gutting Palestinian Authority offices; and stripping Arafat's ministries of their files, computer hard drives, and capacity to govern. He was declared "irrelevant" by Prime Minister Ariel Sharon, who urged the remaking of the Palestinian Authority. Suicide bombings continued. And so on.

Someday, it can be hoped, the unchanging will change, and this book will be pulled from a dusty shelf and read as an artifact of the past.

– DAVID K. SHIPLER

MAY, 2002

THE
HISTORY

DAVID K. SHIPLER

Arab and Jew

J ERUSALEM IS A FESTIVAL and a lamentation. Its song is a sigh across the ages, a delicate, robust, mournful psalm at the great junction of spiritual cultures. Here among the constant ruins and rebuilding of civilizations lies the coexistence of diversity and intolerance.

In Jerusalem, the moment of harmony comes at dawn. The first light sings a pastel tune on ancient stone. As the sun rises from behind the desert mountains across the Jordan and the Dead Sea, the rays touch the curve of the Mount of Olives, then illuminate the creations of man. The sunlight kindles the brilliant gold of the Dome of the Rock, built by Muslims around the massive stone from which the faithful believe Muhammad

DAVID K. SHIPLER, *was Jerusalem Bureau Chief for the* New York Times *from 1979 to 1984. He won the Pulitzer Prize in 1986 for his penetrating reportage of the Middle East conflict in his* book Arab and Jew: Wounded Spirits in a Promised Land, *from which this excerpt is taken.*

departed on his night journey to heaven. Then the adjacent al-Aqsa mosque is lit, followed by the newest blocks of towering stone yeshivas in the Jewish Quarter of the Old City, reconstructed by the Israelis as testimony to the revival of the Jewish state and to the holiness of Jerusalem to the Jews. The light catches the dome and eclectic superstructure of the Church of the Holy Sepulcher, built over the centuries by Christian denominations on the site determined by the mother of Constantine, Queen Helena, to have been the place of the crucifixion, the burial, and the resurrection of Jesus.

The new sun casts a rose glow on the sawtoothed top of the wall that encloses the Old City. Practically every ruler of Jerusalem has added to the city wall, changing its configuration, building on the levels of earlier epochs. And as the sun climbs, the illumination descends along the courses of stone, working its way back through time, lighting first the repairs made by the Israelis, as the city's latest conquerors, to the uppermost ramparts erected by the Turkish sultans of the Ottoman Empire, then teasing color out of the layers placed by the Byzantines, the Crusaders, King Herod, and finally, at the southeast corner, blocks that may have been laid during the time of Nehemiah, following the exile of the Jews in Babylon.

Within the walls, light slowly penetrates the narrow alleys and secluded courtyards where small communities of Jews, Muslims, Armenians, Greek Orthodox, Roman Catholics, and other ethnic and religious groups reside with intense devotion to their traditions and their faiths.

Below al-Aqsa and the Dome of the Rock, the freshening day softens the shadow thrown by the massive blocks of Herodian stone that makes up the revered Wailing Wall or Western Wall, which is the western retaining wall of the Temple Mount, or Mount Moriah, the plateau on which the Muslim shrines now stand, where the Temple of Solomon once stood, and where no Jewish place of worship has existed since the Second Temple was burned by the Romans in A.D. 70.

In most cities of the world, the first to wake are the servants and workers and merchants—the bus drivers, the garbagemen, the cooks, the calloused men and women who bear their produce to early-morning market. But in Jerusalem it is the pious who greet the dawn—the Muslims, Jews, and Christians who sacrifice sleep for prayer. Their calls and chants in the eerie half light of the Old City mingle in an overlapping minor key like separate strains of the same plaintive melody. At the wall, Hasidic rabbis daven, their sidecurls swinging as they pray, "*Shma Yisrael* [Hear, O Israel]. *Adonai Eloheinu* [The Lord our God]. *Adonai Ehad* [The Lord is one]." Deep inside the ornate sepulcher a few hundred yards away, the air is still laden with the heavy incense of an Armenian service just completed. Under the church's schedule of worship, which has remained unchanged since the Crusades, three Franciscan monks follow the Armenians, taking their places at the tiny altar and singing mass: "Christ has died. Christ has risen. Christ will come again." And reverberating among the arches and domes and cobbled courtyards comes the thin wail of the muezzin's call to prayer from loudspeakers on al-Aqsa: *"Allahu akbar* [God is most great]! *La ilaha illa Allah* [There is no god but God]. *Al-salat khayr min al-naum* [Prayer is better than sleep]!" Like the Dead Sea, saturated with rich and poisonous salts and minerals, this small quarter of Jerusalem holds a concentration of congested traditions and convictions of beauty and rage.

Shadows move among the narrow, twisting alleyways. Orthodox Jews in broad-brimmed black hats, long black coats, black trousers, full beards, walk quietly to and from the wall, passing Arabs who wear white keffiyahs, the kerchiefs draped gracefully over their heads and held by circular thongs. The eyes of the Jews and of the Arabs slide past each other. Perhaps one gives a slight, silent nod to the other as they pass in the final moments of the night.

When the sun is high, and the flush of day is upon the city, the harmony of light becomes a dissonance of movement. Children scamper, shouting, using sticks to roll the rims of bicycle wheels along the cobblestones. Donkeys saddled with sacks of cement plod through the alleys. Arab merchants emerge, shouting morning greetings, throwing up the corrugated metal doors of their shops with an echoing clatter. They put out their cheap jewelry and their sheepskin rugs, their weavings and their brasswork, their trays of baklava and halva, their sacks of chick-peas and cardamom. The alleys begin to fill with the smells of leather and coffee and sweets, and of the bitter herbs that grow in the Judean Hills.

In my final weeks in Jerusalem, I walked as much as I could through the narrow alleys of the Old City to cling to the clashing sensations of time and history and belief. It was Ramadan, the Muslim month of fasting. Transistor radios, tuned to Radio Damascus, blared calls to prayer and commentaries on the Koran. I sat with my camera outside Damascus Gate, where curved stone steps rise like bleachers that put the throngs onstage as they flow in and out beneath the arch that opens a breach in the northern wall. In the gathering quiet of a Friday afternoon, when the preparations for the Jewish Sabbath overlap with the Muslim holy day, cross-currents of Jews and Arabs intersect through Damascus Gate, each person wearing his uniform, his badge of identity: Arab men in glistening white or checked keffiyahs, religious Muslim women, their heads bound tightly with shawls; Orthodox Jewish women covering their heads in the same tradition; Hasidic Jews wearing the black of the European shtetl, Orthodox Jews in plain yarmulkes as an expression of pious modernity. Israeli soldiers in loose-fitting olive-drab fatigues stroll laconically in pairs, Uzi submachine guns or M-16 automatic rifles slung casually on webbed straps across their shoulders; they are more alert than they seem. Young Arab students in jeans, Arab businessmen in dark suits and ties, Jews in shirts opened halfway down their chests, Franciscan monks in soft brown habits, Greek Orthodox priests in black cassocks, Scandinavian and American tourists—all raise a babble of languages a they move in and out through the gate. The Arabs and the Jews walk among one another, but they seem not to see each other. An Arab boy leads a lamb on a rope. Another boy prods a donkey along with a stick until they pass through the gate and disappear into the darkness of the twisting alleys inside.

I sat on the stone steps with my camera as often as I had time before I left. This was the finest theater in Jerusalem, and I didn't want to let go. All the characters in the drama of conflict were portrayed here in the swirling throngs, and I needed somehow to see them again with a fresh eye, to watch them through a telephoto lens and focus on their faces, one by one, instant after instant, and then to put the camera aside for a while and soak up the sensations of sight and sound that had become part of me, but which were now about to drift out of my daily life.

A bizarre calm, an odd absence of tension, enveloped the mingling of Arabs and Jews beneath Damascus Gate, as if each side moved comfortably within its category of self-containment. That this could be the case, that Jerusalem could be a tranquil island of workaday coexistence and also the spiritual heart of the competing Jewish-Arab claims to the this land, testified to the ancient ambivalence of the city.

The name of Jerusalem in Hebrew is Yerushalayim— "City of Peace." In Arabic it is al-Quds, "The Holy." Since its first appearance in manuscripts as a Canaanite city-state in the Bronze Age nearly 4,000 years ago—and all through a succession of conquerors and rulers from King David and King Solomon and the Kings of Judah through the Babylonians, Macedonians, Egyptians,

Seleucids, Greeks, Jewish Hasmoneans, Romans, Byzantines, Persians, Umayyads, Abbasids, Fatimids, Ayyubids, Crusaders, Mameluks, Ottoman Turks, British, Jordanians, and now again the Jews—Jerusalem has known no line between warfare and religion. It is a center of conflicting absolutes, of certainty, of righteousness. Its lofty refinement of intellect and theology has given enlightenment to its violence, mixing the wisdom of the ages into eternal bloodshed.

Jerusalem is located on a ridge of rolling hills that have historically divided two fundamentals of human society—the desert and the farm, the nomadic encampment and the sedentary village, the land of milk and the land of honey. On the east, the land runs down into the stark, dry Judean Desert and its milk-producing herds of goats tended by semi-nomadic tribesmen. On the west, the hills descend onto the coastal plains along the Mediterranean, with the sweet orchards and lush fields of the settled villagers. The land of milk and honey is thus two lands, merging and grinding at one another, shaping the nature of Jerusalem, which stands between the fertile and the arid, the rooted and the wanderer. And Jerusalem in turn has zealously nurtured both the worldly and the parochial, the scholar and the bigot. The thick walls surrounding the Old City keep nothing out and nothing in, but bear witness to the flow of faiths and hatreds through the great gates.

The lands of milk and honey no longer divide peoples with quite the clarity of ancient times. Since centuries before the idea of Zionism brought Jews to Palestine,

Arabs have terraced the slopes and farmed the land in the valleys and on the seaward side of the Judean Hills, their villages often growing into small cities and spawning an urban population that has included writers, doctors, teachers, lawyers, and tradesmen. Jews since the 1967 war have gone eastward into the parched desert of the Jordan Valley to establish farms and fields with the modern tools of drip irrigation and plastic sheeting. Many Bedouins have stopped moving their goat-hair tents with the seasons, and live somewhat permanently in ramshackle shelters of plywood and corrugated tin among the desert hills outside the city. For the most part, the distinction that some scholars make between the ancient, roaming tribes of desert Arabs and the ancient, sedentary Jews has disappeared. In its place, a passion for the land—as divinely given, as a mystical force, as a symbol of peoplehood and nationality, as a place of origin and security—now governs the conflict and fuels the violence between the two peoples.

Spiritually and geographically, Jerusalem lies at the heart of the small area—the sliver of territory reaching some fifty to eighty miles form the Jordan Rift on the east to the Mediterranean on the west, and 256 miles from Lebanon in the north to Egyptian Sinai in the south. Scarcely more than a smudge on a map of the Middle East, this is the land most burdened and enriched by ancient history, most scarred and coveted by the Jews and Arabs who now face each other in combat, in distaste, in regard, in accommodation, in strange affinity. They and their perceptions of each other are the subject here, for the 5 million Jews and 4 million Arabs who live in Israel, the West Bank, the Gaza Strip, and the Golan Heights stand at the point of contact between the military, ethnic, and religious forces of the region.

Both peoples are victims. Each has suffered at the hands of outsiders, and each has been wounded by the other.

The Jews have come from scattered regions of a great Diaspora where they have rarely been able to enjoy unbridled pride and flourishing contentment in their Jewishness. At best, even in the most open societies where they have lived as a minority and have excelled in the dominant culture, Jews have been made to feel at least slightly alien when they have observed their holidays, followed their traditions, practiced their religion, and embraced their Jewishness. At worst, they have been subordinated, despised, vilified, imprisoned, and slaughtered. Throughout their history, they have been haunted by a corrosive sense of illegitimacy that transcends individual spasms of brutality, of which the exterminations of the Holocaust are the most recent and most monstrous example. And they have stood and fallen alone. Nobody has rescued them except incidentally, as the Allies liberated many from the concentration camps after defeating Hitler's Germany. World War II was not fought to save the Jews.

The hardships of the Palestinian Arabs in modern history bear no resemblance in scope or depth to those of the Jews. Subjected to Turkish brutality under the Ottoman Empire, British rule under the Mandate created by the

League of Nations, political arrest by the Jordanian monarchy, and tough controls under Israel, the Arabs from this crucial slice of Palestine have suffered power-lessness and deprivation of liberty but never genocide. Their sense of distinctiveness as a Palestinian people has come not from an ancient source but largely in reaction to the creation and growth of Israel on part of the land where they lived. Their Palestinian awakening, even with its pre-state origins, was heightened by the upheavals of Israel's birth in 1948 and the refusal of the Arab governments to accept the presence of the tiny Jewish state on the edge of Arab territory. It gained further impetus when Israel cap-tured East Jerusalem, the West Bank, and the Gaza Strip—along with the Sinai and Golan Heights—during the Six-Day War of 1967. The struggles generated a new subculture of Arabs divorced from their own land. In con-temporary, personal terms, then, many Palestinian Arabs have been the victims of expulsion, displacement, and war. They have found themselves scattered and rejected in the Arab world at large, excluded from full participation in the Arab countries where many have settled, and con-fined to squalid refugee camps, often by the venal politics of their own leaders.

The feeling of aloneness is heavy on both sides. The wounds rub raw. An encounter between two victims, as one Israeli Jew observed, is "like fire and kerosene," a chemistry made especially volatile by the fact that both Arabs and Jews are minorities and majorities at once, their positions and roles intersecting and overlapping as the scope of the landscape shifts. The Jews historically have been a minority wherever they have gone, and they are a tiny minority in the vast Middle East. The Palestinians are part of the Arab majority in the region, but they are also a minority subgroup in the Arab world. In the territory under examination here, the Jews have finally become a majority, and have embraced the role with such alacrity that their official jargon refers to the Arabs under their control as "the minorities," as indeed they are within those boundaries.

History in the Middle East has a marvelous elasticity. It is easily stretched, twisted, compressed in the hands of its custodians, squeezed to fit into any thesis of righteous cause or pious grief. But it also has a way of springing back into an inconvenient form, a shape made of hard reminders. Certain features of the past remain as immutable as the ancient stones in Jerusalem—the Western Wall of huge Herodian blocks, the outcropping of bedrock form which Muhammad is said to have ascended to heaven, the stone core of Calvary now encased in ornate grillwork and marble in the Church of the Holy Sepulcher. The stones are cool to the touch, to the lips, to the Jewish, Muslim, and Christian fingers that tremble as they reach out in faith. The people are imprisoned by history.

To draw the boldest outlines of the past is to make Israel's basic case. To sketch the present is to see the Arabs' plight.

According to Genesis, this was the land that God gave to Abraham and his seed, and some of the Jews of modern

Israel have articulated their biblical claim by returning to the Old Testament names of the places they now control: the West Bank Arab city of Nablus they call "Shechem"; the nearby Jewish settlement they call "Elon Moreh"; the West Bank they prefer to see rendered as "Judea and Samaria." Those Jews who rely on the biblical deed to the land take their history from the ancient period of 4,000 years or so ago, skipping easily over the centuries of Muslim rule that followed; those Arabs who regard history as their ally tend to begin with the Muslim conquests in the seventh century A.D., blithely ignoring the Jewish kingdoms that existed here 2,000 years before Muhammad made his appearance.

Jewish history has been molded by yearning. The promise of a sweet land drew the ancient Israelites in their exodus from Egypt and in their wandering through Sinai. Their attachment to Jerusalem, where they dwelled under King David and built their first Temple under King Solomon, then remained a source of abiding faith after they were crushed, enslaved, and exiled into Babylon in 587 B.C. There they sang and dreamed of returning to the holy city. And from there they did return to build and restore. Under Herod they erected their Second Temple, which survived until the Romans destroyed it by fire in A.D. 70 on a day still mourned by Jews who keep the firm traditions. They made memory a part of ritual, holding their devotion to Jerusalem as the city changed hands again and again in blood, as Muslim conquerors were ejected by the Crusaders in 1099 and then in turn drove out the Crusaders in 1187. The Muslims—through the

Ottoman Turks—held Jerusalem until the end of World War I, when the British took over and set the stage for the reestablishment of a Jewish nation.

The Crusaders murdered, enslaved, or ousted the Jews of Jerusalem, but Jews began to return to the city under the Muslims, and during most of the intervening centuries between ancient and modern Israel, Arabs and Jews lived intermingled or in their own neighborhoods of Jerusalem, Hebron, Tiberius, Safed, and other towns. The Jews, most of them extremely religious, were wedded to the places by piety, not nationalism. Not until Zionism evolved as a movement in the nineteenth century—largely in reaction to pogroms in Russia—did significant numbers of European Jews begin to migrate to Ottoman-controlled Palestine. By 1845, Jews formed the largest single community in Jerusalem, the vanguard of an influx that gathered momentum after Great Britain endorsed the creation of a Jewish homeland through the Balfour Declaration of 1917. The migration gained urgency as Hitler came to power, promulgated anti-Jewish laws in Germany in the 1930s, then rounded up Jews in Germany and in the expanding sphere of German-occupied countries, restricted them to ghettos, shot them, deported them to concentration camps, and exterminated an estimated 6 million of them in the cause of racial purity. Out of this Holocaust grew the international compassion for the purpose of a new Israel as a sanctuary for the Jews.

Local Arab resistance to the Zionist enterprise began well before the formal creation of the Jewish state. As more and more Jews came to Palestine, a communal war commenced. Conducted from Arab towns and villages against nearby Jewish settlements, it fragmented the early Arab-Jewish relationships into a strange mosaic of clashes and coexistence. By the mid-1930s, Arabs in Palestine had endorsed the principle of "armed struggle" and in 1936–39 conducted the "Arab revolt," a futile series of riots and killings aimed at breaking the bonds of the British Mandate to block the coming of Israel.

Decimated by the catastrophe in Europe, weakened by war, the Jews who came to perch on the edge of the vast Arab region of the Middle East were idealistic pioneers, but they felt vulnerable enough not to exaggerate their capacity to demand, control, and govern. They pushed the British to make good on the promise of the Balfour Declaration—and some used terrorism as a weapon—but their mainstream was also ready for compromise. The Jewish Agency, as the precursor of the Israeli government, expressed its willingness to settle for only half of the land. It was prepared to accept a division of British-ruled Palestine west of the Jordan into two states—one Jewish, the other Arab. (The present Kingdom of Jordan, to the east, had been established on a large tract of Mandatory Palestine that Britain designated as an emirate in 1921.) The Jewish Agency's partition plan of 1946, followed by the United Nations plan of 1947 internationalizing Jerusalem and drawing boundaries between a Jewish and an Arab state, was less generous to the Jews than the final armistice lines that followed the 1948 war. If one looks today at the map of the Jewish

Agency plan, it is a striking lesson in the fickle nature of compromise, recalcitrance, and history. Had the Arabs accepted partition, Israel would have ended up with considerably less territory than it gained through their rejection. But when the Arabs refused to tolerate a Jewish state in their midst, opposed the U.N. plan, continued the communal war against Jewish settlements, and then invaded as soon as Israel declared its independence in 1948, they provided the Jews with the most severe motive in battle: survival. When the fighting was done, the Israelis had won half of Jerusalem, parts of Galilee, and areas of the Negev Desert that they had been willing, on paper, to relinquish.

The patterns of the wars that followed in 1956, 1967, 1973, and 1982 gave license to hatred and ground to extremists on both sides. Israel's capture of the West Bank after Jordan entered the 1967 fighting, and the subsequent unwillingness of the Arabs to negotiate peace for territory, allowed zealous Israeli Jews to settle and secure a hold on the West Bank, where about 750,000 Palestinian Arabs reside, making compromise more difficult and prolonging the hardships of the Palestinians who remained under Israeli military occupation in an atmosphere of violent lawlessness. Only in 1979 did Egypt find the key to winning back territory bloodlessly by signing a peace treaty with Israel in exchange for the Sinai. But gradually through these years, some moderate elements among both the Palestinians and the larger Arab world seemed to be approaching a pragmatic reconciliation with the fact of Israel's existence. A formal peace existed with

Egypt, a de facto peace with Jordan, a tense standoff with Syria. Inside Israel and its occupied territories, the shadings of Arab-Jewish attitudes and interactions retained a somber complexity.

This is the broad sketch of history against which the mutual perceptions of Arabs and Jews have emerged. The resulting stereotypes and images possess a durability beyond the rapid events in which they have been nurtured. They do not change as quickly as the political alignments in Israel and the Arab world. They are not as fluid as the forces of battle. And they are less susceptible to peace treaties than might be wished, for now they have been insinuated like indelible stains into the respective cultures, literatures, and languages.

The relationships between Arabs and Jews are examined here in three dimensions: First, the broad forces that contribute to aversion, namely the engines of war, nationalism, terrorism, and religious absolutism. These form the milieu of the Middle East, the environment of tension and yearning in which hatred is mobilized, in which minds are scarred. Second, the catalogue of images, each of the other, some held in parallel, some unique to the Arab-Jewish relationship, some reminiscent of stereotypes between other groups in other societies. Third, the complexities of interaction, from cultural and religious affinity to the idealistic efforts of a few Jews and Arabs to reach across the gap of ignorance.

In none of these dimensions do Arabs and Jews confront each other as two monoliths, for each side is multifaceted, itself torn by tensions along ethnic, class, and religious lines. The Jews have gathered in Israel from the Western cultures of the United States and Europe, from the Islamic countries of the Middle East, from India and Argentina and the Soviet Union, from among the impoverished black villages of Ethiopia and the white affluence of South Africa. Culturally they range along the entire far-flung spectrum of human civilization, finding only their Jewishness in common. Politically they are angrily diverse, from slavishly pro-Soviet communists to liberal democrats to militant right-wing authoritarians. Religiously they endure a mutual hostility of a high pitch, for they include the extreme Orthodox who reject Zionism, the modern Orthodox who embrace it with zeal, the nonreligious who resent the imperious efforts of the fundamentalists to impose religious strictures on the secular majority. The more and less religiously observant do battle against one another in the political arena. Regional differences also create variations in attitude, with many Jews in Haifa, for example, living nearer to Arabs and having easier relations with them than do many Jews of the Tel Aviv area, who can reside in a wholly Jewish environment.

The Arab population is diverse as well. Among the Arabs who live between the Jordan and the Mediterranean, the boundaries of belonging—and friction—are defined by clan, village, region, religion, and the larger concepts of peoplehood: Palestinian and Arab. The tensions among them lie along the layers of identity. The extended family, for example, remains a powerful determinant of status and influence in a village, and revengeful blood feuds are still occasionally fought between clans. The village itself is an important focus of loyalty. Families and the descendants of those who fled from one town to another nearby during the war of 1948 say they are still known as "refugees," a label, used by other Arabs native to their place of sanctuary, that assigns to them the unending status of outsiders.

Conflicts run along the lines of armistice, politics, and religion. Arabs inside Israel are often considered suspect by Arabs outside; those who endorse compromise with the Jews are often detested by those who support a steadfast Palestinian nationalism. Muslims and Christians often express a mutual distaste that prevents them from cooperating even in village political affairs. Sedentary Arabs have little contact with semi-nomadic Bedouins, and the small Druse minority exists in cultural, religious, and geographical separation from the larger sweep of the Arab population. To the north of Israel, in Lebanon, these religious and ethnic divisions have erupted into a long civil war with Palestinians and Lebanese Druse, Christians, and Muslims slaughtering each other as they pull back into their enclaves of distinctiveness and separateness.

The labels of nationality are determined in part by where the Arabs live between the Jordan and the Mediterranean. Those who reside inside Israel proper—that is, within the pre-1967 boundaries of the Jewish state—are citizens of Israel with the rights to vote in local and nation-

al elections, to equal protection under the law, to the judi-
cial system's due process, and the like. The vast majority of
them are sedentary and are commonly known as "Israeli
Arabs." Only a fraction are semi-nomadic Bedouins. All
the Bedouins and more than three quarters of the sedentary Arabs are Muslim; the rest are Christian Arabs and
Druse, the Druse practicing a religion whose secret tenets
have roots in Islam and Christianity.

Those who live in East Jerusalem, the Arab half of the
city captured by Israel during the Six-Day War, have for
the most part retained their Jordanian citizenship, having
declined the offer of Israeli citizenship after East
Jerusalem was annexed to Israel in 1967. But even non-
Israelis are allowed to vote in the Jerusalem municipal elections held every five years, and a growing minority of them
are doing so.

The Arabs on the West Bank are almost all Jordanian
citizens, although many, as Palestinians, are hostile to the
Hashemite regime of King Hussein, who is of Hijazi origin; since the West Bank residents have lived under Israeli
military occupation since 1967, they have not been
offered, nor have they sought, Israeli citizenship, and they
are subject to a system of military decrees and military
courts resembling martial law. Most of he West Bank
Arabs are Muslim, with a minority of Christians among
them. Those in the occupied Gaza Strip are stateless, having been formerly occupied by Egypt, which never granted
them Egyptian citizenship. The Druse on the Golan
Heights, which Israel captured from Syria in 1967 and

annexed in 1981, have also generally refused to accept Israeli citizenship, fearing retribution against their relatives in Syria or against their villages should Syria return to power in the Golan.

Every one of these categories of Arabs has a different relationship with the Israeli Jews, politically, legally, and attitudinally. The Druse inside Israel are generally accommodating, the Druse on the Golan Heights antagonistic. Israeli Arabs—those living inside Israel proper and enjoying Israeli citizenship—come to the relationship on a theoretically equal legal footing, whereas those living under military law on the West Bank and the Gaza Strip understandably display more antipathy and resistance to Israeli rule. Add to these variations the array of Israeli relationships with neighboring Arab countries—the peace and open border with Egypt, the quiet and selectively open border with Jordan, the confrontation and closed border with Syria, the alliances and hostilities with different Lebanese factions—and you have an Arab-Jewish interaction of enormous complexity.

Whatever happens in war or diplomacy, whatever territory is won or lost, whatever accommodations or compromises are finally made, the future guarantees that Arabs and Jews will remain close neighbors in this weary land, entangled in each other's fears. They will not escape from one another. They will not find peace in treaties, or in victories. They will find it, if at all, by looking into each other's eyes.

The time has passed when Jews and Arabs could face

each other in simple conflict. They live together now in rich variety. There is no single Arab-Jewish relationship; they are many, and they require an elusive tolerance that must somehow run against the forces of war, nationalism, terrorism, and religious certainty. . . .

Spring is a fleeting season in Israel. Fresh from the winter rains, hills and pastures are cloaked in a lushness that passes quickly. Wild flowers burst into a riot of color, then vanish, and the desert, momentarily brushed with a tint of green from wisps of new grass, lies burnished again by a relentless sun. The sky takes on its summer tone of cloudless, pastel blue. Not a drop of rain will fall again until November.

In the spring, Israel marks a double holiday divided by a dramatic shift in moods, two days in a row fixed in the Hebrew calendar to observe the sorrow of war and the joy of rebirth. First comes the Day of Remembrance to honor the country's fallen soldiers, a solemn, moving, mournful time. Then, at sundown, the sadness is cast aside and the streets come alive in a festive air as Independence Day begins; the Israelis who have spent the daylight hours in cemeteries form circles in the streets and dance into the night. The main thoroughfares become great promenades for strolling couples and clusters of teenagers; parking lots are floodlit and bathed in music; across makeshift counters, grilled Middle Eastern delicacies and games of chance are offered. And the next morning many go into the brief abundance of spring for picnics and songs and story-telling with their old army friends from the 1948 War of Independence, the 1956 Sinai Campaign, the Six-Day War of 1967, the War of Attrition with Egypt in 1969–71, the Yom Kippur War of 1973, or the Lebanon War of 1982.

Six wars and nearly 15,000 Israeli deaths have scarred the landscape of this ancient land. The gravestones on Mount Herzl, the military cemetery at the edge of Jerusalem, are marching down the terraced hillside, cutting into the forest that was planted by Jewish pioneers as a gesture of reclaiming faith and return.

This hillside is where the journey into Arab-Jewish attitudes must begin, for war is the soil that nourishes those tangled weeds of hatred. All that happens in men's minds here happens on the ground of war—all the toughness, all the gentleness, all the fear, all the longing, all the shrinking back in anger, and all the reaching out in hope. War has hardened and softened, embittered and mellowed. Even during peaceful intervals its presence can be felt, scratching at the soul of Jerusalem.

For both Jews and Arabs, war has produced its own sorrow and glorification. The Jews have confronted it mostly through combat, mourning their dead, nursing their wounded, extolling their heroes, praying for peace and victory. The process of war has become a business with budgets and economists and scientists; it brings serious pleasure to some and provides an outlet for cruelty. Battle has its thrills as well as its regrets. But somehow was has not generated the lust in Israeli Jews that it has among some other peoples at other times. When it comes, it does not arrive with the clamor of stirring oratory or the jingoistic exhortations to conquer all. It comes instead with a quiet strain of melancholy.

War has not been precisely the same experience for the Arabs. In those countries that have sent their armies against Israel again and again, the battle has not consumed the entire nation as it has for the Jews: Each Arab country has been large enough to absorb defeat. But the dead have included many more civilians than in Israel; Arab industry has been wrecked more thoroughly by a skillful Israeli air force, etching deeply in Arab minds the image of Israel as a rabid juggernaut bent on grinding up and taking over Arab lands. In addition, the battle has been given religious connotation through the Islamic concept of *jihad*, or holy war against the infidel. And as Israeli peace activists lament, the Arab side has lacked a parallel peace movement. War, it seems, is integral to the conduct of human affairs. To speak or to act against it requires the courage of an Anwar Sadat, who then pays the price of his life, or the subtlety of a King Hussein, who survives as long as he takes only half steps.

For many of the Palestinian Arabs who live, or once lived, between the Jordan and the Mediterranean, war has meant something else: displacement from their home villages. That has been their central experience of war; except for those who have been struck directly by Israeli planes or naval vessels while in refugee camps in Lebanon, for example, they have not been touched by actual combat.

War has come to them not as a clap of thunder, suddenly destroying, but as a corrosive cause that eats within. Their sorrow and glorification follow a different formula—a sorrow in defeat and a glorification in resistance. A young lad from a West Bank refugee camp who goes off to join the guerrillas of the Palestine Liberation Organization stirs mixed feelings among his family and friends—a dread of loss to his parents in many cases, a heroic portrait among his peers.

The enormous impact of war on Arab and Jewish perceptions of each other and of their own positions in the conflict was documented by a study of eleven-year-old children in Israel and the West Bank. Although both groups of youngsters expressed intense patriotism and loyalty to their own sides, the Palestinian Arabs saw their struggle in an idealistic, romantic light, whereas the Israeli Jews gave war a pragmatic connotation. Nearly all the Arab children—94 percent—said that war was good if you defeated your enemy; the Jewish youngsters were divided, with 53 percent agreeing that war was justified by victory. Among a sample of American youngsters used as a control group, only 35 percent saw virtue in war.

More accord between the Arab and Jewish children was revealed on other points, however. A large majority within both groups believed that war was always necessary (81 percent of the Arabs, 71 percent of the Jews, and 54 percent of the Americans). High levels of anxiety were found among both the Arab and Jewish children, with the Jews fearing terrorist attacks, that "father will be called up for reserve duty," and that "father won't return home." The West Bank Arabs expressed the worry that their fathers would be arrested or their houses demolished by Israeli authorities, a standard technique used against the families of those branded as terrorists.

At eleven o'clock on the morning of the Day of Remembrance, sirens sound to honor the dead, and all of Israel comes heavily to a halt. Downtown in West Jerusalem, cars pull over, their drivers and passengers climb out and stand at attention, pedestrians stop in their tracks, storekeepers pause behind their counters, and the man who sells newspapers at the corner of King George and Ben Yehuda Street interrupts his lilting call, falling silent while the sirens wail. In classrooms, children stand at their desks. In offices and factories, in fields and hospitals, Israelis are joined for two minutes in suspended reflection and homage, a rare moment of concord in a common grief.

On Mount Herzl, thousands of mourners move slowly through the cemetery gates in a broad river of sadness, their faces sculptures of suffering. They carry wreaths, bouquets, or small clusters of wild flowers they have picked along the way. They or their fathers have come to this place from Poland and Yemen, Morocco and Greece, Argentina and Belgium, India and the United States—scholars with soft hands, farmers with hard hands, wealthy and poor, men who pray and men who don't, mothers and fathers and brothers and sons and sisters and wives and friends of those who lie in the graves. All of Israel is here, every piece of the mosaic. There is an old, weathered man who saw the earliest days before the state. There is a delicate girl in army uniform sitting on an old gravestone, touching it with her hand, weeping without tears for a father she scarcely knew. There are small children who abandon their frolicking amid the heaviness, not knowing exactly why.

When the sirens sound, the flow of mourners shuffles to a stop, and the people stand in dignity and sorrow, held in their private thoughts, their flowers by their sides, as the sirens' solemn note holds high, then slides and wails down and dies. And the people move forward again, dividing as they go along the pathway into the sections of the cemetery devoted to their respective wars. A salute is fired, a bugle sounds, an army rabbi moves from grave to grave to chant the melancholy prayer for the dead. A weeping mother stretches face down on the long tombstone of her son; she clutches at it and cries some mangled words as if grabbing and calling to him to come back. The father stands stooped, then bends to put a hand on her shoulder.

In the newest section, the graves and the grief are as fresh as the turned earth. The mourners cluster among the gravemarkers, and at the far end, two cleanly dug rectangular holds stand open, waiting for the victims of the Lebanon war. Elsewhere, in the sections for the older battles, the survivors' agony is less raw, more subdued, scarred by time. There, at the grave of Yaacov Walzer, who was saved from the Nazis in Belgium at the age of two and killed in the fighting for Jerusalem at the age of twenty-seven, a small group of middle-aged adults stand, composed. Yaacov's brother Aryeh and sister Nellie Kremer raised him practically as parents after their mother and father disappeared from their home in Belgium into the Auschwitz concentration camp. The three children were taken in at great risk by a Christian family, which hid them for two years.

"He was two years old, and I was twelve," his brother says. "He was a boy who didn't understand anything, who didn't understand why, when Nazi troops came to search, he couldn't make any noise, couldn't say anything. I had to push a cloth into his mouth because he wanted to laugh, and I kept it there until he started to turn blue, then just at the last moment I took it out. From then on he knew. In 1948 we came to Israel. He went to Hebrew University, prepared for a doctorate in physics. He was a brilliant student. He had work published in an American physics journal. It's difficult to explain. We remained three children, three orphans. But we brought him up as a little child. He was our pride. We did everything to make it possible for him to continue his studies. I saw in him what I'd like to be, but I couldn't because of the circumstances. So my sister and I did everything possible so he could be somebody. He was so near to the goal. And in the Six-Day War he fell in Jerusalem. You can see here the destiny of a Jewish child who was saved by Gentile people who risked their lives to save Jewish children. Afterward he came to his homeland, Israel, and here he fell in the liberation of Jerusalem." The liberation of Jerusalem, the conquest of Jerusalem.

The mourners stand among the graves, talking softly, filling cups and jars with water for the fresh flowers. Rivka Fass sits weakly on the stone of her son's tomb, stroking it, kissing it. Another Yaacov, he died in Sinai in 1967. Now hard-won Sinai is given back to Egypt: "We are all afraid of war," says Yaacov's sister Hanni Zalmona. "We had these awful experiences. We don't have any sentiments for Sinai. We have sentiments for peace. He died for peace." A man approaches, Yaacov's best friend. He shakes hands with the father, silently, the way men do when they are at the edge of tears. He goes to the mother and embraces her. No words are spoken.

The impact of war looks simple from a distance. It should twist emotions into straightforward anger, weld hatred into the bones, seal off understanding. Not always so. At close view, war nurtures a somber complexity. An honest man who goes into battle confronts himself. His doubts gnaw; he broods on his fears; his pleasures enjoy a revived freshness. Sometimes he reaches out and touches.

Where Syrian and Israeli troops faced each other across a narrow ravine in Lebanon's Bekaa valley a year after the hard battles of the Lebanon war, they occasionally called and waved and sang to each other. Once, when the Israelis were lounging around without helmets or flak jackets, a state of relaxation contrary to regulations, the Syrians, who held slightly higher ground and could see well behind the Israeli position, started jumping and waving and yelling to get the Israelis' attention. The Syrians shouted in Arabic to Arabic-speaking Israeli soldiers that a high-ranking Israeli officer was driving up in a jeep. Well warned, the Israelis scrambled for their equipment and got into complete battle dress by the time their superior arrived.

In Sinai after peace was signed between Egypt and Israel, soldiers from the two sides visited each other routinely at an isolated checkpoint, greeted each other warmly, threw parties for each other in their tents, and simply became human beings in the vastness of the wilderness. The Israelis took water to the Egyptians, whose army was inefficient about supplies; the Egyptians, grateful but nervous about getting into trouble for having such friendly relations, asked that their names not be mentioned or their faces shown when we photographed them with Israeli troops.

Near the Strait of Tiran in Sinai the morning of January 27, 1982, a sturdy, muscular man in khaki shorts, a white T-shirt, and sandals drove his dusty white Saab through a twisting desert track that wound among old mine fields marked by tumbled barbed-wire fences. He pulled up to the wreck of a Mustang P-51, a propeller plane that had crashed three wars ago and had been made into a monument of sorts by encircling it with low posts. The plane still had a yellow stripe on the wing; the blue Star of David had faded to white, and the number "73" was still faintly visible after the years of bleaching sun and blowing sand. The man, his wife, and their three children got out of the car and looked at the wreck. From another direction, a tour bus full of Israeli girls lumbered up. Their teacher, a young man, had them gather around while he told the story of this lonely ruin in the desert.

It was during the Sinai Campaign of '56, the teacher explained to his students, and the plane had come to attack an Egyptian unit. As it flew low from out of the sun, to strafe with its six machine guns, it was hit, and crash-landed. The Israeli pilot, Jonathan Etkes, survived, was captured by the Egyptians, and was then released at the end of the war. As the teacher spoke and the girls listened, the man in the khaki shorts stood listening also, his arms crossed. He had a thick neck, and his thinning hair was cropped razor short.

When the teacher had nearly finished, the man stepped forward, climbed onto a wing of the plane, and said, "Excuse me. I'm Jonathan Etkes." His timing was masterful, and he loomed above them like some heroic apparition. "Oh!" the teacher shouted, and shook his hand. The girls gasped. A student who had stayed drowsily in the bus heard the commotion and called to her classmates, asking what was going on. "It's the pilot!" they screeched. And the pilot, Jonathan Etkes, told his story, correcting only a few details of the teacher's version. "They had thirty-seven-millimeter radar guns, Russian guns," he said, and went on to explain that the Egyptians had shot down a jet aircraft, a Mystère 41. "Benny Peled was the pilot; he later became commander of the air force. I started to see all the ack-ack, the puff. As long as you see it, it's good," he laughed. "The one that hits you, you don't see," and he laughed again as he continued his account. "Benny Peled, he fell, and in order that he wouldn't be captured, I remained to do some strafing, and he ran to the mountains. The sun was south, and we came from the south strafing." He made his hand go like a plane, diving, soaring, turning. "I went to sea, pulled up, and came from the south again. I suddenly saw shooting on the left side. They got me here, see?" He pointed to the scar on his leg. He looked down into the array of fresh faces upturned in rapture. "I wanted to run, but my legs didn't want to run, so I was running in my imagination, lying here. I lost consciousness. At five o'clock they took me." When he had finished, the girls crowded around him for a while, then were herded back into their bus, which rumbled off into the silence of the desert.

The day that Etkes visited his crash site had heavy meaning for him. It was on that date, twenty-five years before, that he had been released in a prisoner exchange, and the anniversary had become his private holiday. After Israel regained Sinai in the 1967 war and he could simply drive down from his home in Tel Aviv, he had brought his family to the crash site every January 27. This was the last time; Sinai was going back to Egyptian control three months hence in what he felt would be a bitter peace. After Sadat's 1977 visit to Jerusalem, Etkes was honored, as a former prisoner of war, by being selected as one of three Israeli pilots to fly the first El Al plane to Cairo, carrying a party of officials to prepare for a return visit by Menachem Begin. But Etkes was gloomy about the future. "To be honest, I have very, very bad feelings," he told me as we stood in the sun. "How many times can the enemy fool you? I really hope that this peace remains, though personally I'm pessimistic."

His little girl, Tal, climbed into the cockpit while his

wife, Mira, snapped pictures. Etkes strolled quietly around the aircraft tapping the wings and poking the ailerons. The dry desert is kind to machinery, and the ruins of warfare last well after the names of those who perished have been forgotten.

The Egyptians had tortured him as a prisoner. "They were very rough, but I was lucky to be in Egypt rather than Syria," he said. "They burned me with cigarettes." He pointed to a white spot on his cheek. "All my lips were burned, my nose, eyebrows, and ears. This was the easy part. They put surgical clamps on my tongue and started to turn them as you would open a sardine can, until you can't breathe anymore." They used syringes to give him shots all over his body, of what he did not know. They cut away dead flesh from his wounded leg without using anesthetic. "My head was as big as a watermelon. Electric shocks. I was completely naked. They put water on me to have good connections."

The interrogators wanted to know about a planeload of high-ranking Egyptian officers that Israeli fighters had shot down just before the war; the Egyptians were worried that the officers had been taken prisoner. But "they were so full of hate," Etkes recalled, "all they wanted was to see me suffer, and they didn't pay attention to the information. They deserve some credit for the amount of hatred and the amount of satisfaction they drew from the torture." His eyes burned intensely beneath his bushy eyebrows. Then suddenly he guffawed as he remembered the positive side. After his release, a false rumor circulated that the Egyptians had castrated him, he said. A lot of Israeli women wanted to find out firsthand whether it was true.

The experience of Etkes hardened his politics and his perception of Arabs' attitudes. "The heart of the conflict is the lack of acceptance of Jews here by Arabs," he declared. "This is the heart of the problem, not the Palestinians. I want to live. In order to live, I have to be the one to decide what's good for me. If you push me back to the wall too far, I won't be responsible for what I do." He had an old claim here: his children were the eighth generation on his mother's side to live in Palestine, he noted. "When Napoleon was defeated in Moscow, they were in Hebron already," he said of his wife's ancestors. "So my friend Arafat can't tell me that this isn't my home."

When Jonathan Etkes had finished talking, I had a few words with his son, Dori, a pleasant lad of sixteen. "It's my father's story," he said. "I've heard the story many times. I don't feel much, to tell you the truth. I'm going into the army in a few years, and maybe then I'll start to understand. . . ."

Virtually everyone in Israel has known war. Many have seen combat, and almost all know the experience of waiting for word from a loved one in battle. Every Cabinet in the country's brief history has contained men who were once warriors, men who have killed. And this brings a continuity of calloused wisdom to the mood of Israel, a hardness to the dreams.

To deny war is to deny reality, to embrace a supremely

sane insanity. When Israeli soldiers during the 1982 Lebanon invasion began to suffer combat fatigue—the mental stress that often leads to withdrawal from the reality of battle—psychiatrists and other trained professionals moved in to render aid. The worst cases were evacuated to special bases set up for treatment. One man of thirty-five collapsed after seeing comrades blown apart by artillery shells, and he sat and stared in silence at a single spot at his feet. He refused to touch a rifle. Another spent twenty-four hours crying, yelling, rolling on the floor and crawling around, trying to piece together what he imagined were the parts of a friend's dismembered body. Some became blind, deaf, paralyzed. "Shell shock," "battle fatigue"; now, in the growing trend toward euphemism, it is called "combat reaction." And the treatment was given at a place with the manly, matter-of-fact name Combat Fitness Retraining Unit. The patients were never called "patients," and they were told that before they left they would overcome their gun phobia and be shooting on the rifle range. They laughed derisively at the idea, for almost none of them—in their temporary, so-called craziness—ever wanted to touch a weapon again. So the army exposed them gently and slowly to guns, first letting them look at gun parts on a table, then putting a bolt or a trigger assembly in their pockets to be carried around for a day or so. Gradually, the soldiers would return to reality. They would touch the parts of the gun; they would touch the gun; they would shoot the gun. And with few exceptions, they were cured; they were brought back from their demented state in which guns were repulsive objects to be shunned. They were ready to move back into the stable, sensible, sane world in which guns are embraced as the tools of a necessary trade.

In the wasteland of warfare are buried little nuggets of fondness for years long gone, when Arab and Jew lived more as neighbors than as enemies. These memories of the days before 1948 are cupped in the ruins of suffering, guarded gently, given a gloss that lends them a beauty they probably do not deserve. They surface now and then, especially in conversation with Arabs who need to remember the time before the Jewish state as a time of abundant happiness. Thus did Jamil Ahmed, survivor of Deir Yassin, speak with nostalgia, saying, "Before that, we had very good relations with the Jews. We used to visit each other until the foreign Jews came." He meant the Jews whose ancestry could be traced back for generations in Palestine were somehow of this land, unlike the alien interlopers who arrived later from Europe, North America, and Arab countries. Thus did the Arabs of Kfar Kassem, one year after the massacre, agree with the Jews to hold a *sulha*, a traditional Arab ceremony and meal to unite the families of murderer and murdered and resolve the outstanding grievance. About 400 attended in the Arab village, where the army's catering service provided an Arab-style meal. The chief rabbi of the nearby Jewish town of Petah Tikvah sent a message of goodwill. The village sheikh quoted a Muslim precept that "none fall, even by a killer's hand, until their allotted span has been completed." And an eighty-seven-year-old founder of Petah Tikvah, presiding over the ceremony, pleaded for the restoration of the good feeling that had existed for decades, noting that he had represented the Jews at many *sulhas* for murders in which Jews had been victims.

Jews such as Dov Yermiya, born in Palestine before the Jewish state, also remember the decent relations that emerged out of conflict. He fought the Arabs, then befriended them. There were troubles in '21–'22, he said, in '29, and from '36 to '38. "When I settled in a kibbutz in the Galilee, we were fired upon by the Arabs who didn't want us there, in '38. But as soon as the troubles ceased, or stopped for a while, I managed to make good friends with the Arabs, and this friendship—not only did I enjoy it, it proved strong in the times of war that came afterwards. So my experience is that not only is it necessary, it's also possible."

Acts of terrorism and war, then, become the benchmarks of the Middle East, more definite than the fleeting seasons or the regularity of the calendars in measuring the distances between times of hatred, times of accord. They divide memory as precisely as the ticking of a clock.

Before 1948, before the first Arab-Jewish war, Jamil Hamad, now a journalist in the West Bank Arab village of Bethlehem, lived in a small town in Palestine called Rafat, near the Jewish town of Beit Shemesh. Rafat no longer exists; it was demolished in the 1948 war, when he and his family fled to the West Bank. But the memories exist strongly, and they are good ones. "To me, to all members of my family, the Jews were friendly," Jamil recalled. "We had very friendly relations. I never felt the mistrust. We played football. We would take them to our fields, give them presents—

grapes, melons, eggs. They used to stay at our house. We used to stay at their houses." As a boy, he sometimes spent Friday nights with a Jewish friend in the next village. "I remember Shabbat evening," he said. "I loved to see them lighting the candles, praying in a language which I didn't understand. It was something I didn't have as a Muslim. I used to go back to my mother and father and ask, 'Why don't we have that?' To this very day I have a weakness for candles. I buy them frequently. When I have guests for dinner, I put a candle on the table and light it."

KAREN ARMSTRONG

Three Faiths, One City

I N JERUSALEM, more than in any other place I have visited, history is a dimension of the present. Perhaps this is so in any disputed territory, but it struck me forcibly the first time I went to work in Jerusalem in 1983. First, I was surprised by the strength of my own reaction to the city. It was strange to be walking around a place that had been an imaginative reality in my life ever since I was a small child and had been told tales of King David or Jesus. As a young nun, I was taught to begin my morning meditation by picturing the biblical scene I was about to contemplate, and so conjured up my own image of the Garden of Gethsemane, the Mount of Olives, or the Via Dolorosa. Now that I was going about my daily business among

KAREN ARMSTRONG *is one of the world's foremost scholars on the history of religion. This piece, which traces the history of Judaism, Christianity and Islam in Jerusalem, is from her book* Jerusalem: Three Faiths, One City *(1996). Armstrong is the best-selling author of books such as* The History of God *and* The Battle for God.

these very sites, I discovered that the real city was a far more tumultuous and confusing place. I had, for example, to take in the fact that Jerusalem was clearly very important to Jews and Muslims too. When I saw caftaned Jews or tough Israeli soldiers kissing the stones of the Western Wall or watched the crowds of Muslim families surging through the streets in their best clothes for Friday prayers at the Haram al-Sharif, I became aware for the first time of the challenge of religious pluralism. People could see the same symbol in entirely different ways. There was no doubting the attachment of any of these people to their holy city, yet they had been quite absent from *my* Jerusalem. Still, the city remained mine as well: my old images of biblical scenes were a constant counterpoint to my firsthand experience of twentieth-century Jerusalem. Associated with some of the most momentous events of my life, Jerusalem was somehow built into my own identity.

Yet as a British citizen, I had no political claim to the city, unlike my new colleagues and friends in Jerusalem. Here again, as Israelis and Palestinians presented their arguments to me, I was struck by the vivid immediacy of past events. All could cite, in sometimes minute detail, the events leading up to the creation of the State of Israel in 1948 or the Six-Day War in 1967. Frequently I noted how these depictions of the past centered on the question of who had done what *first*. Who had been the first to resort to violence, the Zionists or the Arabs? Who had first noticed the potential of Palestine and developed the country? Who had lived in Jerusalem first, the Jews or the Palestinians? When they discussed the troubled present, both Israelis and Palestinians turned instinctively to the past, their polemic coursing easily from the Bronze Age through the Middle Ages to the twentieth century. Again, when Israelis and Palestinians proudly showed me around *their* city, the very monuments were drawn into the conflict.

On my first morning in Jerusalem, I was instructed by my Israeli colleagues how to spot the stones used by King Herod, with their distinctively beveled edges. They seemed ubiquitous and a perpetual reminder of a Jewish commitment to Jerusalem that could be dated back (in this case) to the first century B.C.E.—long before Islam appeared on the scene. Constantly, as we passed construction crews in the Old City, I was told how Jerusalem had been utterly neglected by the Ottomans when they had ruled the city. It had come to life again only in the nineteenth century, thanks, large, to Jewish investment—look at the windmill built by Sir Moses Montefiore and the hospitals funded by the Rothschild family. It was due to Israel that the city was thriving as never before.

My Palestinian friends showed me a very different Jerusalem. They pointed out the splendors of the Haram al-Sharif and the exquisite *madāris*, Muslim schools, built around its borders by the Mamluks as evidence of the Muslim commitment to Jerusalem. They took me to the shrine of *Nebī Mūsā* near Nericho, built to defend Jerusalem against the Christians, and the extraordinary Umayyad palaces nearby. When we drove through Bethlehem once, my Palestinian host stopped the car beside Rachel's roadside tomb to point out passionately that the Palestinians had cared for this

Jewish shrine for centuries—a pious devotion for which they had been ill rewarded.

One word kept recurring throughout. Even the most secular Israelis and Palestinians pointed out that Jerusalem was "holy" to their people. The Palestinians even called the city al-Quds, "the Holy," though the Israelis scornfully waved this aside, pointing out that Jerusalem had been a holy city for Jews *first*, and that it had never been as important to the Muslims as Mecca and Medina. But what did the word "holy" mean in this context? How could a mere city, full of fallible human beings and teeming with the most unholy activities, be sacred? Why did those Jews who professed a militant atheism care about the holy city and feel so possessive about the Western Wall? Why should an unbelieving Arab be moved to tears the first time he stood at the Mosque of al-Aqsā? I could see why the city was holy to Christians, since Jerusalem had been the scene of Jesus's death and resurrection: it had witnessed the birth of the faith. But the formative events of both Judaism and Islam had happened far away from Jerusalem, in the Sinai Peninsula or the Arabian Hijaz. Why, for examples, was Mount Zion in Jerusalem a holy place for Jews instead of Mount Sinai, where God had given the Law to Moses and made his covenant with Israel? Clearly, I had been wrong to assume that the holiness of a city depended on its associations with the events of salvation history, the mythical account of God's intervention in the affairs of humanity.

What I have discovered is that even though the word "holy" is bandied around freely in connection with

Jerusalem, as though its meaning were self-evident, it is in fact quite complex. Each one of the three monotheistic religions has developed traditions about the city that are remarkably similar. Furthermore, the devotion to a holy place or a holy city is a near-universal phenomenon. Historians of religion believe that it is one of the earliest manifestations of faith in all cultures. People have developed what has been called a sacred geography that has nothing to do with a scientific map of the world but which charts their interior life. Earthly cities, groves, and mountains have become symbols of this spirituality, which is so omnipresent that it seems to answer a profound human need, whatever our beliefs about "God" or the supernatural. Jerusalem has—for different reasons—become central to the sacred geography of Jews, Christians, and Muslims. This makes it very difficult for them to see the city objectively, because it has become bound up with their conception of themselves and the ultimate reality—sometimes called "God" or the sacred—that gives our mundane lives meaning and value.

There are three interconnected concepts that recur. First is the whole notion of God or the sacred. In the Western world, we have tended to view God in a rather anthropomorphic and personalized manner, and as a result, the whole notion of the divine frequently appears incoherent and incredible. Since the word "God" has become discredited to many people because of the naive and often unacceptable things that have been asserted and done in "his" name, it may be easier to use the term "sacred" instead. When they have contemplated the world, human beings have always experienced a transcendence and mystery at the heart of existence. They have felt that it is deeply connected with themselves and with the natural world, but that it also goes beyond. However we choose to define it—it has been called God, Braham, or Nirvana—this transcendence has been a fact of human life. We have all experienced something similar, whatever our theological opinions, when we listen to a great piece of music, or hear a beautiful poem and feel touched within and lifted, momentarily, beyond ourselves. We tend to seek out this experience, and if we do not find it in one setting—in a church or synagogue, for example—we will look elsewhere. The sacred has been experienced in many ways: it has inspired fear, awe, exuberance, peace, dread, and compelling moral activity. It represents a fuller, enhanced existence that will complete us. It is not merely felt as a force "out there" but can also be sensed in the depths of our own being. But like any aesthetic experience, the sense of the sacred needs to be cultivated. In our modern secular society, this has not always been a priority, and so, like any unused capacity, it has tended to wither away. In more traditional societies, the ability to apprehend the sacred has been regarded as of crucial importance. Indeed, without this sense of the divine, people often felt that life was not worth living.

This is partly because human beings have always experienced the world as such a painful place. We are the victims of natural disasters, of mortality, extinction, and human injustice and cruelty. The religious quest has usually begun with the perception that something has gone wrong, that, as the Buddha put it, "Existence is awry." Besides the common shocks that flesh is heir to, we all suffer personal distress that makes apparently unimportant setbacks overwhelmingly upsetting. There is a sense of abandonment that makes such experiences as bereavement, divorce, broken friendship, or even losing a beloved object seem, sometimes, part of an underlying and universal ill. Often this interior dis-ease is characterized by a sense of separation. There appears to be something missing from our lives; our existence seems fragmented and incomplete. We have an inchoate feeling that life was not meant to be thus and that we have lost something essential to our well-being—even though we would be hard put to explain this rationally. This sense of loss has surfaced in many ways. It is apparent in the Platonic image of the twin soul from which we have been separated at birth and in the universal myth of the lost paradise. In previous centuries, men and women turned to religion to assuage this pain, finding healing in the experience of the sacred. Today in the West, people sometimes have recourse to psychoanalysis, which has articulated this sense of a primal separation in a more scientific idiom. Thus it is associated with memories of the womb and the traumatic shock of birth. However we choose to see it, this notion of separation and a yearning for some kind of reconciliation lies at the heart of the devotion to a holy place.

The second concept we must discuss is the question of myth. When people have tried to speak about the sacred or about the pain of human existence, they have not been able to express their experience in logical, discursive terms but have had recourse to mythology. Even Freud and Jung, who were the first to chart the so-called scientific quest for the soul, turned to the myths of the classical world or of religion when they tried to describe these interior events, and they made up some new myths of their own. Today the word "myth" has been rather debased in our culture; it is generally used to mean something that is not true. Events are dismissed because they are "only" myths. This is certainly true in the debate about Jerusalem. Palestinians claim that there is absolutely no archaeological evidence for the Jewish kingdom founded by King David and that no trace of Solomon's Temple has been found. The Kingdom of Israel is not mentioned in any contemporary text but only in the Bible. It is quite likely, therefore, that it is merely a "myth." Israelis have also discounted the story of the Prophet Muhammad's ascent to heaven from the Haram al-Sharif in Jerusalem—a myth that lies at the heart of the Muslim devotion to al-Quds—as demonstrably absurd. But this, I have come to believe, is to miss the point. Mythology was never designed to describe historically verifiable events that actually happened. It was an attempt to express their inner significance or to draw attention to realities that were too elusive to be discussed in a logically coherent way. Mythology has been well defined as an ancient form of psychology, because it describes the inner reaches of the self which are so mysterious and yet so fascinating to us. Thus the myths of "sacred geography" express truths about the interior life. They touch on the obscure sources of human pain and desire and can thus unleash very powerful emotions. Stories about Jerusalem should not be dismissed because they are "only" myths: they are important precisely *because* they are myths.

The Jerusalem question is explosive because the city has acquired mythical status. Not surprisingly, people on both sides of the present conflict and in the international community frequently call for a rationalized debate about rights and sovereignty, divorced from all this emotive fiction. It would be nice if this were possible. But it is never safe to say that we have risen above our need for mythology. People have often tried to eradicate myth from religion in the past. Prophets and reformers in ancient Israel, for example, were extremely concerned to separate their faith from the mythology of the indigenous Canaanites. They did not succeed, however. The old stories and legends surfaced again powerfully in the mysticism of Kabbalah, a process that has been described as the triumph of myth over the more rational forms of religion. In the history of Jerusalem we shall see that people turned instinctively toward myth when their lives became particularly troubled and they could find no consolation in a more cerebral ideology. Sometimes outer events seemed so perfectly to express a people's inner reality that they immediately assumed mythical status and inspired a burst of mythologized enthusiasm. Two such events have been the discovery of the Tomb of Christ in the fourth century and the Israeli conquest of Jerusalem in 1967. In both cases, the people concerned thought they had left this primitive way of thinking far behind, but the course of events proved too strong for them. The catastrophes which have befallen the Jewish and the Palestinian people in our own century have been of such magnitude that it has not been surprising that myth has once again come to the fore. For good or ill, therefore, a consideration of the mythology of Jerusalem is essential, if only to illuminate the desires and behavior of people who are affected by this type of spirituality.

The last term that we must consider before embarking on the history of Jerusalem is "symbolism." In our scientifically oriented society, we no longer think naturally in terms of images and symbols. We have developed a more logical and discursive mode of thought. Instead of looking at physical phenomena imaginatively, we strip an object of all its emotive associations and concentrate on the thing itself. This has changed the religious experience for many people in the West, a process that, as we shall see, began in the sixteenth century. We tend to say that something is *only* a symbol, essentially separate from the more mysterious reality that it represents. This was not so in the premodern world, however. A symbol was seen as partaking in the reality to which it pointed; a religious symbol thus had the power of introducing worshipers to the sacred realm. Throughout history, the sacred has never been experienced directly— except, perhaps, by a very few extraordinary human beings. It has always been felt in something other than itself. Thus the divine has been experienced in a human being—male or female—who becomes an avatar or incarnation of the sacred; it has also been found in a holy text, a law code, or a doctrine. One of the earliest and most ubiquitous symbols of the divine has been a place. People have sensed the sacred in mountains, groves, cities, and temples. When they have walked into these places, they have felt that they have entered a different dimension, separate from but compatible with the physical world they normally inhabit. For Jews, Christians, and Muslims, Jerusalem has been such a symbol of the divine.

This is not something that happens automatically. Once a place has been experienced as sacred in some way and has proved capable of giving people access to the divine, worshipers have devoted a great deal of creative energy to helping others to cultivate this sense of transcendence. We shall see that the architecture of temples, churches, and mosques has been symbolically important, often mapping out the inner journey that a pilgrim must take to reach God. Liturgy and ritual have also heightened this sense of sacred space. In the Protestant West, people have often inherited a mistrust of religious ceremonial, seeing it as so much mumbo-jumbo. But it is probably more accurate to see liturgy as a form of theater, which can provide a powerful experience of the transcendent even in a wholly secular context. In the West, drama had its origins in religion: in the sacred festivals of ancient Greece and the Easter celebrations in the churches and cathedrals of medieval Europe. Myths have also been devised to express the inner meaning of Jerusalem and its various shrines.

One of these myths is what the late Romanian-American scholar Mircea Eliade has called the myth of eternal return, which he found in almost all cultures. According to this mode of thought, all objects that we encounter here on earth have their counterpart in the divine sphere. One can see this myth as an attempt to express the sense that our life here below is somehow incomplete and separated from a fuller and more satisfactory existence elsewhere. All human activities and skills also have a divine prototype: by copying the actions of the gods, people can share in their divine life. This *imitatio dei* is still observed today. People continue to rest on the Sabbath or eat bread and drink wine in church—actions which are meaningless in themselves—because they believe that in some sense God once did the same. The rituals at a holy place are another symbolic way of imitating the gods and entering their fuller and more potent mode of existence. The same myth is also crucial to the cult of the holy city, which can be seen as the replica of the home of the gods in heaven; a temple is regarded as the reproduction of a particular deity's celestial palace. By copying its heavenly archetype as minutely as possible, a temple could also house the god here on earth.

In the cold light of rational modernity, such myths appear ridiculous. But these ideas were not worked out first and then applied to a particular "holy" location. They were an attempt to explain an experience. In religion, experience always comes before the theological explanation. People first felt that they had apprehended the sacred in a grove or on a mountain peak. They were sometimes helped to do so by the aesthetic devices of architecture, music, and liturgy, which lifted them beyond themselves. They then sought to explain this experience in the poetic language of mythology or in the symbols of sacred geography. Jerusalem turned out to be one of those locations that "worked" for Jews, Christians, and Muslims because it did seem to introduce them to the divine.

One further remark is necessary. The practices of religion are closely akin to those of art. Both art and religion try to make some ultimate sense of a flawed and tragic world. But religion is different from art because it must have an ethical dimension. Religion can perhaps be described as a moral aesthetic. It is not enough to experience the divine or the transcendent; the experience must then be incarnated in our behavior toward others. All the great religions insist that the test of true spirituality is practical compassion. The Buddha once said that after experiencing enlightenment, a man must leave the mountaintop and return to the marketplace and there practice compassion for all living beings. This also applies to the spirituality of a holy place. Crucial to the cult of Jerusalem from the very first was the importance of practical charity and social justice. The city cannot be holy unless it is also just and compassionate to the weak and vulnerable. But sadly, this moral imperative has often been overlooked. Some of the worst atrocities have occurred when people have put the purity of Jerusalem and the desire to gain access to its great sanctity before the quest for justice and charity.

All these underlying currents have played their part in Jerusalem's long and turbulent history. . . .

One of the inescapable messages of the history of Jerusalem is that, despite romantic myths to the contrary, suffering does not necessarily make us better, nobler people. All too often, quite the reverse. Jerusalem first became an exclusive city after the Babylonian exile, when the new Judaism was helping Jews to establish a distinct identity in a predominantly pagan world. Second Isaiah had proclaimed that the return to Zion would usher in a new era of peace, but the Golah simply made Jerusalem a bone of contention in Palestine when they excluded the Am ha-Aretz. The experience of persecution at the hands of Rome did not make the Christians more sympathetic to the suffering of others, and al-Quds became a much more aggressively Islamic city after the Muslims suffered at the hands of the Crusaders. It is not surprising, therefore, that the State of Israel, founded shortly after the catastrophe of the Holocaust, has not always implemented policies of sweetness and light. We have seen that the fear of destruction and extinction was one of the main motives that impelled the people of antiquity to build holy cities and temples. In their mythology the ancient Israelites told the story of their journey through the demonic realm of the wilderness—a nonplace, where there was no-one and no-thing—to reach the haven of the Promised Land. The Jewish people had endured the annihilation on an unprecedented scale in the death camps. It is not surprising that their return to Zion during the Six-Day War shook them to the core and led some of them to believe that there had been a new creation, a new beginning.

But today, increasingly, Israelis are beginning to contemplate the possibility of sharing the Holy City. Sadly, however, most of the committed people who are working for peace are seculars. On both sides of the conflict, religion is becoming increasingly belligerent. The apocalyptic spirituality of extremists who advocate suicide bombing, blowing up other people's shrines, or driving them from their homes is pursued by only a small minority, but it engenders hatred on a wider scale. On both sides, attitudes harden after an atrocity, and peace becomes a more distant prospect. It was the Zealots who opposed the Peace Party in 66 C.E. who were chiefly responsible for the destruction of Jerusalem and its Temple, and it was Reynauld of Chatillon, convinced that any truce with the infidel was a sin, who brought down the Crusader kingdom. The religion of hatred can have an effect that is quite disproportionate to the numbers of people involved. Today religious extremists on both sides of the conflict have been responsible for atrocities committed in the name of "God." On February 25, 1994, Baruch Goldstein gunned down at least forty-eight Palestinian worshipers in the Cave of the Patriarchs in Hebron: today he is revered as a martyr of Israel by the far right. Another martyr is the young woman member of the Islamic group Hamas, who died in a suicide bombing of a Jerusalem bus on August 25, 1995, killing five people and injuring 107. Such actions are a travesty of religion, but they have been frequent in the history of Jerusalem. Once the possession of a land or a city becomes an end in itself, there is no reason to refrain from murder. As soon as the prime duty to respect the divinity enshrined in other human beings is forgotten, "God" can be made to give a divine seal of absolute approval to our own prejudices and desires. Religion then becomes a breeding ground for violence and cruelty.

On November 4, 1995, Prime Minister Yitzhak Rabin was murdered after speaking at a peace rally in Tel Aviv. To their horror, Israelis learned that the assassin was another Jew. Yigal Amir, the young student who fired the fatal shots, declared that he had acted under God's direction and that it was permissible to kill anybody who was prepared to give the sacred land of Israel to the enemy. The religion of hatred seems to have a dynamic of its own. Murderous intransigence can become such a habit that it is directed not only against the enemy but also against co-religionists. Crusader Jerusalem, for example, was bitterly divided against itself, and the Franks were poised on the brink of a suicidal civil war at a time when Saladin was preparing to invade their territory. Their hatred of one another and their chronic feuding was a factor in their defeat at Saladin's hands at the battle of Hattin.

The tragic murder of Rabin was a shocking revelation to many Israelis of the deep fissures in their own society—divisions which tell then they had tried to ignore. The Zionists had come to Palestine to establish a homeland where Jews would be safe from the murderous *goyim*. Now Jews had begun to kill one another for the sake of that land. All over the world, Jews struggled with the painful realization that they were not merely victims but could also do harm and perpetrate atrocity. Rabin's death was also a glaring demonstration of the abuse of religion. Since the time of Abraham, the most humane traditions of the religion of Israel had suggested that compassion to other human beings could lead to a divine encounter. So sacred was humanity that it was never right to sacrifice another human life. Yigal Amir, however, subscribed to the more violent ethic of the Book of Joshua. He could see the divine only in the Holy Land. His crime was a frightening demonstration of the dangers of such idolatry.

Kabbalistic myth taught that when the Jews returned to

Zion, everything in the world would fall back into its proper place. The assassination of Rabin showed that the return of the Jews to Israel did not mean that everything was right with the world. But this mythology had never been meant to be interpreted literally. Since 1948 the gradual return of the Jewish people to Zion had resulted in the displacement of thousands of Palestinians from their homeland as well as from Jerusalem. We know from the history of Jerusalem that exile is experienced as the end of the world, as a mutilation and a spiritual dislocation. Everything becomes meaningless without a fixed point and the orientation of home. When cut off from the past, the present becomes a desert and the future unimaginable. Certainly the Jews experienced exile as demonic and destructive. Tragically, this burden of suffering has now been passed by the State of Israel to the Palestinians, whatever its original intentions. It is not surprising that Palestinians have not always behaved in an exemplary manner in the course of their own struggle for survival. But, again, there are Palestinians who recognize that compromise may be necessary if they are to regain at least part of their homeland. They have made their own hard journey to the Oslo Accords: that Palestinians should give official recognition to the State of Israel would once have seemed an impossible dream. In exile, Zion became an image of salvation and reconciliation to the Jews. Not surprisingly, al-Quds has become even more precious to the Palestinians in their exile. Two peoples, who have both endured an annihilation of sorts, now seek healing in the same Holy City.

Salvation—secular or religious—must mean more than

the mere possession of a city. There must also be a measure of interior growth and liberation. One thing that the history of Jerusalem teaches is that nothing is irreversible. Not only have its inhabitants watched their city destroyed time and again, they have also seen it built up in ways that seemed abhorrent. When the Jews heard of the obliteration of their Holy City, first by Hadrian's contractors and then by Constantine's, they must have felt that they would never win their city back. Muslims had to see the desecration of their beloved Haram by the Crusaders, who seemed invincible at the time. All these building projects had been intent on creating facts, but ultimately bricks and mortar were not enough. The Muslims got their city back because the Crusaders became trapped in a dream of hatred and intolerance. In our own day, against all odds, the Jews have returned to Zion and have created their own facts in the settlements around Jerusalem. But, as the long, tragic history of Jerusalem shows, nothing is permanent or guaranteed. The societies that have lasted the longest in the holy city have, generally, been the ones that were prepared for some kind of tolerance and coexistence in the Holy City. That, rather than a sterile and deadly struggle for sovereignty, must be the way to celebrate Jerusalem's sanctity today.

PAUL JOHNSON

A History
of the Jews

T
HE HOLOCAUST and the new Zion were organically connected. The murder of six million Jews was a prime causative factor in the creation of the state of Israel. This was in accordance with an ancient and powerful dynamic of Jewish history: redemption through suffering. Thousands of pious Jews sang their profession of faith as they were hustled toward the gas chambers because they believed that the punishment being inflicted on the Jews, in which Hitler and the SS were mere agents, was the work of God and itself proof that He had chosen them. According to the Prophet Amos, God had said: "You only have I known of all the families of the earth, therefore I will punish you for all your

PAUL JOHNSON, *a philosopher and historian, is the author of numerous bestsellers, including* A History of the American People *and a Penguin biography of Napoleon. This piece on the history of Zionism comes from his highly regarded 4,000-year survey of Jewish thought,* A History of the Jews *(1987).*

iniquities." The sufferings of Auschwitz were not mere happenings. They were moral enactments. They were part of a plan. They confirmed the glory to come. Moreover, God was not merely angry with the Jews. He was also sorrowful. He wept with them. He went with them into the gas chambers as he had gone with them into Exile.

That is to state cause and effect in religious, metaphysical terms. But it can also be stated in historical terms. The creation of Israel was the consequence of Jewish sufferings. We have used the image of the jigsaw puzzle to show how each necessary piece was slotted into place. As we have seen, the great eastern massacres of 1648 led to the return of a Jewish community to England, and so to America, thus in time producing the most influential Jewry in the world, an indispensable part of the geopolitical context in which Israel could be created. Again, the massacres of 1881 set in motion a whole series of events tending toward the same end. The immigration they produced was the background to the Dreyfus outrage, which led directly to Herzl's creation of modern Zionism. The movement of Jews set in motion by Russian oppression created the pattern of tension from which, in 1917, the Balfour Declaration emerged, and the League of Nations Palestine mandate was set up to implement it. Hitler's persecution of the Jews was the last in the series of catastrophes which helped to make the Zionist state.

Even before the Second World War, Hitler's anti-Jewish policy had the unintended effect of greatly strengthening the Jewish community in Palestine. Hitler eventually came to see the Jewish state as a potential enemy, a "second Vatican," a "Jewish Comintern," a "new power-base for world Jewry." But for a time in the 1930s the Nazis actively assisted the emigration of German Jews to Palestine. Not only did 60,000 German Jews thus reach the national home, but the assets of these German Jews played an important part in establishing an industrial and commercial infrastructure there. It was the war, bringing with it not only Hitler's outright physical assault on the Jews as his prime enemy, but the chance for Jews to hit back at him with the Allies, which activated the last phase of the Zionist program. From the outbreak of war in 1939, the creation of the Israeli state, at the earliest possible moment, became the overriding object of the Zionists and spread gradually to the majority of the world Jewish community. The obstacles to a Zionist fulfillment were still considerable. It was not enough to defeat Hitler. It was also necessary to remove any objections from the three victorious Allies, Britain, the United States, and Soviet Russia. Let us look at each in turn.

Initially, Britain was the most important, because it was the power in possession. Moreover, the 1939 White Paper policy had, in effect, repudiated the Balfour Declaration and projected a future in which no predominantly Jewish Palestine could emerge. The Jews were Britain's ally in the war. But at the same time they had to overthrow British policy for Palestine. Ben Gurion thought the aims were compatible: "We must fight Hitler as though there were no White Paper, and fight the White Paper as though there were no Hitler." He was right, provided the British would allow the Jews to fight the war as a coherent unit, which could later be used to determine events in Palestine. The British authorities, military, diplomatic, and colonial, were hostile to the idea for this very reason. Indeed, after the Alamein victory late in 1942 removed the German threat from the Middle East, British HQ there looked with suspicion on any Jewish military activity. But the Jews had one powerful defender: Churchill. He favored Weizmann's proposal to form a Jewish striking-force from existing small-scale Jewish units. The British army repeatedly blocked the scheme, but Churchill eventually got his way. "I like the idea," he minuted to the Secretary of State for War, July 12, 1944, "of the Jews trying to get at the murderers of their fellow countrymen in Central Europe. It is with the Germans that they have their quarrel. . . . I cannot conceive why this martyred race scattered about the world and suffering as no other race has done at this juncture should be denied the satisfaction of having a flag." Two months later, the Jewish Brigade, 25,000 strong, was formed. Without Churchill, the Jews would never have got it, and the experience of working together at this formation level was critical to the Israeli success four years later.

All the same, the British had no intention of reversing their Palestine policy. Overthrowing Hitler impoverished them and made their Middle Eastern oilfields more, not less important; they had no intention of permitting a level of Jewish immigration which would turn the Arab world implacably hostile. Nor were they ready to move out of Palestine until they could do so in a manner which retained their Arab friendships. So they prevented illegal Jewish immigrants from landing, and if they got through efforts were made to capture and deport them. In November 1940, the *Patria*, about to set sail for Mauritius with 1,700 deportees on board, was sabotaged by the Haganah. It sank in Haifa Bay and 250 refugees were drowned. In February 1942 the *Struma*, a refugee ship from Romania, was refused landing permission by Britain, turned back by the Turks, and sank in the Black Sea, drowning 770.

These tragic episodes did not shake Britain's resolve to maintain her immigration limits throughout the war and even after, when there were 250,000 Jews in DP camps. Nor did the accession to power in 1945 of the British Labour Party, theoretically pro-Zionist, make any difference. The new Foreign Secretary, Ernest Bevin, bowed to the arguments of the diplomats and generals. At that time, Britain still ruled a quarter of the earth's surface. She had 100,000 men in Palestine, where the Jews numbered only 600,000. There was no material reason why the Zionists should get their way. Yet eighteen months later Bevin threw in his hand. As Evelyn Waugh, in his book on Jerusalem, bitterly observed of British conduct: "We surrendered our mandate to rule the Holy Land for low motives: cowardice, sloth, and parsimony. The vision of Allenby marching on foot where the Kaiser had arrogantly ridden, is overlaid now by the sorry spectacle of large, well-found force, barely scratched in battle, decamping before a little gang of gunmen." How did this happen?

The answer lies in yet another Jewish contribution to the shape of the modern world: the scientific use of terror to break the will of liberal rulers. It was to become commonplace over the next forty years, but in 1945 it was new. It might be called a by-product of the Holocaust, for no lesser phenomenon could have driven even desperate Jews to use it. Its most accomplished practitioner was Menachem Begin, former chairman of Betar, the Polish youth movement. He was a man in whom the bitterness generated by the Holocaust had become incarnate. Jews formed 70 percent of his hometown, Brest-Litovsk. There had been over 30,000 of them in 1939. By 1944 only ten were left alive. Most of Begin's family were murdered. The Jews were forbidden even to bury their dead. That was how his father died, shot on the spot digging a grave for a friend in the Jewish cemetery. But Begin was a born survivor, and a revenger. Arrested in Lithuania, he was one of the very few men to survive, unbroken, an interrogation by Stalin's NKVD. At the end of it, his interrogator said with fury: "I never want to see you again." Begin commented later: "It was my faith against his faith. I had something to fight for, even in the interrogation room." Begin was sent to a Soviet slave-camp in the Arctic Circle near the Barents Sea, building the Kotlas-Varkuta railway. He survived that too, benefited from an amnesty for Poles, walked through Central Asia and made his way to Jerusalem as a private in the Polish army. In December 1943 he took over control of the Revisionists' military arm, the Irgun. Two months later he declared war on the British administration.

Among the Jews there were three schools of thought about the British. Weizmann still believed in British good faith. Ben Gurion, though skeptical, wanted to win the war first. Even after it he drew an absolute distinction between resistance and terrorism, and this was reflected in Haganah policy. On the other hand there was an extremist breakaway from the Irgun, known as the Stern Gang after its leader Avraham Stern. He disobeyed Jabotinsky's instructions for a ceasefire with the British on the outbreak of war, and was killed in February 1942. But his colleagues, led by Yizhak Shamir and Nathan Yellin-Mor, carried on an unrestricted campaign against Britain. Begin took a third course. He thought the Haganah too passive, the Stern Gang crude, vicious, and unintelligent. He saw the enemy not as Britain but the British administration in Palestine. He wanted to humiliate it; make it unworkable, expensive, ineffective. He had 600 active agents. He rejected assassination but he blew up CID offices, the immigration building, income-tax centers, and similar targets.

Relations between the three groups of Jewish activists were always tense and often venomous. This had grave political consequences later. On November 6, 1944, the Stern Gang murdered Lord Moyne, the British Minister of Middle East Affairs. Haganah, appalled and infuriated, launched what was called the Saison against both Sternists and Irgun. It captured some of them and held them in underground prisons. Worse, it handed over to the British CID the names of 700 persons and institutions. At least 300 and possibly as many as 1,000 were arrested as a result of information supplied by the Zionist establishment. Begin, who got away, accused Haganah of torture too, and issued a defiant statement: "We shall repay you, Cain." But he was too shrewd to get into a war with Haganah. It was during these months, when he was fighting both the British and his fellow Jews, that he created an underground force almost impervious to attack. He believed Haganah would have to join him to get rid of Britain. He was proved right. On October 1, 1945, Ben Gurion, without consulting Weizmann, sent a coded cable to Moshe Sneh, the Haganah commander, ordering him to begin operations against the British forces. A united Jewish Resistance Movement was formed. It began its attacks on the night of October 31, blowing up railways.

Even so, disagreements on targets remained. The Haganah would not employ terror in any form. It would employ force only in what could plausibly be called a military operation. Begin always rejected murder, such as the cold-blooded killing by the Sternists of six British paratroopers in their beds on April 26, 1946. He repudiated, then and later, the label "terrorist." But he was willing to take moral risks, as well as physical ones. How could the Promised Land have been secured in the first place without Joshua? And was not the Book of Joshua a disturbing record of how far the Israelites were prepared to go to conquer the land which was theirs by divine command?

Begin was a leading figure in two episodes which were instrumental in inducing Britain to quit. On June 29, 1946, the British made a dawn swoop on the Jewish Agency. Some 2,718 Jews were arrested. The object was to produce a more moderate Jewish leadership. It failed. Indeed, since Irgun was untouched, it strengthened Begin's hand. He got Haganah to agree to blow up the King David Hotel, where part of the British administration was housed. The agreed

object was to humiliate, not to kill. But the risk of mass murder was enormous. Weizmann got to hear of the plot and
threatened to resign and tell the world why. Haganah told
Begin to call it off but he refused. At lunchtime on July 22,
1946, six minutes ahead of schedule, about 700 pounds of
high explosive demolished one wing of the hotel, killing
twenty-eight British, forty-one Arabs, and seventeen Jews,
plus five other people. A sixteen-year-old schoolgirl gave a
warning phone call as part of the plan. There is a conflict of
evidence over what happened next. Begin always insisted
that adequate warning was given and blamed the British
authorities for the deaths. He mourned the Jewish casualties
alone. But, in such acts of terror, those who plant the explo-
sives must be held responsible for any deaths. That was the
view taken by the Jewish establishment. The Haganah commander Moshe Sneh was forced to resign. The Resistance
Movement broke up into its component parts. Nevertheless
the outrage, combined with others, achieved its effect. The
British government proposed a tripartite division of the
country. Both Jews and Arabs rejected the plan. Accordingly,
on February 14, 1947, Bevin announced that he was handing over the whole Palestine problem to the United Nations.

That did not necessarily mean a rapid British withdrawal,
however. So the terror campaign continued. A further
episode, for which Begin was again responsible, proved decisive. He was opposed to Sternist-type assassinations but he
insisted on Irgun's moral right to punish members of
the British armed forces in the same way as Britain punished
Irgun members. The British hanged and flogged. Irgun

would do the same. In April 1947 three Irgun men were put on trial for an attack on the Acre prison-fortress, which freed 251 prisoners. Begin threatened retaliation if the three were convicted and hanged. They were, on July 29. A few hours later two British sergeants, Clifford Martin and Mervyn Paice, who had been captured for this purpose, were hanged on Begin's instructions by Irgun's operations chief, Gidi Paglin. He also mined their bodies. This gruesome murder of Martin and Paice, who had committed no crime, horrified many Jews. The Jewish Agency called it "the dastardly murder of two innocent men by a set of criminals." (It was even worse than it seemed at the time, for it emerged thirty-five years later that Martin had a Jewish mother.) It caused unrestrained fury in Britain. A synagogue was burned down in Derby. There were anti-Jewish riots in London, Liverpool, Glasgow, and Manchester—the first in England since the thirteenth century. These in turn produced critical changes in British policy. The British had assumed that any partition would have to be supervised and enforced by them; otherwise the armies of the Arab states would simply move in and exterminate the Jews. Now they decided to get out as quickly as possible and leave Arabs and Jews to it. Thus Begin's policy succeeded, but it involved appalling risks.

The extent of the risks depended to some extent on the two superpowers, America and Russia. In both cases the Zionists benefited from what might be called luck or divine providence, according to taste. The first was the death of Roosevelt on April 12, 1945. In his last weeks he had turned anti-Zionist, following a meeting with King Ibn Saud after the Yalta Conference. The pro-Zionist presidential assistant, David Niles, later asserted: "There are serious doubts in my mind that Israel would have come into being if Roosevelt had lived." F.D.R.'s successor, Harry S. Truman, had a much more straightforward commitment to Zionism, part emotional, part calculating. He felt sorry for Jewish refugees. He saw the Jews in Palestine as underdogs. He was also much less sure of the Jewish vote than of Jewish organizations in swing-states such as New York, Pennsylvania, and Illinois. Once the British renounced their mandate, Truman pushed for the creation of a Jewish state. In May 1947 the Palestine problem came before the U.N. A special committee was asked to submit a plan. It produced two. A minority recommended a federated binational state. The majority produced a new partition plan: there would be Jewish and Arab states, plus an international zone in Jerusalem. On November 29, 1947, thanks to Truman's vigorous backing, it was endorsed by the General Assembly, thirty-three votes to thirteen, with ten abstentions.

The Soviet Union and Arab states, followed by the international left in general, later came to believe that the creation of Israel was the work of a capitalist-imperialist conspiracy. But the facts show the reverse. Neither the American State Department nor the British Foreign Office wanted a Jewish state. They foresaw disaster for the West in the area if one were created. The British War Office was equally strong in opposition. So was the U.S. Defense Department. Its Secretary, James Forrestal, bitterly denounced the Jewish lobby: "No group in this country should be permitted to influence our policy to the point where it could endanger our national security." The British and American oil companies were even more vehement in opposing the new state. Speaking for the oil interests, Max Thornburg, of Cal-Tex, said that Truman had "extinguished the moral prestige of America" and destroyed "Arab faith in her ideals." It is impossible to point to any powerful economic interest, in either Britain or in the United States, which pushed for the creation of Israel. In both countries, the overwhelming majority of her friends were on the left.

Indeed, if there was a conspiracy to create Israel, then the Soviet Union was a prominent member of it. During the war, for tactical reasons, Stalin suspended some aspects of his anti-Semitic policies. He even created a Jewish Anti-Fascist Committee. From 1944, for a brief period, he adopted a pro-Zionist posture in foreign policy (though not in Russia itself). His reason seems to have been that the creation of Israel, which he was advised would be a socialist state, would accelerate the decline of British influence in the Middle East. When Palestine first came before the United Nations in May 1947, Andrei Gromyko, the Soviet Deputy Foreign Minister, caused surprise by announcing that his government supported the creation of a Jewish state, and by voting accordingly. On October 13, Semyon Tsarapkin, head of the Soviet delegation to the U.N., offered members of the Jewish Agency the toast, "To the future Jewish state," before voting for the partition plan. At the decisive General Assembly vote on November 29 the entire Soviet bloc voted in the Israeli interest, and thereafter the Soviet and American delegations worked closely together on the timetable of

British withdrawal. Nor was this all. When Israel declared its independence on May 14, 1948, and president Truman immediately accorded it *de facto* recognition, Stalin went one better and, less than three days later, gave it recognition *de jure*. Perhaps most significant of all was the decision of the Czech government, on Stalin's instructions, to sell the new state arms. An entire airfield was assigned to the task of air-lifting weapons to Tel Aviv.

Timing was absolutely crucial to Israel's birth and survival. Stalin had the Russian-Jewish actor Solomon Mikhoels murdered in January 1948, and this seems to have marked the beginning of an intensely anti-Semitic phase in his policy. The switch to anti-Zionism abroad took longer to develop but it came decisively in the autumn of 1948. By this time, however, Israel was securely in existence. American policy was also changing, as the growing pressures of the Cold War dissolved her mood of postwar idealism and forced Truman to listen more attentively to Pentagon and State Department advice. If British evacuation had been postponed another year, the United States would have been far less anxious to see Israel created and Russia would almost certainly have been hostile. Hence the effect of the terror campaign on British policy was perhaps decisive to the entire enterprise. Israel slipped into existence through a fortuitous window in history which briefly opened for a few months in 1947–48. That too was luck; or providence.

However, if Begin's ruthlessness was responsible for the early British withdrawal, it was Ben Gurion who brought the state into being. He had to take a series of decisions, each of which could have produced catastrophe for the Jewish people of Palestine. Once the U.N. partition vote was taken the Arabs were bent on destroying the Jewish settlements and began to attack them immediately. Azzam Pasha, secretary-general of the Arab League, said on the radio: "This will be a war of extermination and a momentous massacre." The Jewish commanders were confident but their resources were small. By the end of 1947 the Haganah had 17,600 rifles, 2,700 stern-guns, about 1,000 machine guns, and between 20,000 and 43,000 men in various stages of training. It had virtually no armor, heavy guns, or aircraft. The Arabs had collected a Liberation Army of considerable size but with a divided leadership. They also had the regular forces of the Arab states: 10,000 Egyptians, 7,000 Syrians, 3,000 Iraqis, 3,000 Lebanese, plus the 4,500-strong Arab Legion of Transjordan, a formidable force with British officers. By March 1948 over 1,200 Jews had been killed, half of them civilians, in Arab attacks. The Czech arms were beginning to arrive and were deployed over the next month. The British mandate was not due to end until May 15. But early in April Ben Gurion made what was probably the most difficult decision in his life. He ordered the Haganah on to the offensive to link up with the various Jewish enclaves and to consolidate as much as possible of the territory allotted to Israel under the U.N. plan. The gamble came off almost completely. The Jews occupied Haifa. They opened up the route to Tiberias and the eastern Galilee. They took Safed, Jaffa, and Acre. They established the core of the state of Israel and in effect won the war before it started.

Ben Gurion read out the Scroll of Independence on Friday May 14, in the Tel Aviv museum. "By virtue of our national and intrinsic right," he said, "and on the strength of the resolution of the United Nations General Assembly, we hereby declare the establishment of a Jewish state in Palestine, which shall be known as the State of Israel." A provisional government was formed immediately. Egyptian air raids began that night. The next day, simultaneously, the last British left and the Arab armies invaded. They made little difference, except in one respect. King Abdullah's Arab League took the Old City of Jerusalem for him, the Jews surrendering it on May 28. This meant that Jewish settlements east of the Holy City had to be evacuated. Otherwise the Israelis made further gains.

A month's truce was arranged on June 11. During it the Arab states heavily reinforced their armies. But the Israelis secured great quantities of heavy equipment, not only from the Czechs but from the French too, who provided it chiefly to anger the British. When the fighting resumed on July 9, it quickly became apparent that the Israelis were in control. They took Lydda, Ramleh, and Nazareth and occupied large areas of territory beyond the partition frontiers. The Arabs agreed to a second truce within ten days. But there were occasional outbreaks of violence, and in mid-October the Israelis launched an offensive to open the road to the Negev settlements. It ended in the capture of Beersheba. By the close of the year the Israeli army was 100,000 strong, and properly equipped. It had established a military paramountcy in the area it has never since lost. Armistice talks were opened in Rhodes on January 12, 1949, and were signed with Egypt (February 14), Lebanon (March 23), Transjordan (April 3) and Syria (July 20). Iraq made no agreement at all, and the five Arab states remained in a formal state of war with Israel.

The events of 1947–48, which established Israel, also created the Arab-Israeli problem, which endures to this day. It has two main aspects, refugees and frontiers, best considered separately. According to U.N. figures, 656,000 Arab inhabitants of mandatory Palestine fled from Israeli-held territory: 280,000 to the West Bank of the Jordan, 70,000 to Transjordan, 100,000 to Lebanon, 4,000 to Iraq, 75,000 to Syria, 7,000 to Egypt, and 190,000 to the Gaza Strip (the Israelis put the total figure rather lower, 550,000–600,000). They left for four reasons: to avoid being killed in the fighting, because the administration had broken down, because they were ordered to or misled or panicked by Arab radio broadcasts, and because they were stampeded by an Irgun-Stern Gang massacre at the village of Deir Yassin on April 9, 1948.

The last merits scrutiny because it is relevant to the moral credentials of the Israeli state. From 1920 until this point, the Jews had refrained from terrorist attacks on Arab settlements, though the innumerable Arab ones had sometimes provoked heavy-handed reprisals. When the fighting began in the winter of 1947–48, Deir Yassin, an Arab quarrying village of less than 1,000 people, made a non-aggression pact with the nearby Jerusalem suburb of Givat Shaul. But two Jewish settlements nearby were overrun and destroyed, and the Jewish desire for revenge was strong. The Stern Gang proposed to destroy Deir Yassin to teach the Arabs a lesson. A senior Irgun officer, Yehuda Lapidot, testified: "The clear aim was to break Arab morale and raise the morale of the Jewish community in Jerusalem, which had been hit hard time after time, especially recently by the desecration of Jewish bodies which fell into Arab hands." Begin agreed to the operation but said a loudspeaker van must be used to give the villagers a chance to surrender without bloodshed. The local Haganah commander also gave his reluctant approval, but laid down further conditions. There were eighty Irgun and forty Sternists in the raid. The loudspeaker van fell into a ditch and was never used. The Arabs chose to fight and were actually stronger and better armed. The Irgun-Sternists had to send for a regular platoon with a heavy machine-gun and two-inch mortar, and it was these which ended Arab resistance.

It was at this point that the raiding force moved into the village and went out of control. A Haganah spy who was with them described what followed as "a disorganized massacre." The raiders took twenty-three men to the quarry and shot them. An Arab eye-witness said ninety-three others were killed in the village, but other accounts put the figure of those killed as high as 250. Begin, before he knew the details of the battle, sent out an order of the day in the spirit of the Book of Joshua: "Accept my congratulations on this splendid act of conquest. . . . As at Deir Yassin, so everywhere we will attack and smite the enemy. God, God, thou has chosen us for conquest." News of this atrocity, in exaggerated form, spread quickly and undoubtedly persuaded many Arabs to flee over the next two months. There is no evidence that it was designed to have this effect. But in conjunction with the other factors it reduced the Arab population of the new state to a mere 160,000. That was very convenient.

On the other hand, there were the Jews encouraged or forced to flee from Arab states where, in some cases, Jewish communities had existed for 2,500 years. In 1945 there were over 500,000 Jews living in the Arab world. Between the outbreak of the war on May 15, 1948, and the end of 1967, the vast majority had to take refuge in Israel: 252,642 from Morocco, 13,118 from Algeria, 46,255 from Tunisia, 34,265 from Libya, 37,867 from Egypt, 4,000 from Lebanon, 4,500 from Syria, 3,912 from Aden, 124,647 from Iraq, and 46,447 from the Yemen. With a total of 567,654 Jewish refugees from Arab countries were thus not substantially smaller in number than Arab refugees from Israel. The difference in their reception and treatment was entirely a matter of policy. The Israeli government systematically resettled all its refugees as part of its national-home policy. The Arab governments, with the assistance of the U.N., kept the Arab refugees in camps, pending a reconquest of Palestine which never came. Hence, as a result of natural increase, there were more Arab refugees in the late 1980s than there had been forty years before.

This contrasting attitude toward refugees itself sprang from a fundamentally different approach towards negotiations. The Jews had been for two millennia an oppressed minority who had never possessed the option of force. They had therefore been habitually obliged to negotiate, often for bare existence, and nearly always from a position of great weakness. Over the centuries they had developed not merely negotiating skills but a philosophy of negotiation. They would negotiate against impossible odds, and they had learned to accept a negotiated status, however lowly and underprivileged, knowing that it could later be improved by further negotiations and their own efforts. The paramountcy of settlement, as opposed to force, was built into their very bones. That was one reason they found it so difficult, even when the evidence became overwhelming, to take in the magnitude of Hitler's evil: it was hard for them to comprehend a man who wanted no settlement at all with them, just their lives.

The Arabs, by contrast, were a conquering race whose sacred writings both inspired and reflected a maximalist position toward other peoples, the despised *dhimmi*. The very concept of negotiation toward a final settlement was to them a betrayal of principle. A truce, an armistice might be necessary and was acceptable because it preserved the option of force for use later. A treaty, on the other hand, appeared to them a kind of surrender. That was why they did not want the refugees resettled because it meant the final disposal of a moral asset. As Cairo Radio put it: "The refugees are the cornerstone in the Arab struggle against Israel. The refugees are the armaments of the Arab and Arab nationalism." Hence they rejected the 1950 U.N. plan for resettlement without discussion. Over the subsequent quarter century they refused even to receive repeated Israeli proposals for compensation. The result was disastrous for the refugees themselves and their progeny. It was a source of instability for the Arab states also. It came near to destroying Jordan in the 1960s. It did destroy the finely balanced structure of Lebanon in the 1970s and 1980s.

The different approach to negotiating played a still more important part in determining Israel's frontiers. For Jews there were three possible ways of looking at their recreated country: as a national home, as the Promised Land, and as the Zionist state. The first can be quickly disposed of. If all the Jews wanted was a place where they could be safe, it might be anywhere: Argentina, Uganda, Madagascar, for instance, were all proposed at one time or another. But it quickly became clear that few Jews were interested in such schemes. The only one with the slightest practical appeal was the El Arish proposal, precisely because it was near Palestine.

So we move on to the second notion: the Promised Land. In one way or another, this had a theoretical appeal to all Jews, secular and religious, except to pious Jews who insisted that any return to Zion must be part of a messianic event, and assimilated Jews who had no intention of returning anywhere. But what exactly was this land? As we have already noted, when God gave it to Abraham he did not define it with any precision. Was it then to consist of the territories the Israelites had actually occupied? If so, at what period? There had in fact been two commonwealths as well as two temples, the Davidic and the Hasmonean. Some Zionists saw (and see) the state as the Third Commonwealth. But to which was it the successor-state? David's kingdom (but not Solomon's) had included Syria. The Hasmoneans had also ruled at one time over a vast territory. Both ancient commonwealths had been mini-empires at their greatest extent, and had included subject people who had been only semi-Jewish or not Jewish at all. They could scarcely serve as models for a Zionist state whose primary purpose was to provide a national home for Jews. On the other hand there was a strong emotional belief in the Jews' right to claim those parts of Palestine where they had been predominant in antiquity. This found expression in the plan put forward by the Zionists to the Paris Peace Conference in 1919. It gave the Jews the whole coast from Rafah to Sayda and both banks of the Jordan, the eastern frontier running just west of the Damascus-Amman-Hijaz railway. The plan, as expected, was turned down, but its claims lingered on in the program of Jabotinsky's Revisionists.

We turn then to the Zionist state as such, the territory which in practice Jews could acquire, settle, develop, and defend. This empirical approach was the one the main Zionist bodies adopted and which became in practice the policy of the state itself. It was a sensible approach because it offered the widest possible scope to Jewish negotiating skills. It allowed the Jewish leaders to say that they would settle for any frontiers which included the areas occupied by Jews and which were themselves coherent and defensible. Hence at every stage, during the mandate and after, the Jews were flexible and willing to accept any reasonable partition proposal put to them. In July 1937 the Peel Commission Partition Plan offered them only Galilee from Metulla to Afula, and the coastal strip from a point twenty miles north of Gaza up to Acre, the later being broken by a corridor to a British-held enclave round Jerusalem. The Jews were reluctant but they accepted it. The Arabs, who would have been given three-quarters of Palestine, turned it down without discussion.

City of Stone

O N MONDAY, September 4, 1995—the ninth day of the month of Elul in the year A.H. 5755 (according to the Jewish calendar)—the Israeli prime minister Yitzhak Rabin officially opened the celebrations marking the 3,000th anniversary of the establishment of Jerusalem as capital of the Kingdom of Israel. Lasting fifteen months, the festivities focused on the founder of the House of David, who conquered the Jebusite city of Jerusalem and made it the temporal and spiritual capital of his people. "King David's many-faceted personality—musician, warrior, statesman, poet, singer, and dancer, as well as king and lover—," stated the official provide the inspiration for an entire

MERON BENVENISTI *is the former deputy mayor of Jerusalem and author of numerous volumes on Israel, including* City of Stone: The Hidden History of Jerusalem. *The book, from which this piece is taken, is a compelling insider look at the political, architectural, social, cultural, and religious history of the holy city.*

year of cultural events." Prime Minister Rabin stood on
the stage erected for the occasion at the recently opened
archeological park in "David's City" and declared:
"Jerusalem is the celebration of the glory of the Jewish people from the day it was created in the Image of God. She is
its heart and the apple of its eye; and our festivities here
today are only meant to once again elevate Jerusalem
'above our chiefest joy,' as was the custom of our fathers
and forefathers."

The information sheets distributed to the invited
guests stated: "No other people designated Jerusalem as
its capital in such an absolute and binding manner—
Jerusalem is the concrete historical expression of the Jewish religion and its heritage on the one hand and of the
independence and sovereignty of the Jewish people on the
other. Jerusalem's identity as a spiritual and national symbol at one and the same time has forged the unique and
eternal bond between this city and the Jewish people, a
bond that has no parallel in the annals of the nations.
Israel's rule over the united city has allowed her to bloom
and prosper, and despite the problems between the communities within her, she has not enjoyed such centrality
and importance since her days as the capital of the Kingdom of Israel."

The ceremony that launched the events marking the
"3,000 Years of Jerusalem, City of David" took place in the
presence of some 200 invited guests, all of them members of
the Jewish establishment from Israel and abroad. For "security reasons" a solid wall of security personnel barred entry

to the residents of the Arab neighborhood in which the park is situated. After all, the site of the City of David is located in the heart of Silwan, an Arab neighborhood with a population of 30,000. Ironically, the houses nearest to the site where the opening ceremonies took place have recently been the scene of sporadic violent confrontations between Jews and Arabs, and in 1991–92 a group of Jewish fanatics, assisted by the police, took over several Arab buildings and forcibly ejected their inhabitants.

One Arab resident of Silwan, who had Jewish settlers forced upon him as neighbors, watched the proceedings in bewilderment. He had no idea of the nature of the sudden visit by the prime minister and the mayor. An Israeli journalist who was recording the reactions of the Arab population to the "Jerusalem 3,000" celebrations explained the meaning of the ceremony to him. The Arab, an employee of an East Jerusalem research institute, pulled out a Palestinian history book and read the following passages aloud:

> The Philistines, who came from Crete and Asia
> Minor, merged with the Canaanites, who originat-
> ed from the Arabian peninsula, and gave the land
> its name, Falastin. The Jebusites, a Canaanite peo-
> ple, are the ancestors of the Palestinians. Abraham
> was neither a Jew nor a Christian, but a "believer in
> one God." The twelve sons of Jacob fled to Egypt,
> interbred with the Egyptians there and became
> numerous. Moses and his followers wandered in
> the desert; they were not endowed with any scien-
> tific or artistic talents and made no cultural

achievements whatsoever. Hence they were influenced by the Canaanites and imitated their religious beliefs. . . .

Warfare between the Israelites and the Philistines (Palestinians) continued for hundreds of years, and the Bible confirms that the land's inhabitants, who were of Arabian origin, succeeded in zealously maintaining their independence and culture. Jerusalem has been the capital of our Palestinian Arab homeland ever since it was built by our ancestors, the Jebusites and the Arab Canaanites, in the heart of Falastin. The Arab presence in Jerusalem was never interrupted, in contrast to the Jewish presence, which disappeared. The Arabs tenaciously remained under the Babylonians, the Persians, the Greeks, the Romans, and the Byzantines. There has been Arab rule in Jerusalem and in Palestine ever since the seventh century (except for the Crusader period). The Arab-Muslim tradition was preserved, and flourished under the Muslim Arab dynasties—the Amayyads, the Abassids, the Fatamids, the Seljuks, the Mamluks, the Ottomans . . . until the British conquest of 1917.

"Even your prophets say that you and your king, David, were foreign occupiers," commented the Arab. "This is what the prophet Ezekiel says: "'Thus saith the Lord God to Jerusalem: Thy birth and thy nativity is of the land of Canaan; thy father was an Amorite and thy mother a Hittite'" (Ezek. 16:3).

Had circumstances been reserved and had Jerusalem been under Palestinian sovereignty, the authorities would have been organizing a "Jebusite Festival" to mark Jerusalem's 5,000th anniversary. During this festival, they would have depicted their historical myths in speech and music, exactly as the Israelis did with their celebration of 3,000 years of the City of David. Who is right? The question is superfluous. The chronicles of Jerusalem are a gigantic quarry from which each side has mined stones for the construction of its myths—and for throwing at each other. . . .

"The problem of Jerusalem"—demanding a political, religious, and communal solution secured in international agreements—arose at the close of the First World War, when, following centuries of Ottoman sovereignty, the city was occupied by Great Britain. This was not the first time in modern history that Jerusalem had been the object of international contention. A hundred years before, European states had clashed with one another over the holy places; however, those international disputes were not related to the question of sovereignty over Jerusalem, but arose from religious disputes that served as a pretext for increasing the spheres of influence of the international powers outside the city. Communal strife, too, was dormant until the British occupation. The various communities residing in Jerusalem differed in religious identity only. The Jewish community, which constituted the majority of the city's population by the mid-nineteenth century, uncomplainingly accepted the favored status accorded the Muslim Arabs and contented itself with religious autonomy. Muslim ascendancy was conspicuous in all areas of life in Jerusalem.

The disintegration of the Ottoman Empire exacerbated the problems. Immediately preceding and following the British occupation, the European powers sought to solve the problem of sovereignty by proposing the imposition of international rule over Jerusalem. The Sykes-Picot agreement of 1916 specified that, following the division of the Ottoman Empire, the region between Dan and Beersheba (biblical Palestine) would be placed under "international administration," but this treaty was never implemented. With the conclusion of the war and the dismemberment of the Ottoman Empire, Great Britain received a League of Nations Mandate granting it rule over Palestine, including Jerusalem. This was the solution to the sovereignty problem. The European powers and other interested parties attempted to resolve the issue of the holy places as well. Long and tortuous negotiations were conducted over an international agreement regarding the holy places, which, if signed, would have imposed certain restrictions on British sovereignty in Jerusalem. The negotiations collapsed, however, and in late 1924 it was decided that the British administration would also be responsible for the holy places, without the involvement of outside elements. This was the solution to the religious problem. The problem of Jerusalem ceased, for the time being, to be an object of international concern. The city reverted to being simply the capital of a political entity under British sovereign rule.

It was the ongoing intercommunal conflict that returned the problem of Jerusalem to the international arena. The Jewish and Arab (Muslim and Christian) communities embarked upon a prolonged, tangled, and bloody struggle for national hegemony in Palestine. Throughout the years of the British Mandate, Jerusalem was the principal point of contention and main arena in this struggle. Conflicting interests came to light in all areas of the city's life: municipal administration, economics, the holy places, national symbols, transportation, commerce, construction, and land ownership. The principal political struggle focused on municipal government. From the time of the municipality's inception during the Turkish period, a Muslim Arab had always served as mayor, and the Arabs demanded the continuation of this practice. However, Jews constituted a majority of the city's population, and they demanded the democratic election of the mayor and members of the city council. The British searched for a compromise solution, but in the end they decided in favor of continuing the status quo.

No one was satisfied with this arrangement. The Jews developed their own elaborate system of municipal and communal services, but the existence of separate communal organizations only increased the polarization and tension. The conflict was reflected in the economic and commercial spheres as well—essentially in every aspect of the city's life.

Intercommunal strife in Palestine peaked in the mid-thirties. With the outbreak of the Arab Revolt in 1936, all hope for reconciliation and coexistence evaporated. The British government drew the logical conclusion and for the first time proposed partitioning the country into Jewish and Arab states, in keeping with the recommendations of the Peel Commission (1936). According to this plan, Jerusalem was to remain united and to come under a permanent British Mandate. Elections would be conducted based on ethnically determined electoral districts and voters' lists. In 1938 another commission (the Woodhead Commission) was appointed to implement the partition plan.

Plans to implement partition were suspended in the atmosphere of increasing tension leading up to the Second World War. In May 1939, a White Paper was issued in which the British declared their intention to establish a unified Palestinian state at the end of ten years. In this state a two-thirds Arab majority would be guaranteed by means of restrictions on Jewish immigration, and Jerusalem would have no special status apart from the guaranteed freedom of access to its holy places. Understandably, the Jews rejected the White Paper of 1939; but so did the Arabs.

Meanwhile, the Second World War broke out, and as a result the problem of Jerusalem was temporarily marginalized, even though intercommunal tensions persisted. During the last days of the war and especially in 1946–47, Jerusalem was the scene of violent clashes between Jewish underground organizations and British authorities, which reached a climax with the July 1946 bombing of the British governmental offices in the King David Hotel.

In 1947, the Palestine problem again returned to the international stage. As in 1917, the questions requiring resolution concerned sovereignty, the holy places, and municipal administration. On November 29, 1947, the United Nations General Assembly approved a proposal for the partition of Palestine into two states, Jewish and Arab. The Jerusalem district would become a *corpus separatum*, under U.N. Trusteeship. A representative of the United Nations was to be designated as responsible for the holy places, whereas municipal administration would be divided between the Jews and Arabs. However, the internationalization of Jerusalem was never accomplished. In the wake of the U.N. decision, Jews and Arabs embarked upon a war that rapidly expanded into an armed conflict between the Arab countries and the nascent State of Israel.

In the weeks following the proclamation of the state on May 14, 1948, the Israeli government had no time for political decisions that did not relate directly to the most important problem of the hour: the conduct of the war. No steps were taken to define the legal status of those portions of Jerusalem that fell to the Israeli Defense Forces (IDF). The government refrained from political actions liable to provoke the various countries with interests in Jerusalem, even at the price of lack of clarity regarding the form of civilian government in the city.

At that time David Ben-Gurion defined the question of who would govern Jerusalem as "a question of military ability." This was not a decree based on principles, but an interim decision of a practical nature. At that time Israel had not yet abandoned the effort to conquer the entire city. Only in July 1948, when the second cease-fire came into effect, did the Jewish community's leaders begin a process of adjustment to the bitter reality that the Old City would remain outside Israeli jurisdiction. The sole official step taken by the government at that time in Jerusalem was the application of Israeli law to those portions of the city under Israeli control, which was not perceived as an attempt to annex the area to the State of Israel, but as a way to create a "controlled territory" subject to military administration. This step by the government was acceptable to the international community, whose representatives in Jerusalem began referring to the Israeli military governor as "the military governor of Israeli-occupied Jerusalem."

Throughout the summer of 1948 the Israeli government continued to vacillate on the question of Jerusalem. There were three options to choose from: internationalization of the entire city, as demanded by the partition resolution of 1947; partition of the city between Israel and Transjordan, along the military lines established in the aftermath of the war; and occupation of the remainder of the city.

In late August 1948, the Israeli cabinet convened to deliberate the question and decided—by a majority of one (five to four)—that given the choice between the partition and the internationalization of the city, the latter option was preferable, electing to relinquish its sovereignty over Jerusalem entirely rather than divide the city. This decision aroused the ire of the Jewish residents of Jerusalem. Their spokesperson, the military governor Dov Joseph, stated, "It is hard for me to understand the brand of political thinking that says that instead of the Arabs having something it is better that neither they nor we have anything."

David Ben-Gurion laid the military option before the cabinet. He proposed launching a campaign beginning with "storming Latrun and continuing from there north to Ramallah and to Jericho and the Jordan, so as to liberate the Hebron district and the whole area between Latrun and Ramallah and all the way to Jericho and the Dead Sea." He was careful not to mention the Old City explicitly. Foreign Minister Moshe Sharett expressed the opposite opinion: "I am certain that the lesser of the evils is part of Jerusalem for the Arabs—if absolutely essential—rather than international rule over all of Jerusalem."

The final debate, held on September 26, 1948, concluded with two historic votes. Ben-Gurion's proposal regarding a renewed military campaign was rejected by a seven to five majority; and the cabinet decided, with a seven to four majority and two abstentions, that "should the partition [of Jerusalem] be necessary, the [Israeli] delegation to the United Nations would agree."

These decisions defined Israel's policy regarding

Jerusalem: first, it must accept the partition of the city as a fact and strive for stabilization of the political-military status quo, while maintaining dialogue with the Transjordanians and opposition to the internationalization of the city; second, the military status quo must not be altered by force via preemptive military action, even with a good chance of success.

Faithful to these decisions, Ben-Gurion initiated the renewal of secret contacts with Transjordan, which went on intensively throughout November and December of 1948. Early in 1949, Israeli army officers proposed a plan to capture Judea and Samaria in a lightning attack lasting three days; however, the prime minister rejected it. Even so, Israel still refrained from publicly announcing its official stance on the future of Jerusalem. In accordance with a motto coined by Ben-Gurion, "Declaration—no; deeds—yes," Israel embarked upon a series of vigorous steps to consolidate its rule and its legal status in the city and to make it the capital of the state in practice. In February 1949, military administration of Jerusalem was abolished, and a government decision stated the intent "to implement [in Jerusalem] all the governing arrangements customary elsewhere in the State of Israel." In December 1949, the Knesset began holding its sessions in Jerusalem, and on the sixteenth of that month Ben-Gurion moved his office to the city, designating the beginning of January 1950 as the date when the remaining governmental offices, with the exception of the Foreign Ministry, the Ministry of Defense, and the National Police Headquarters, must make the move. The final step in Israel's effort to establish political faits accomplis in Jerusalem was taken on July 12, 1953, when the spokesperson for the Foreign Ministry announced that "in accordance with the government's decision and following the completion of arrangements for the accommodation of the ministry and its employees, the Foreign Ministry will today move to Jerusalem." The foreign diplomatic missions in Israel reacted lukewarmly to this latest step by the government. Some boycotted the ministry's Jerusalem offices, but only briefly, and ever since 1954, all foreign diplomats have presented their credentials to the president of Israel at his Jerusalem residence and have paid a visit to the Foreign Ministry.

By the time of the 1967 war, there were twenty-three diplomatic missions in Jerusalem. Most missions, however, including all of the major embassies, did not relocate from Tel Aviv. In any case, the prolonged process of creating political "facts" and turning Jerusalem into the capital of the state continued for some six years, concluding in 1954.

The Arab Legion—Transjordan's British-commanded army—entered the battle for Jerusalem on May 18, 1948, thereby preventing the complete collapse of the Arab-Palestinian military campaign in the city and determining the position of the front lines, which, in the form of armistice lines, have remained more or less stationary since then. After a relatively short period of military rule of East Jerusalem, King Abdullah convened the Jericho Conference, at which 2,000 Palestinian public figures expressed their desire for "the unification of Palestine and Transjordan as a step toward full Arab unity." The Jericho Conference proclaimed "His Majesty Abdullah as King of all Palestine." On December 7, 1948, the Transjordanian government declared its intention to implement "the unification of the two sister countries . . . legally and internationally, when the time is ripe." On that day the name Transjordan was abolished and the kingdom renamed "the Hashemite Kingdom of Jordan." Abdullah was forced to postpone the annexation of the West Bank because of vehement opposition from the other Arab countries, but not for long. All the inhabitants of Palestine residing in the West Bank became citizens of the Hashemite Kingdom. The post of Governor General of the Jordanian-occupied territory was abolished and its civilian administration brought under the jurisdiction of the minister of the interior in Amman. In April 1950 parliamentary elections were held with the participation of all the citizens of the kingdom, from both banks of the Jordan River. The unified parliament, made up of twenty representatives of the East Bank and twenty representatives of the West Bank, was called upon to ratify the formal unification of the two banks. The following decision was passed with a large majority and no votes in opposition, several Palestinian delegates having absented themselves before the vote: "Full unification between the two sides of the Jordan Valley, the eastern and the western, and their merger into one state, the Hashemite Kingdom of Jordan." Thus, in mid-1950 East Jerusalem, and with it the West Bank, became an integral part of the Hashemite Kingdom of Jordan.

By late 1948 Israel and Jordan were ripe for negotiations regarding the future of Jerusalem. The Israelis had ratified a decision to accept in principle the partition of the city, and were seeking allies in their struggle to prevent its internationalization. King Abdullah had institutionalized his rule in the West Bank, and at the Jericho Conference assured himself some public support for annexing it to his kingdom. There was room, therefore, to assume that political dialogue between the partners in ruling Jerusalem would bear fruit. These were not the first political negotiations between Jews and the Bedouin king. Throughout the winter and spring of 1948 talks had taken place between representatives of the Jewish Agency and King Abdullah, and there was no difficulty reviving them. Negotiations were resumed in November 1948 and continued without interruption until early 1951. They revolved around military issues, such as the terms of the armistice agreement, the future of the West Bank, a nonaggression pact, and a peace agreement. Concerning Jerusalem, the two sides agreed to regard the ceasefire lines determined in November 1948 as agreed-upon boundaries. The Jordanian negotiators did indeed, from time to time, demand the return of Arab neighborhoods in the western part of the city, but these claims were rejected by the Israelis and King Abdullah did not press the matter. On February 22, 1949, the king stated to the Israeli delegation: "I have no demands with regard to new, that is, West Jerusalem, but I will not agree to hand over the Old City to the Jews or accept its internationalization." The Israelis did not challenge the

Old City's remaining in Arab hands; this would have meant an end to the negotiations. What they did want was a guarantee of free access to the holy places, the use of the ancient Jewish cemetery on the Mount of Olives and of the Hebrew University campus on Mount Scopus, and the restoration of the flow of water in the pipeline from Rosh Ha'ayin to Jerusalem via Latrun, then in the hands of the Arab Legion.

The rapid progress being made in the negotiations prompted the Israelis and Jordanians to view these matters as minor details that could be resolved easily and that need not delay the signing of the armistice agreement. In any case they figured that this agreement was just a step on the way to a comprehensive settlement. The two sides therefore agreed that resolution of the remaining issues would be worked out by a special committee appointed in accordance with Article 8 of the Israeli-Jordanian Armistice Agreement. However, this committee's deliberations went badly from the very beginning. It became clear that the sides had conflicting interests. Israel was relatively satisfied with the territorial division that had been settled upon, being interested, as mentioned, chiefly in free access to the holy places and Mount Scopus.

Jordan, by contrast, was not interested in freedom of access but in territorial changes. The pressing issue for the Israelis was their being cut off from the Western Wall and the Israeli sector of Mount Scopus. For the Jordanians it was the tens of thousands of Palestinian refugees who had left the Arab neighborhoods in the "new" city. The Israelis refused to link freedom of access to the return of the refugees, and the Jordanians claimed that the "restoration of normal life," upon which the demand for freedom of access was based, meant the return of the refugees to their homes. The committee's deliberations continued until the end of 1950, but nothing practical came of them. Jerusalem remained divided in half between Israel and Jordan along the cease-fire lines of November 1948, and from the point of view of both states, the question of sovereignty over the city remained open. The Armistice Agreement states categorically that "no provision of this Agreement shall in any way prejudice the rights, claims, and positions of either side hereto in the ultimate peaceful settlement of the Palestine question" (Art. 3). On the basis of this article of the agreement, the Arab states maintained—throughout the years that the armistice remained in force—that the entire agreement was temporary and did not abolish the state of belligerency between Israel and Jordan, that the boundaries designated in the agreement were merely military lines, and that Arabs' signing the document in no way implied their recognition of permanent borders.

The Israelis' argument was the reverse. Israel's version was that the Armistice Agreement had indeed created a permanent situation. Government positions stated in the Knesset make it clear that Israel also did not regard the annexation of the West Bank by Jordan as illegal. As to Jerusalem—there Israel and Jordan accepted each other's de facto rule. Indeed, throughout the years that the armistice held (1948–1967), there were continuous incidents, both minor and major. However, on the whole it may be said that the two sides strove to the best of their abilities to refrain from provoking each other, both being guided by the desire to maintain the status quo as far as possible. During the nineteen years that the city was divided, the two sides essentially sought to cover up the fact that the final outcome of the military campaign for Jerusalem had not been decided, and by drafting the series of agreements and set-ting up the proper administrative bodies, this was accomplished. As long as neither side violated the status quo by deliberately attempting to capture territory, the armistice in Jerusalem could be preserved.

On the Israeli side of the city, a sense of forced acquiescence to its division prevailed. The sadness and longing caused by being cut off from the sacred places of the nation were from time to time expressed in works of literature or in emotional outbursts, but these never developed into any political initiative calling for the conquest of the Old City. On the Arab side of Jerusalem, there were severe political tensions between the local people and the Jordanian regime. Jerusalem, more than any other city in the West Bank, was a gathering place for those factions who regarded the Jordanian regime as an invader that had destroyed their hopes for independence. Through violent demonstrations and terrorist acts they attempted to disrupt the plans of those who adopted the idea of integration with Jordan. The regime fought these factions, which were centered around the Mufti Hajj Amin al-Husseini and the leftist parties. The Arab Legion jailed them or banished them from the city. The Jordanians cultivated and fostered the rivals of the Husseinis. On the assumption that diplomatic support for the strengthening of Jerusalem as the political center of the West Bank would promote the Palestinian separatist cause, the Jordanians persistently and vigorously worked to establish Amman's status as the sole political and economic center of the kingdom. They purposely held back Jerusalem's development, deprived the city of any political power base, abolished its limited administrative independence, and turned it into a backward provincial town. The Palestinians followed these actions angrily, but were powerless to oust the regime. They persevered in their protests against Jerusalem's backward and neglected state, but bowed to the superior force of the Jordanians. Thousands of Jerusalemites emigrated to settle in Amman. The Palestinians continued to clash with the Jordanian authorities over one issue only: the latter's attitude in relation to Israel and Jerusalem. The Arab residents of the city did not accept its division as a fait accompli. Many of them supported the activities of Palestinian infiltrators to Israel and grumbled over the Jordanian army's harsh repression of attempts to provoke Israel. For some twenty years there was continuous tension between the people, whose attitude toward Israel was relatively extreme, and the government, which knew that any ill-considered act on its part was liable to provoke the Israelis to murderous retaliatory attacks. Despite the massive exodus of 1948-era refugees from the city to all parts of the Arab world, thousands remained there whose homes were in West Jerusalem. Many of these people, who had not managed to take their belongings with them when they fled, still zealously guarded their house keys.

The partition of the city separated the warring communities. The struggle for control that had characterized Jerusalem during the Mandatory period ceased. The two sections of the city became homogeneous districts, separated from each other by a fortified border, bristling with barbed wire and roadblocks. Separate municipal governing bodies were established in West and East Jerusalem respectively. The first municipal elections were held in West Jerusalem in 1950, and in East Jerusalem in 1951.

The problem of the holy places was not solved, and as long as the sovereignty question remained unanswered, it was impossible to find a lasting solution. Jordan, in whose custody most of the holy places remained, took legal and practical steps to protect them. In January 1951, a "custodian of the holy places" was appointed and the Jordanians assiduously preserved the status quo there. Locations sacred to the Jews—particularly the Western Wall and the cemetery on the Mount of Olives—remained closed to worshipers for nineteen years.

In June 1967, the status quo that had prevailed in Jerusalem for nineteen years was violently upset. The Jordanian attempt to capture the former British High Commissioner's mansion in no-man's-land—which was the first attempt by either side to take territory by force since 1948—launched an inevitable chain of events that necessarily decided the city's fate. Israel, which had not initiat-

ed the war with Jordan—and had even tried to prevent it—
was left in control of the whole city. The Israeli government's original perception of the Six-Day War as a defen-
sive war with no territorial objectives changed after its
occupation of the West Bank. And the first practical
expression of this change, of course, pertained to the Old
City of Jerusalem. Less than one week after the end of the
war, the cabinet had already approved a decision to annex
it to Israel.

The Israeli occupation reopened the question of sovereignty in all its intensity. The obliteration of the border
restored Jerusalem's physical integrity; however, it
revived both the national conflict and the struggle on the
local front over the economy, development, resources, and
land. The reunification of the city did not bring an agreed-
upon settlement on the question of the holy places any
closer.

The occupation and the reunification of Jerusalem
altered not the parties to the conflict but the character of
the struggle. During the British Mandate, the Jews and
Arabs had fought each other while both were subject to the
domination of a third party. The major part of the struggle
had not been carried on between these two communities
themselves, but via the efforts of both to achieve their
objectives through pressure and influence on the colonial
regime. With the ouster of the British, the struggle had
assumed the character of a military confrontation that had
concluded in a temporary compromise. The Israeli occupation created a new situation. The ongoing conflict was now

between one community, which ruled over the entire city, and another, which had been vanquished and had become a subject minority.

The international competition over sovereignty also assumed a different character. In 1949 two national states, Israel and Jordan, had reached a (temporary) agreement on the division of the city and had cooperated in thwarting the attempt by Christian states (albeit with the participation of other elements, including Arab ones) to impose the rule of an international religious patron on the city. The agreement between the partner-rivals had made it possible for them to stand together against the Christian religious interests; to challenge and defeat them; and then to prove that they were capable of finding their own solution without compromising their national sovereignties. In 1967 an entirely new state of affairs came into being. One of the two ruling states had upset the delicate balance in the city, and because of this strategic error, Jordan had lost control of its part of Jerusalem. Yesterday's partner was today's ruler of the entire city; the renewed national conflict had culminated in the victory of one side. But now Israel faced two contenders in the campaign for Jerusalem: international Christian interests (as in 1949), and Arab and Muslim interests.

Israel's success in blocking the internationalization of Jerusalem had been due not only to its cooperation with Jordan, but also to the world powers' view of the Jerusalem issue as marginal in 1949. The political conditions that came into being following the Six-Day War were substantively different from those that had prevailed during the period when the city was divided, and international pressure on Israel assumed new dimensions.

The Jews' return to the actual sites of the historical events that had forged their nationhood was a unique experience, the intensity of which had seldom been paralleled, even in the history of so ancient a people. As a sovereign state, Israel was obliged to give concrete expression to the profound connection between the people and the capital city. To this end, the government enacted of a series of legislative actions and administrative measures that were later called "the reunification of Jerusalem." It was inevitable that the reunification legislation—smelted in the furnace of such a profound spiritual experience—would be regarded as eternal and irreversible from the moment of its enactment. Even the boundaries of the unified city, drawn in accordance with military and demographic considerations, took on profound political and symbolic significance: they too, like the reunification legislation, became an unchallengeable part of the national myth. Israel's policy regarding the political future of Jerusalem was formulated in a variety of ways, but the overwhelming majority of Israelis agreed that the reunified city, with the boundaries determined in 1967, would "eternally" remain under exclusive Israeli sovereignty, and that no compromise would be allowed granting sovereign status in the city to any other state. Yet for many years the Israeli government accepted a policy formulation that committed it to conduct negotiations "with no preconditions" with any Arab state that consented to sit down at the negotiating table. When asked how their uncompromising stance on Jerusalem could be reconciled with this commitment, the Israelis explained that the official Israeli policy formulation did not contradict it. For example, in a letter to U.N. Secretary General U. Thant in 1967, Foreign Minister Abba Eban wrote that, "The term *annexation* is out of place." In 1978, the foreign minister Moshe Dayan stated, in an address to the U.N. General Assembly, that "one of the subjects that will undoubtedly be discussed [in peace negotiations] is problems regarding Jerusalem." In Israel's view, there was no contradiction, said Dayan, between "absence of preconditions" and "demands that each side might bring up."

The official Israeli stance, which enjoyed wide-ranging support within the Jewish population of Israel as well as in the diaspora, was one of emphasizing unwillingness to make any compromises regarding sovereignty over reunified Jerusalem. This fact disquieted Israeli policymakers. With their thorough knowledge of the Arabs' no less determined stance, they were particularly aware of the necessity of introducing fresh ideas with regard to the future of Jerusalem and of the danger that, if this did not happen, the problem could become an obstacle blocking any chance of a settlement. However, since they did not dare deviate from the national consensus, they concentrated their efforts on making proposals that did not clash with the principle of total Israeli sovereignty.

The Israeli proposals were directed at finding ways to satisfy the religious and communal needs of Jerusalem's non-Jewish residents and to solve the problem of the holy places. For example, Israel suggested granting extraterritoriality to the Christian holy places, self-administration to the Muslim holy places, and autonomy of religious jurisdiction to all of the city's religious communities. Ideas such as the decentralization of Jerusalem's municipal government and the establishment of an Arab submunicipality in the context of an overall Israeli municipality were proposed. None of them ever came to anything since it was clear, from sounding out the Jordanians and Palestinians on the subject, that these ideas could not provide a basis for negotiations. In any case, no meaningful negotiations concerning Jerusalem were taking place, so priority was not given to political planning on that issue. Instead, Israel's position was expressed in practical terms by the establishment of demographic and physical "facts" in East Jerusalem. A massive building program totally changed the face of the annexed areas. The Israelis had faith that in this way, physical facts would create political ones. They supposed that as time went by, the international community would grow used to the new situation and would moderate its opposition to the unilateral measures Israel was taking.

The Israeli occupation dealt an immeasurably powerful blow to the Palestinians, paralyzing them totally. When political activity finally began to revive, one policy line united all Palestinian streams—that of ending the occupation. No agreed-upon political program outlining the manner of achieving this objective was in evidence. The ouster of the Israelis was, in effect, an ideal that they did not know how to realize. The possibilities they explored were armed insurrection, active nonviolent resistance, feigned acquiescence (while exploiting the enforced "rules of the game" to their own ends), and complete dependency on Jordan and the Arab states. The possibility of negotiating an agreement with the Israelis was not considered. As far as the Palestinians were concerned, the "abolition of the results of aggression" was not a matter for negotiation, and certainly not one on which there could be compromise. Moreover, there was no agreement about what the character of Palestinian relations with Israel should be after the termination of the occupation. Opinions were divided as to the political future of the West Bank and Jerusalem.

As a result, no clear Palestinian position regarding the solution of the problem of the occupied territories was formulated. The only common denominator to be found was refusal to recognize Israel as a legitimate negotiating partner. In the aftermath of the Yom Kippur War of October 1973, there began a process of political consolidation, reflected in the universal acceptance of the PLO as the sole representative of the Palestinian national movement. However, because this organization was a coalition, the disagreements continued. A moderate minority within the PLO supported the establishment of Palestinian rule in any territory of Palestine that became liberated, as an interim phase on the way to "the liberation of all of Palestine," and acknowledged that this objective could only be attained politically. In contrast, a majority opposed any political course of action and did not agree to the political objective of establishing a mini-state that would live in peace, even temporarily, with Israel.

Jordan's stance passed through a number of permutations. In the period following the 1967 war, King Hussein uncompromisingly demanded the restoration of his total control over East Jerusalem. Late in 1971, he began hinting at a willingness to be satisfied with sovereignty over just part of it: in conversations with the Israelis, he proposed leaving the Jewish Quarter and the Western Wall in Israel's hands. He supported the principle of an "open city," meaning the physical reunification of Jerusalem. Despite these signs of flexibility regarding a territorial settlement, the Jordanian king stood by his demand for the restoration of his country's sovereign status in at least part of Jerusalem. He regarded himself as ordained by fate to preserve the Arab character of Jerusalem, and to hold it in trust for all Muslims. Hussein could not take any stance that would make him responsible for "the loss of the Holy City." In the plan for a Jordanian-Palestinian federation that he published in 1971, Hussein designated Jerusalem as the capital of the Palestinian province "of the federated United Arab Kingdom." His position became more rigid after the Yom Kippur War, but in March 1976 he declared: "In the context of a peace agreement, if Arab sovereignty is restored to (the Eastern) part of the city, I see no reason that the city should be divided. Jerusalem must be the city of all believers."

Ever since 1948, the United States has found itself in a strange position. It has been the principal supporter and promoter of the legal fiction called the "internationalization of Jerusalem," despite actively opposing it and cautioning others against its adoption. In 1949, when the U.N. General Assembly was debating the ratification of a resolution calling for the installation of an international regime in Jerusalem, the American representative warned that approval of the plan would involve the United Nations in countless difficulties in an attempt to attain objectives that were not all pertinent to the international community. The Americans maintained that the resolution did not take into account the interests of the city's inhabitants and that it endangered international interests in Jerusalem. The General Assembly ratified the internationalization resolution despite U.S. opposition. That same year, the United States supported a Swedish proposal for the functional internationalization of the holy places, in place of territorial internationalization. On that occasion also, the U.S. position was rejected. In spite of taking this stand, the United States adhered to the legalistic position that it was bound by the General Assembly resolutions regarding the internationalization of Jerusalem. Officially, it recognized Israeli and Jordanian rule in Jerusalem as de facto only.

In the first weeks of Israeli occupation (in 1967), the United States took political stands favorable to Israel. It headed the bloc that thwarted a Soviet-Arab proposal wherein the General Assembly would have declared Israel an "aggressor" and ordered it to unconditionally withdraw from Jerusalem. The United States thereby prevented the Israeli occupation's being defined as illegal in international law. It acknowledged Israel's right of "belligerent occupation," a form of occupation whose legality is recognized in international law as extending until the time a peace treaty is signed. When Israel took measures to annex East Jerusalem, the United States was critical. The official American position was formulated by Arthur Goldberg, U.S. Ambassador to the United Nations, as follows: "The United States does not accept or recognize these measures [Israeli annexation] as altering the status of Jerusalem. My government does not recognize that the administrative measures taken by Israel on 28 June 1967—the passing of the Reunification Law—can be regarded as the last word on the matter . . . [but can only be interpreted as] interim and provisional, and not as prejudging the final and permanent status of Jerusalem."

That is, Israeli claims notwithstanding, this was how the United States related to the Reunification Law. This critical stance was convenient for Israel because it expressed only moderate censure and left an opening for discussion of the "measures" themselves. Ambassador Charles Yost reiterated this position on July 1, 1969: "The United States considers that the part of Jerusalem that came under the control of Israel in the June 1967 war, like other areas occupied by Israel, is occupied territory and hence subject to the provision of international law governing the rights and obligations of an occupying power. . . . We have consistently refused to recognize those measures as having anything but a provisional character."

These declarations, as we shall see further on, were

re-iterated on various occasions, and represented the official U.S. policy on Jerusalem. Their verbal gymnastics, however, en-abled the United States to take a moderate position in regard to Israel's massive construction activity in East Jerusalem.

The visit of President Sadat to Jerusalem in the fall of 1977 ushered in a new era in the history of the conflict over Jerusalem. The fact that the Egyptian president visited the city and spoke before the Knesset was interpreted by the Israelis as recognition of Jerusalem's status as Israel's capital. However, it quickly became clear that the problem had not been miraculously solved. The question of Jerusalem was raised at every bilateral encounter between Israel and Egypt, and at Camp David it even threatened to scuttle the entire conference: the Egyptian president brought up the issue and offered several draft proposals, but the Israelis refused to discuss any alteration to the status quo and objected to any reference being made to the problem of Jerusalem in the text of the documents of the accords. The Americans tried, under pressure from Sadat, to find some sort of symbolic solution—such as flying Muslim flags on the Temple Mount—but their suggestions were vehemently rejected by the Israelis. When it became clear that there was no chance of arriving at any agreement, the conference participants agreed to mention the Jerusalem problem only in letters that would be exchanged among the delegation heads—Carter, Begin, and Sadat— and appended to the body of the Camp David Accords. President Sadat, as one interested in a change in the

Jerusalem situation, initiated the correspondence. In his letter to President Carter, Sadat made the following points:

1. Arab Jerusalem is an integral part of the West Bank. Legal and historical rights in the city must be respected and restored.

2. Arab Jerusalem should be under Arab sovereignty.

6. The holy places of each faith may be placed under the administration and control of their representatives.

7. Essential functions in the city should be undivided and a joint municipal council composed of an equal number of Arab and Israeli members can supervise the carrying out of these functions. In this way the city shall be undivided.

These formulations reflected a noticeable effort on the part of the Egyptians to adopt a moderate stance, similar to the official American position, as well as a clear attempt to present themselves as not opposing the physical unity of the city. Even so, the Egyptian position was completely contradictory to that held by the Israelis, who regarded political division and physical unity as diametric opposites. Prime Minister Begin wrote to President Carter: "On 28 June, Israel's parliament [the Knesset] promulgated and adopted a law. . . . On the basis of this law, the government of Israel decreed in July 1967 [sic] that Jerusalem is one city, indivisible, the capital of Israel."

President Carter replied to the Egyptian president's letter, saying that "the position of the United States regarding Jerusalem remains as stated by Ambassador Goldberg to the United Nations General Assembly on 14 July 1967, and subsequently by Ambassador Yost, to the U.N. Security Council on 1 July 1969."

The position taken by President Sadat at Camp David did not differ greatly from that of King Hussein, nor was it more moderate with regard to Arab demands. However, the fact that Sadat agreed to sweep the Jerusalem problem aside and sign a document that made no reference to it upset the Saudis and was one of the main factors contributing to the tension between the two countries. The fact that the issue of Jerusalem was not part of the peace process was also one of the factors given by Jordan as a reason for its nonparticipation. The Palestinians took a negative position vis-à-vis the peace process as a whole, as a matter of principle. And unlike the Egyptians, Jordan and Saudi Arabia were unwilling to agree to continued Israeli sovereignty even over West Jerusalem.

Differences of opinion regarding the application of the Camp David Accords to Jerusalem arose immediately with the start of negotiations concerning Palestinian self-rule. At every meeting the Egyptians demanded that the matter of Jerusalem be discussed and the Israelis rejected the demand. Each side based its stand on the Camp David Accords and accused the other of deviating from them. The argument mainly revolved around the Egyptian demand that the residents of East Jerusalem be granted the right to vote in elections to choose the Palestinian self-governing authority. In the early stages of the negotiations, Foreign Minister Moshe Dayan was not opposed to this demand; however, after a short while the Israeli government officially stated that it would not agree to the demand, since doing so would set a precedent for Jerusalem's being considered part of the "occupied territories" where autonomy was to be implemented.

This continual reference to the problem of Jerusalem was contrary to the scenario to which the Camp David participants had agreed, wherein Jerusalem was to have been last on the political agenda. The Israelis, Egyptians, and Americans all recognized the centrality of the Jerusalem problem, but since they also knew that this was the most complex and delicate of all the problems in the Middle East conflict, they sought to isolate it and agreed not to seek a resolution to it until other, smaller obstacles had been removed from the road to a comprehensive settlement. There was much logic to this position, except that the Egyptians and Israelis did not succeed in operating in accordance with it, and the Jerusalem problem was quickly moved to the center of the deliberations.

A number of factors combined to bring this about. Those who opposed Camp David—the "rejectionist front" in the Arab states and extremist elements in Israel and Egypt—stubbornly insisted on raising the question of Jerusalem in hopes that discussing it would sabotage the autonomy talks and perhaps the entire process of normalization of diplomatic relations between Israel and Egypt.

Within the Egyptian administration itself, opinion was becoming increasingly strong that their not mentioning the issue of Jerusalem would be construed as meaning they were neglecting it. The Americans, who were striving to expand the scope of the peace negotiations and to end Egypt's isolation, saw a need to help create the conditions necessary for the integration of Jordan and Saudi Arabia into the peace process. In Israel there was a new school of thought—at variance with the conventional wisdom that Israel must work to the postpone the resolution of the Jerusalem problem—whose adherents demanded its being placed at the top of the agenda. However, Israeli statesmen had always considered leaving Jerusalem for last to be an extremely important tactical objective, since postponement of the debate would enable Israel to continue establishing faits accomplis in the city, thereby reinforcing its status.

The debate over Jerusalem took on the character of recurrent conflagrations, flaring up with increasing frequency and intensity. Positions became polarized and additional players were drawn into the fray. The Egyptians intensified the dispute by accentuating positions that they had always held but that they had blurred and downplayed in the past. The Israeli government reacted by establishing physical "facts" (through land confiscations and construction of government offices in East Jerusalem) and by making strong statements that were construed as closing the door on further negotiations. The Israeli reactions, unlike the Egyptian positions, made real alterations in the situation in the city, and Israel was thus blamed for the intensification of the dispute. Every Israeli reaction led to a counterreaction, and an unending cycle of escalating extremism resulted. A salient example of this process was the Knesset's ratification of the Law of Jerusalem— Capital of Israel. This law was introduced as a private member's bill in July 1980 by Knesset members opposed to the peace agreement, with the announced objective of scuttling it. The Likud cabinet, which agreed with the wording of the proposed law (merely a reiteration of the prime minister's formulations from Camp David), dared not oppose it. The opposition likewise did not dare stand against it, for fear of being accused of "destroying the national unity over Jerusalem." Following the ratification of the law, Egypt withdrew from the autonomy talks, and Sadat publicly initiated an exchange of angry letters with the Israeli prime minister. Even countries friendly toward Israel were convinced that the law had altered the status of Jerusalem and therefore reacted by removing the few embassies remaining there.

This reaction to the Jerusalem Law provoked an Israeli counterreaction, which again took the form of establishment of a physical presence in the city. The endless chain of reactions and counterreactions resulted in increasingly entrenched positions on all sides. Chances of arriving at a solution to the problem seemed more remote than ever.

The Lebanon War (1982) and, in its aftermath, Israel's massive settlement activities and the construction of gigantic Jewish neighborhoods surrounding Jerusalem, led to the intensification of Palestinian protests, and Jerusalem became the focus of demonstrations and acts of terrorism. The sporadic rebellion, which was accompanied by efforts to improve the standard of living in Arab East Jerusalem, obscured the accumulation of rage by the Arab populace of Jerusalem from many observers until it erupted all at once toward the end of 1987. The Intifada totally altered day-to-day reality in Jerusalem. Months of commercial strikes, demonstrations, murders, stone throwing, and car torching caused Israelis to cease visiting East Jerusalem; the intercommunal rift deepened and became an abyss. The impact of the Intifada internationally forced all parties to the conflict to realize the necessity of embarking on diplomatic initiatives, and these directly affected Jerusalem.

In July 1988, King Hussein announced that he was cutting all legal and administrative ties with the West Bank. The king understood that there was no longer any chance of returning to the status quo ante of the unity of the two banks that his grandfather, King Abdullah, had created in 1948. Even so, Hussein maintained a direct connection with the Muslim holy places in Jerusalem and continued to finance the activities of the Muslim institutions in the city. In November 1988, the Palestine National Council declared the establishment of "the state of Palestine, in the land of Palestine, with its capital at Jerusalem."

In May 1989, the Israeli government published a "peace plan," the gist of which was the holding of elections for representatives who would carry on negotiations with Israel regarding an interim settlement and self-rule. This initiative foundered, one major reason being Israel's refusal to permit the Arab residents of East Jerusalem to vote in the elections on the grounds that the city was part of the State of Israel and not of the West Bank. The issue became a point of contention inside Israel, when the Likud-led government (and, following the election of a Labor-led coalition in 1992, the right-wing opposition) opposed the Jerusalem Arabs' voting, whereas the Labor government agreed to it under specific conditions.

In October 1990, the intercommunal tensions—which had increased in the face of the political paralysis, the continuing Intifada, and the Iraqi invasion of Kuwait—erupted again. The Temple Mount massacre, in which seventeen Palestinians were killed in clashes with Israeli security forces (police and border guards) in and around the compound of the Al-Aqsa Mosque, was the most serious episode in the twenty-three years of Israeli occupation. It, in turn, generated a chain of serious acts of violence that continued until the convening of the peace conference in Madrid (October 1991).

In the discussions preceding the Madrid conference, the question of Jerusalem occupied a central place. Israel demanded that the city not be mentioned in the official invitations to the conference and that the Palestinian participants (within the Jordanian-Palestinian delegation) not be residents of East Jerusalem. The Palestinians, on the other hand, demanded that the United States issue them a letter of assurance in which it would reiterate its known (though downplayed) position regarding nonrecognition of the annexation of Jerusalem, whose future would be determined by negotiation. The Americans solved the problem by not mentioning Jerusalem in the letters of assurance it sent to the Israelis, but by giving the Palestinians what they had requested in theirs. Thus, the Israelis and Palestinians both went to Madrid thinking that their (contradictory) preconditions had been met, and this anomaly was not discovered during the conference.

However, immediately following the conclusion of the ceremonial event and with the commencement of the bilateral talks in Washington, the dispute over Jerusalem erupted openly. The Palestinians stuck by their claim that Jerusalem was an inseparable part of the occupied territories and that therefore all of the agreements in the interim settlement that applied to the West Bank must apply to Jerusalem as well, and that Jerusalem must become the capital of the Palestinian state in the context of the permanent settlement. Israel vehemently opposed any discussion of East Jerusalem, even though the ban on East Jerusalemite Faisal al-Husseini's participation in the deliberations of the Israeli-Palestinian committee was lifted in the wake of Labor's ascent to power (in mid-1992). The Americans recommended postponing discussion of the question of Jerusalem until after the negotiations for the permanent settlement, but the Palestinians refused, since "Israel is establishing physical and other sorts of 'facts' that could potentially predetermine the situation and leave nothing to discuss in the future." When the talks reached a stalemate (and there are those who claim that this was a deliberate tactic on the part of PLO Chairman Yasir Arafat), it was suddenly revealed that the Madrid process was merely a diversionary tactic, and that the real deliberations had been conducted in Oslo in complete secrecy.

In the Israeli-Palestinian Declaration of Principles signed in September 1993, the Palestinians agreed to what they had rejected at the bilateral talks in Washington, namely the removal of discussion of Jerusalem from the context of the interim agreement: "Jurisdiction of the [Palestinian] Council [self-governing authority] will cover the West Bank and Gaza Strip territory except for issues that will be negotiated in the permanent status negotiations: Jerusalem, settlements, etc."

Right-wing circles in Israel regarded Israel's willingness to discuss Jerusalem at all as undermining its status as "Israel's unified capital," but as we have seen previously, the Likud government headed by Menachem Begin had also been prepared to discuss the issue of Jerusalem in the context of peace negotiations. The Declaration of Principles also stated that "Palestinians of Jerusalem who live there will have [the] right to participate in the election process." Both sides exhibited apparent flexibility on issues regarding Jerusalem. The Israelis agreed to a liberal interpretation of the passive and active voting rights of the Palestinians (i.e., the right to vote and to be elected)— an issue that had been a source of disagreement for years— leaving the way open for interpretations defining Jerusalem as a part of the West Bank. The Palestinians relented on their principal demand for immediate discussion of the Jerusalem issue and agreed to postpone it despite the fact that they well knew the Israelis were energetically at work establishing irreversible "facts" in East Jerusalem. However, this mutual flexibility was not actually an indication that their polarized positions had become less so. The Declaration of Principles and the agreements that were signed in its wake allowed Israel to specify that the Palestinian Authority would be entitled to operate only in the territories turned over to its control, and that it was forbidden to maintain any official institutions in Jerusalem. The Palestinians, for their part, agreed to postpone the discussion of Jerusalem only after Foreign Minister Shimon Peres promised the PLO chairman (in a letter addressed to the Norwegian foreign minister) that the Palestinian institutions in East Jerusalem were very important and would be preserved. All of these institutions, "including economic, social, educational, and cultural institutions as well as Christian and Muslim holy places, fulfill a vital role for the Palestinian population. Needless to say, we shall not interfere with their operation. On the contrary, the fulfillment of this important role merits encouragement." These institutions, and particularly Orient House, which had become the hub of Palestinian political and diplomatic endeavors, stepped up their activities, and this became an embarrassment to the Israeli government. The Palestinian Authority's activities in East Jerusalem became a weapon in the hands of the right—especially Jerusalem's mayor, Ehud Olmert, Teddy

Kollek's successor—who denounced the government for pursuing a policy promoting the redivision of the city and its abandonment to the Palestinians.

Under pressure from the right, the government was compelled, in late 1994, to pass a special law authorizing the police to close any institution connected with the Palestinian Authority, and requiring any activity of the Authority "within the precincts of the State of Israel" (i.e., East Jerusalem) to have the approval of the Israeli authorities. This attempt by the Israeli government to treat the Palestinian Authority like a foreign governing body forbidden to operate outside its area of jurisdiction was indeed based on the Palestinian Authority's commitment not to do so, but was, of course, pathetically futile. No law can sever the Palestinian people's attachment to Jerusalem and make it into a "foreign country." The very fact of Israel's recognition of the Palestinian national collective, embodied in the Declaration of Principles, and the willingness to conduct negotiations regarding the realization of its national rights created an entirely new state of affairs in Jerusalem. It essentially imparted legitimacy to this national collective in Jerusalem as well, and recognized its attachment to the city. The approximately 200,000 Palestinians (who have not taken Israeli citizenship) living in East Jerusalem feel that they are entitled to be a part of their own national body, to organize their communal life, and to unite around their national slogans and the governing institutions they agree upon.

The internal contradiction in the Declaration of Principles between the "principles" component—mutual recognition between Israel and the PLO—and the practical component—the setting up of a Palestinian Authority with limited authority—was temporarily dealt with by postponing discussion about the full extent of Palestinian self-determination. But both sides well knew that no problem had really been solved, and both therefore set out to establish additional "facts" to improve their situation, come the hour of decision.

The Israelis persisted in their policy of establishing a physical presence and accelerated the pace of construction of Jewish neighborhoods in the city and its surrounding areas. They also attempted to hamper the Palestinians' activities by shutting down their institutions in East Jerusalem. However, they were unable to actively prevent the Palestinians from establishing their own presence: the establishment of research institutes and cultural and educational centers, and the transformation of their political center, Orient House, into a virtual foreign ministry, where the prime ministers and foreign ministers of many countries came to pay official visits. The Israelis, of course, enjoyed a clear advantage, having all the force of a sovereign state at their disposal, but they repeatedly were made to realize their limitations: no form of coercion that they could apply was capable of suppressing the Palestinians' collective attachment to Jerusalem and its concrete manifestations. The struggle for Jerusalem has not been decided, and the need to mobilize the rival communities to continue it "till victory" has generated ceremonies like the

"Jerusalem 3,000" on the Israeli side and the commemoration of "5,000 years since the Jebusites" by the Arabs. Nearly 100 years after the problem of Jerusalem arose, it still awaits a solution.

A DAY IN
THE LIFE

DAVID GROSSMAN

The Yellow Wind

O N A DAY OF TURBID rain, at the end of March, I turn off the main road leading from my house in Jerusalem to Hebron, and enter the Deheisha refugee camp. Twelve thousand Palestinians live here in one of the highest population densities in the world; the houses are piled together, and the house of every extended family branches out in ugly cement growths, rooms and niches, rusty iron beams spread throughout as sinews, jutting like disconnected fingers.

In Deheisha, drinking water comes from wells. The only running water is the rainwater and sewage flowing down the paths between the houses. I soon give up picking my way between the puddles; there is something

DAVID GROSSMAN, *a prominent Israeli novelist, ventured deep into the Palestinian refugee camps of Israel in the spring of 1988. What he found caused a sensation. His unflinching reports, excerpted here, first appeared in the* New Yorker, *and in his subsequent book,* The Yellow Wind.

ridiculous—almost unfair—about preserving such refinement here, in the face of a few drops of filth.

Beside each house—a yard. They are small, fenced in
with corrugated aluminum, and very clean. A large *jara*
filled with springwater and covered with cloth stands in
each yard. But every person here will tell you without hesi-
tation that the water from the spring of his home village was
sweeter. "In Ain Azrab"—she sighs (her name is Hadija,
and she is very old)—"our water was so clear and healthy
that a dying man once immersed himself, drank a few
mouthfuls, and washed—and was healed on the spot." She
cocks her head, drills me with an examining gaze, and
mocks: "So, what do you think of that?"

I discover—with some bafflement, I admit—that she
reminds me of my grandmother and her stories about
Poland, from which she was expelled. About the river, about
the fruit there. Time has marked both their faces with the
same lines, of wisdom and irony, of great skepticism toward
all people, both relatives and strangers.

"We had a field there. A vineyard. Now see what a flow-
ering garden we have here," and she waves her brown, wrinkled hand over the tiny yard.

"But we made a garden," murmurs her daughter-in-law,
a woman of wild, gypsy, unquiet beauty. "We made a garden
in tin cans." She nods toward the top of the cinder-block
fence, where several pickle cans bring forth red geraniums,
in odd abundance, as if drawing their life from some far
source of fruitfulness, of creation.

A strange life. Double and split. Everyone I spoke to in

the camp is trained—almost from birth—to live this double life: they sit here, very much here, because deprivation imposes sobriety with cruel force, but they are also there. That is—among us. In the villages, in the cities. I ask a five-year-old boy where he is from, and he immediately answers, "Jaffa," which is today part of Tel Aviv. "Have you ever seen Jaffa?" "No, but my grandfather saw it." His father, apparently, was born here, but his grandfather came from Jaffa. "And is it beautiful, Jaffa?" "Yes. It has orchards and vineyards and the sea."

And farther down, where the path slopes, I meet a young girl sitting on a cement wall, reading an illustrated magazine. Where are you from? She is from Lod, not far from Ben-Gurion International Airport, forty years ago an Arab town. She is sixteen. She tells me, giggling, of the beauty of Lod. Of its houses, which were big as palaces. "And in every room a hand-painted carpet. And the land was wonderful, and the sky was always blue."

I remembered the wistful lines of Yehuda Halevy, "The taste of your sand—more pleasant to my mouth than honey," and Bialik, who sang to the land which "the spring eternally adorns," how wonderfully separation beautifies the beloved, and how strange it is, in the barrenness of the gray cement of Deheisha, to hear sentences so full of lyric beauty, words spoken in a language more exalted than the everyday, poetic but of established routine, like a prayer or an oath: "And the tomatoes there were red and big, and everything came to us from the earth, and the earth gave us and gave us more."

"Have you visited there, Lod?" "Of course not." "Aren't you curious to see it now?" "Only when we return."

This is how the others answer me also. The Palestinians, as is well known, are making use of the ancient Jewish strategy of exile and have removed themselves from history. They close their eyes against harsh reality, and stubbornly clamping down their eyelids, they fabricate their Promised Land. "Next year in Jerusalem," said the Jews in Latvia and in Cracow and in San'a, and the meaning was that they were not willing to compromise. Because they had no hope for any real change. He who has nothing to lose can demand everything; and until his Jerusalem becomes real, he will do nothing to bring it closer. And here also, again and again, that absolute demand: everything. Nablus and Hebron and Jaffa and Jerusalem. And in the meantime— nothing. In the meantime, abandoned physically and spiritually. In the meantime, a dream and a void.

It's all bolitics, the Palestinians say. Even those who can pronounce the "p" in "politics" will say "bolitics," as a sign of defiance, in which there is a sort of self-mocking; "bolitics," which means that whole game being played over our heads, kept out of our hands, crushing us for decades under all the occupations, sucking out of us life and the power to act, turning us into dust, it's all bolitics, the Turks and the British, and the son-of-a-whore Hussein who killed and slaughtered us without mercy, and now all of a sudden he makes himself out to be the protector of the Palestinians, and these Israelis, who are willing to bring down a government because of two terrorists they killed in a bus, and with the considered cruelty of an impeccably meticulous jurist they change our laws, one thousand two hundred new laws they issued, and deprive us of our land and of our tradition and of our honor, and construct for us here some kind of great enlightened prison, when all they really want is for us to escape from it, and then they won't let us return to it ever—and in their proud cunning, which we are completely unable to understand, they bind their strings to us, and we dance for them like marionettes.

"It's all bolitics," laughs the ironic woman, who reminds me slightly of my grandmother, and slightly of the cunning, old, loud Italian from *Catch-22*, the one who explains to proud American Nately why America will lose the war in the end, and poor Italy will not win, but survive. "The strongest weapon the Arabs in the occupied territories can deploy against us," a wise man once said, "is not to change." And it is true—when you walk through the Deheisha camp you feel as if that conception has internalized itself unconsciously here, seeped its way into the hearts of the people and become power, defiance: we will not change, we will not try to improve our lives. We will remain before you like a curse cast in cement.

She suddenly remembers: "There, in the village, in Ain Azrab, we baked bread over a straw fire. Not here. Because here we don't have livestock, and none of their leavings." She falls silent and hugs herself. Her forehead wrinkles repeatedly in a spasm of wonder. The brown, wrinkled fingers go, unconsciously, through the motions of kneading.

Everything happens elsewhere. Not now. In another place. In a splendid past or a longed-for future. The thing most present here is absence. Somehow one senses that people here have turned themselves voluntarily into doubles of the real people who once were, in another place. Into people who hold in their hands only one real asset: the ability to wait.

And I, as a Jew, can understand that well.

"When a person is exiled from his land," a Jewish-American author once said to the Palestinian writer from Ramallah, Raj'a Shehade, "he begins to think of it in symbols, like a person who needs pornography. And we, the Jews, have also become expert pornographers, and our longings for this land are woven of endless symbols." The author was speaking of the Jews of hundreds of years ago, but on the day I went to Deheisha the Knesset was storming in fierce debate over the symbolism of the name "Judea and Samaria," and Knesset member Geula Cohen demanded that this remain the only legal designation, and that the terms "West Bank" and "territories" in all their permutations not be used. "Judea and Samaria" really sounds more significant and symbolical, and there are many among us for whom the phrase activates a pleasant historical reflex, a sort of satisfying shiver reaching into the depths of the past, there spreading ripples of longing for other sleeping phrases as well—the Bashan, the Gilad, the Horan, all parts of the ancient Greater Israel and today parts of Syria and Jordan.

About half a million Palestinian refugees live today in the Gaza Strip. In the West Bank there are about 400,000.

(We are speaking here only of refugees, and not of the entire Arab population under Israeli rule.) In Jordan there are about 850,000. In Lebanon, some 250,000. Syria also has about 250,000. A total of about two and a quarter million refugees. Even if the problem of the refugees living under Israeli rule is solved, the bitterness of their more than a million brothers in the Arab countries, living in no less appalling conditions, will remain. This is why the feeling of despair is so deep among all those who know this problem well. This is why the refugees allow themselves to become addicted to their dreams.

Raj'a Shehade, writer and lawyer, admits that he, too, was a pornographer of views in his youth. Of the view of Jaffa and the coastal plain, about which he has heard stories and legends. When he hikes today over the hills next to Ramallah, it happens that he forgets himself for a minute and he can enjoy the contact with the earth, smell the thyme, gaze upon an olive tree—and then he understands that he is looking at an olive tree, and before his eyes the tree transmutes, and becomes a symbol, the symbol of struggle, of loss, "and at that very same moment the tree is stolen from me," says Shehade, "and in its place is a void, filling up with pain and anger."

The void. The absence, which for decades has been filling with hatred.

A.N., whom I met another time, in Nablus, told me: "Of course I hate you. Maybe at the beginning I didn't hate and only feared. Afterwards, I began to hate." A.N., thirty years old, is a resident of the Balata refugee camp. He spent

ten years of his life in jail (the Ashkelon and Nafha prisons)
after being found guilty of belonging to the Popular Front
for the Liberation of Palestine. ("I didn't actually take part
in operations. They only taught me to shoot.") "Before I
went to jail, I didn't even know I was a Palestinian. There
they taught me who I am. Now I have opinions. Don't
believe the ones who tell you that the Palestinians don't
really hate you. Understand: the average Palestinian is not the
fascist and hating type, but you and the life under your
occupation push him into hatred. Look at me, for example.
You took ten years of my life from me. You exiled my father
in '68. He hadn't done anything. He wasn't even a PLO
supporter. Maybe even the opposite. But you wanted to
kick out anyone who had an opinion about anything. So
that we would be here completely without leaders. Even
without leaders who were a little bit for you. And my mother—for six years you did not allow her to go to visit him.
And I—after prison, you don't let me build a house, or
leave here to visit Jordan, nothing. And you constantly
repeat: See what progress we have brought you. You forget
that in twenty years everything has progressed. The whole
world strides forward. True, you helped us a little, but you
aren't willing to give us the most important thing. True, we
progressed a little, but look how much you progressed
during that time. We remained way behind, and if you
check it out, maybe you'll see that we are even worse off in
a relative sense than we were in '67." (The standard of living may be measured by personal consumption per capita
and GNP per capita. I checked the facts with Dr. Meron

Benvenisti, author of *The West Bank Data Project*. In his study, private consumption per capita in the West Bank is estimated at about 30 percent of that of Israel; GNP per capita in the West Bank is four times smaller than in Israel.)

"Then," the young man from Balata continued, restrained in his expression but transmitting cold, tight-lipped anger, "then you say under the Jordanians it was bad for you. Maybe so. But the Jordanians took only our national identity from us, and you took everything. National identity, and the identity of every one of us who fears you and depends on you for his livelihood, you took everything. You made us into living dead. And me, what remains for me? Only the hatred of you and thoughts of *siyassah* [politics]. That's another evil you brought upon us, that you made every man here, even the most ordinary fellah, into a politician."

I drink tea with three women in Deheisha. One hears the most penetrating things from the women. The men are more afraid of imprisonment and intimidation. It is the women who march at the head of the demonstrations, it is the women who shout, who scream out the bitterness in their hearts before the television cameras. Brown women, with sharp features, women bearing suffering. Hadijah is seventy-five years old, her mind sharp and her narrow body healthy. *"Allah yikhalik,"* I say to her, may God be with you, and she laughs to herself, a thin chuckle of bare gums, and says: "What is it to him?" and explains to me that a man is like a stalk of wheat: when he turns yellow, he bends.

She has lived in this house, a standard refugee house, for forty years. The United Nations Welfare and Relief Agency (UNWRA) built it, and the UN symbol can still be found on the walls and doors. At the head of each refugee camp in the West Bank and Gaza Strip stands an UNWRA-appointed director. He serves as middleman between the agency and the residents. He is himself a former refugee and lives in the camp. He has the authority to distribute food and welfare payments, to grant the right to live in the camp, and to recommend students for university admissions.

The house consists of two small rooms and does not have running water. The electricity is usually out. Today it is raining outside, and the house is almost completely dark. Hadijah and her elderly sister sit on a straw mat and examine the medicines the camp doctor has prescribed for the sister. She suffers from asthma. The teachers and doctors who work in the refugee camps come, in general, from outside, from the nearby cities. The simplest jobs, cleaning and sanitation and construction, are filled by the camp residents. In the house in which I now sit live five people. In the room in which we drink our tea there is one cabinet, a suitcase on top. Half open. As if waiting to move on. A few wooden chairs made by an untrained hand, a few shelves holding vegetables.

The young woman, tense, offers oranges and a paring knife. Another item of furniture found in every house here is the dowry chest of the woman of the house, made from the soft trunk of the Judas tree. Here she keeps her dowry, the bedsheets, the wedding dress, and perhaps some childish luxury, a toy, a pretty handkerchief—after all, she was no more than a girl when she was married.

"And if someone were to offer you today a dunam [one-quarter acre, the standard measure of land in countries once under Turkish rule] of land in a nice place, with light, in the open air?"

Yes, yes—she laughs—of course, but only on my own land. There.

She also declaims this, like the politicians, like those purveyors of her fate over all these years. She, at least, has the right to do so. I try to remember how many times Palestinian leaders missed opportunities to gain themselves a homeland: there was the partition proposal of '36 and the second proposal of '47, and maybe there were other chances. They—in their blindness—rejected them all. We drink silently. The men are at work. On the wall, two nails. They serve as a wardrobe. On one hangs the black 'igal (headband) of a kaffiyeh.

Whoever has served in the army in the "territories" knows how such rooms look from the inside during the night. Whoever has taken part in searches, in imposing curfews, in capturing a suspect at night, remembers. The violent entry into rooms like this one, where several people sleep, crowded, in unaired stench, three or four together under scratchy wool blankets, wearing their work clothes still in their sleep, as if ready at any moment to get up and go wherever they are told. They wake in confusion, squinting from the flashlight, children wail, sometimes a couple is making love, soldiers surround the house, some of them—shoes full of mud after tramping through the paths of the camp—walking over the sleep—warm blankets, some pounding on the tin roof above.

The old woman follows, it seems, my gaze to the bare cement walls, the heating lamp, the wool blankets rolled up on the floor. Suddenly she boils over: "Do we look like gypsies, do we? Miserable, are we? Ha? We are people of culture!" Her sister, the sick woman, nods rapidly, her sharp chin stabbing her sunken chest: "Yes, yes, people of culture!" They fall silent, wheezing. The young woman, of the wild, exotic presence, wants to say something and is silent. Her hand literally clamps her mouth closed. Within the arabesque filigree of manners and considered delicacy, of conversation and the protection of hospitality, the wires suddenly go taut. I am confused. The young woman tries to make amends. Change the subject. Is her mother-in-law willing to tell this Israeli here about, for instance, her childhood in Ain Azrab? No. Is she willing to recall the days when she worked the land? No, no. Salt on a wound. Would you be willing, *ya mama*, to sing the songs the fellahin, the winegrowers, the shepherds sang then? No. She only tightens her cracked lips stubbornly, her balding head shaking, but again, out of the conquering power of absence, her left foot begins to tap to a far-off rhythm, and her body moves silently forward and back, and as she traps my cautious gaze, she slaps her thigh with a trembling hand, and her nose reddens with rage: "Culture! You people don't know that we have culture! You can't understand this culture. It's not a culture of television!"

Suddenly she is completely emptied of her anger: once again her face takes on an expression of defeat, of knowing all, the ancient signs written on the faces of the old: "The world is hard, hard..." She nods her head in bitter sorrow, her eyes close themselves off from the small, dark room: "You can't understand. You can't understand anything. Ask, maybe, your grandmother to tell you."

Again in Deheisha. It is a quiet day today. No demonstrations. No stone throwing. The army can be seen only from afar, riding along the road. A week later there would be riots and demonstrations and rocks would fly, and around Deheisha would rise a six-meter fence, to prevent stones from being thrown on every passing car. Deheisha would become invisible as far as the travelers along the road were concerned, and the fence would become, it seems, a new Palestinian symbol. The rainwater and the sewage still flow in rivulets along the paths. A man lays a heavy stone on a tin roof to prevent the wind from blowing it away. A group of young men build another room onto a house. They are building everywhere here. With determination and without any plan. "Why is Thekla's construction taking such a long time?" Marco Polo asked the hardworking builders in Italo Calvino's book *Invisible Cities*, and they answered him—without pausing for a moment from lifting pails and moving their long brushes up and down: "So that its destruction cannot begin." Do you fear that the minute you take down the scaffolding the city will begin to crumble and fall to pieces? And the residents of the invisible city answered hastily, in a whisper: "Not only the city."

The owner of the little grocery store is surprised at my entry, and rises in concern. The merchandise is scanty and old. For the most part it consists of cigarettes, soft drinks, and cans of pineapple displaying suntanned young women covered with dust. Why bother describing it? We are all acquainted with a store just like it. The storeowner's friend, Abu Hana, checks first to see if I am not from the *mukhabarat*, the intelligence service, and afterwards says that he will speak of anything except bolitics, since bolitics is a science in which it is very difficult to discover anything new, no?

Yes, it would seem.

It is better to remain silent, he says. Then he finds that he cannot hold back, and sounds a hurried whisper: "Napoleon, Bismarck, Hitler," he says. "None of them lasted. They were too strong. It's best to sit quietly and wait."

Wait for what?

I don't know. I'm no genius. What do I know?

And he smiles me a calculated, distancing smile.

I look him over. An Arab dressed in a kaffiyeh and enveloped in a neutral, purposeful expression, against the background of a strongly lined face, engraved by a harsh hand. The bank clerk who told me a week ago, in the voice of one making me party to a secret, "I most hate working on the tenth of the month, when all the *arabushim* get their pay," was thinking, no doubt, of this *arabush*. Or maybe she meant the other *arabushim*, who also wear a mask of ignorance and apathy, to the point that the mask has seeped into their skins.

And on the slope of the hill in Deheisha, I passed a group

of small children racing upward. *Rowda*. An Arab kindergarten. Two teachers (Don't give our names, but you can
quote) and thirty-five children from two to five years old.
The Deheisha kindergarten.

I want to expand a little on this subject: the small children, nameless, with running noses, the ones we see along
the roads, playing by the passing cars. These are the children
who in '67 sold us figs for a *grush* and washed our parents'
cars for ten *grush*. And afterwards they grew up a little and
became the *shbab*, you know, the ones with the look of hate
in their eyes, rioting in the streets and throwing stones at
our soldiers, tying a lasso to the crown of a cypress tree,
bending it to the ground, attaching a Palestinian flag to it,
and freeing the tree—and you, the soldier, go cut down the
moon; and afterwards they grew a little more, and from
among them came the ones who make the Molotov cock-
tails and the bombs. They are the same children from '67.
Nothing has changed in the refugee camps, and their
future is etched on their faces like an ancient, fossilized
record.

For now, they are little children in kindergarten. One
group shouts and cheers, and after making a conscious
effort—necessary, perhaps, for all strangers and for Jews
and Israelis in particular—I begin to differentiate their
faces, their voices, their smiles, their characters, and slowly
also their beauty and delicacy, and this is not easy. It
requires an investment of energy on my part, since I also
have trained myself to look at Arabs with that same
blurred vision which makes it easier for me (only for

me?) to deal with their chiding, accusing, threatening presence, and during this month of encounters with them I must do exactly the opposite, enter the vortex of my greatest fear and repulsion, direct my gaze at the invisible Arabs, face this forgotten reality, and see how—as in the process of developing a picture—it emerges before me slowly, slowly from the emulsion in the darkroom of my fears and my sublimations.

The teachers? They giggle, they blush, they consult each other: yes. They would be happy to take me to see their kindergarten. We stride upward between the boulders and the puddles. In every direction, someone is busy building. Renovating. Painting. The families are large, and more and more must be built. "Where is the plan you are following, the blueprint?" Italo Calvino's Marco Polo asked the citizens of Thekla, and received no answer until night fell and the star-filled heavens were spread above. "There is the blueprint," they answered him.

And on the roof of one of those houses sits a boy, twelve years old perhaps, head shaved and eyes closed, and he plays devotedly on a comb wrapped in paper. Fiddler on the roof.

Between two buildings sits a cement structure, plastered white on the outside. Closed with an iron door on which is the UNWRA emblem. It looks like a public bomb shelter from the fifties. The young teacher opens the iron door, filled with holes, and I enter the Deheisha kindergarten.

First, one has to get used to the dimness. There is no electricity in the kindergarten. I stand in a long, narrow space, divided into two rooms. There is not one picture on the grayish walls; because of the dampness, the wall crumbles if you try to pound a nail into it. In the corner of the room, a metal table and two chairs. And one other piece of furniture: a thin reed mat.

The teacher tells the children to sit, and they do so, crowding onto the mat. They chatter with each other, as children do, until the teacher tells them to be quiet. From that moment on, they are totally silent, not making a sound during the entire conversation. In an Israeli kindergarten the children are unable to remain quiet for a single minute. They jump up from their places, run to the teacher, say what they have to say, argue. They are free children, and you can understand what this blessed, natural freedom is only when you see its opposite. "The children here are so quiet and disciplined," I said to the kindergarten teacher in Deheisha, and she answered with an Arabic proverb: "The gosling floats like the gander"—like father, like son.

"Where are you from?"

"From Zakaria. A village."

"Were you born there?"

She laughs. Really. Even her mother has no memories from there. Mother was five years old when they fled. It is Grandmother who preserves the family tradition. Grandmother, married at the age of seven to a twenty-year-old man. This is what happened: the Turkish Army was at the gates of the country, and the Arabs feared that the Turkish soldiers would take the girls. So they betrothed them while they were still in diapers. Grandfather himself went out to the Great War, and when he returned once on furlough his little wife called him a bad name. He became angry with her, lifted her up in his hands, and threw her far away. That's how little she was!

And the giggly kindergarten teacher bends over with laughter as she tells the story. Today that grandmother has four sons and a daughter in Deheisha. She has survived the Turks, the British, the Jordanians, and the Israelis—four occupations.

She is attractive, the ruddy-cheeked teacher, and looks the way our high-school girls once looked. That anarchist enthusiasm of youth. She is sharp and excitable, and is not afraid to say what is on her mind. She was born in Deheisha, and she supposes she will spend her whole life here. She is engaged to a young man from the camp. How do they enjoy themselves? There isn't much to do here, she answers, we go to friends, to relatives. Even after the wedding, the couple has no place to be alone.

"Where will you build your house?"

"In the camp, over my parents' house."

"And you don't want to leave here for a better place?"

"Only for my homeland. Even if they offer me a palace. Our parents made a mistake when they left their homes. We won't make that mistake."

"And you don't dream sometimes, only dream, that you might live in a better place?"

"Dreams?" She laughs. "I have a responsibility," she says, "to the suffering my parents endured, and to my own suffering."

"And because of responsibility to suffering you won't try to achieve even limited possible happiness?"

"I can't. I don't want to."

"And who will help you return to your village—Arafat?"

"Arafat? Arafat is bourgeois. He drives a Mercedes. He doesn't feel the suffering of the refugees. All the Fatah commanders have houses in Syria and the Gulf states. Arafat has no supporters here. Only we can represent ourselves."

"And if Arafat achieves a political settlement? There is talk now of an international conference, you know."

"Understand. We are against Arafat, because Arafat wants peace. We want a solution by force. What was taken by force will be returned by force. Only thus."

Only thus. I remember the similarity between the symbol of the Irgun and that of the PLO: here a fist grasping a rifle against a map of the land of Israel, and there two fists, holding rifles, against the very same map.

The young and enthusiastic kindergarten teacher was neither the first nor the last person I met during these weeks who voluntarily turned himself into an object, a play toy in the hands of those dealers in life and death, into an impersonal symbol. Into a collective noun. When I stand before such people, I have no idea where to begin unraveling this web of iron.

"And the children, what about them?" I ask.

"The children here know everything," she says, and her friend nods. "Some of the children here are the fourth generation in the camp. On any night the army may enter their house, right into the house, conduct a search, shout, turn over the blankets and slash at them with their bayonets, strip their fathers—here, Naji here—"

Naji is two and a half years old, short for his age, black eyes, curls.

"A month ago they took his father, and he doesn't know where he is, or if he will ever return."

"A little while ago," says the second teacher, somewhat heavy, blue-eyed, and delicately made up, always on the edge of a giggle or a blush, "a little while ago the military governor visited the kindergarten and asked if I teach the children bad things, against Israel and the Jews."

"And what did you say to him?"

"I said that I don't. But that his soldiers do."

"What do you mean?"

"What do I mean? I'll explain. When a child goes for a walk outside and sees a tree, he knows that the tree bears fruit and leaves, right? When he sees a soldier, he knows very well what that soldier does. Do you understand?"

"What do soldiers do?" I ask a girl of about four, called Naima, green-eyed, little gold earrings in her ears.

"Searches and beatings."

"Do you know who the Jews are?"

"The army."

"Are there other Jews?"

"No."

"What does your father do?"

"Sick."

"And your mother?"

"She works in Jerusalem for the Jews. Cleans their houses."

So she answers me, the new little Palestinian problem. "And you"—a chubby boy, somewhat dreamy—"do you know who the Jews are?"

"Yes. They took my sister."

"Where to?"

"To Farah."

(Both his sisters are there, in jail, the teachers explain.)

"What did your sisters do?"

"They did *not* throw stones," he says angrily.

Suddenly a little boy gets up, holding a short yellow plastic stick in his hand, and shoots me.

"Why are you shooting me?"

He runs to the teacher, peeks at me from behind her arm, and laughs. He is two years old.

"Who do you want to shoot?" the teachers ask, smiling, like two mothers taking pride in a smart child.

"Jews."

Their lips make out the answer with him.

"Now tell him why," they encourage the little one.

"Because the Jews took my uncle," he says. "At night they came in and stole him from the bed, so now I sleep with my mother all the time."

"Is this the answer, to bring up another generation and another in hatred? To teach them that this hatred justifies the refusal to work toward a solution? Couldn't you try, maybe, another way?"

"There is no other way," they answer, both of them, each

in her own way, in a whisper or with self-assurance, but the same words.

I stand and listen and try to be neutral. To understand. Not to judge. And also not to be like an American or French correspondent, completely severed from the whole complex of events, and quick to pass judgment. But I also stand here as a reserve soldier in the Israeli Army, and as a human being, rising up against this education in blind hatred, and against such tremendous energy being expended for the preservation of malice, instead of being spent in an effort to get out of this barrenness, this ugliness in which this kindergarten lies, these little children who are so good at hating me.

A boy raises his hand. Needs to make peepee. I accompany him. The bathroom is only a little niche separated from the room by a curtain. In its center, a hole in the ground and a porcelain platter. Little piles of excrement all over, and the urinating boy steps in some. I remember the textbooks full of hate and anti-Israel propaganda found by Israeli soldiers twenty years ago, after the war, in the schools and kindergartens. Those books were confiscated, but their content is now transmitted orally. The oral law. It doesn't matter at all who is really guilty of the refugee camps—we, the Israelis, will pay the price. We, and not the Arab countries or the world. It is us they will hate, these children living their whole lives in a colorless world without happiness, who spend long summer and winter hours in a cold and mildewed kindergarten, which has neither a glass window nor electricity. With the all-pervading stink rising from the "bathroom" a grotesque symbol of their situation.

"What games do you play here?"

"Games like everywhere," says the younger teacher. "Tag. Hide-and-seek. There are toys, too."

Two small cardboard boxes hold the kindergarten's toys: old, faded toys. Someone's donation. Not one toy is whole. None of the cars has wheels. Dolls have missing limbs. There is no mercy.

They also have songs, the kindergarten children in Deheisha. The teachers stand them in a line. "What do we sing when the army goes by? One, two, three, four!" And the children break out in song:

"We went out into the street/We waved the flags/We sang for our country the nicest of songs/a song of freedom and unity/a song of victory through struggle/Bloom, my land/By throwing stones and burning tires we will free the motherland . . . "

I recall the Jewish children who sang patriotic songs when British soldiers passed by. They must also have felt like heroes when they did. It is always the same play, only the players change, and sometimes the roles. It requires a lot of strength to change roles, adapt, learn new lines, inure yourself to the complex significance of the new part.

"And jokes about us," I ask them, as if I am not at all part of the joke, "do you tell jokes about us?"

They think for a minute, astounded that there aren't any. There really aren't. No jokes at all? No slang expression, twenty years old, to describe the border guards, the Shin Bet (the secret security service), the military governor?

We, says the smiling teacher, laugh mostly at ourselves.

Strange that they have no jokes about us. In other places I received the same answer. Really, they asked themselves, how is it that there aren't any jokes? It would be interesting to examine what they do with all that aggression and hatred of us. Who is their Sholem Aleichem? Is it that they unconsciously avoid seeking an outlet in humor? Do they prefer to preserve their hatred and humility unworked, raw, and wild?

"I don't tell the children bad things about Israel," the heavy one says, and adjusts her sweater, "but I tell them stories, stories about animals," she hints.

Like fables.

" . . . like, for example, there were small sparrows on a terebinth tree, playing and having a good time, and suddenly came a cruel black raven who coveted their tree and expelled them from it. They were very sad. They almost died of sorrow, until they got up and gathered together, and flew against him as a great and united group, and so were able to expel him from their tree."

"You made it up?"

"Yes. I have a few stories like that. The children already understand."

"And did they succeed in organizing themselves together, the birds?"

"Yes. They are very wise. They're birds, not Palestinians."

Toward evening I travel to Jerusalem. The roads are lined with rusty cars. Metal ruins, tires stuck on barbed-wire fences, old hot-water tanks, discarded doors, walls dirtied with half-erased graffiti, old shoes...everything left bare and harsh along the road, everything preserved, awakening pent-up melancholy: all this abandoned, like a rebellion and cry against a destroyed, corrupt, irreparable circumstance.

At six in the evening I arrive at the Ben Yehuda mall in downtown Jerusalem to buy *Dear Brothers*, a book about the Jewish underground by one of its members, Haggai Segel. The evening is gray and misty, and the people are burdened with their civilian matters, isolated so much from the hate and the danger, as I walked among them like the bearer of evil tidings among the unaware. In the thin fog and with the light of the yellow streetlamps it is possible to succumb to illusions and see behind every person a halo, a sort of double peeking out for a split second, the identical twin of this man, his double from Nablus, and that young woman, whose unknown twin I met this morning at Deheisha, that same walk and same smile and same quiet sensuality, and for every child there was a double, and none of them knew, and none of them guessed a thing.

What do the Arabs dream about? And what do Jewish children dream about? Is it possible to hope that the dreams of the Jews and the Arabs provide some sort of escape and easing and refinement of the harsh and cruel reality of life—or are dreams only a direct continuation of it?

And why should the mirror mold of dreams not create some sort of closeness, a dialogue unknown to its participants, anti-grammar, unexpectedly creating a new language?

It will not happen.

Dr. Yoram Bilu, a lecturer in psychology at the Hebrew University of Jerusalem, examined with the help of his students, Yussuf Nashef and Tehila Blumenthal, the dreams of eleven-to-thirteen-year-old children in different parts of Israel and the West Bank. Part of his study concerned the children of the Kalandia refugee camp, and the children of Gush Etzion and Kiryat Arba, Jewish settlements in the West Bank.

Every child who took part in the study received a colored notebook and was asked to record four dreams immediately upon wakening. The age of the subjects was fixed so that they would be old enough to write down their dreams but not old enough to be bothered by sexual dreams.

And one other important comment: the children in the refugee camp did not know that the study was for the Hebrew University. The notebooks were given to them through UNWRA and afterwards were carefully translated. What dreams do they dream?

Seventeen percent of the dreams of the Jewish children dealt with meetings with Arabs. (To the attention of those who wish at any price to prevent such meetings. And by the way: does the law recently passed by the Knesset making it illegal for Israelis to meet with PLO members include dream meetings? Check.) In contrast, 30 percent of the children in the Kalandia refugee camp dreamed during the brief period of the study at least one dream involving some sort of meeting with a Jew. The meaning of this, according to Dr. Bilu, is that the children in the Kalandia camp "are obsessively involved with the conflict."

But whom exactly do Jews and Arabs meet on moonless nights?

Among 328 dreams of meetings (Jews and Arabs) there is not one character identified by name. There is not a single figure defined by a personal, individual appearance. All the descriptions, without exception, are completely stereotyped; the characters defined only by their ethnic identification (Jew, Arab, Zionist, etc.) or by value-laden terms with negative connotations (the terrorists, the oppressors, etc.). The Arabs do not try to refine their stereotyped characters. The Jews make some sort of effort—in general, the word "Arab" is associated for them with the word "criminal." "I lived in an Arab city, full of criminals," wrote an eleven-year-old from Kiryat Arba. "I entered the grocery store and two men, an Arab and a gangster, attacked me there," dreamed another boy from the same town. "We have to educate the Arabs, so that they will be good, law-abiding citizens," declared another young citizen from among the Jewish settlers in Hebron. "I taught them to write in Hebrew, until they became good people, and then they freed them from the jail, and they didn't make any more problems."

The Arabs often find escape in apocalyptic dreams, in which the final, decisive battle is held, and the Arab armies, dressed in shining white, are ranged against the Jewish heretics, wrapped in black. The battle is always won by the good guys.

Jewish children also have trouble facing the constant struggle, offering no escape, and they find release in imagination and transference: Kiryat Arba children told, for example, of a colored flying saucer which landed on the border between Israel and "the land of the enemy"; of soldiers from Uganda who attacked a Jewish child, and a twelve-year-old went the farthest when he dreamed that he was walking, minding his own business, in the heart of Hebron and was cruelly attacked from the back, "and I turned around and managed to see that it was a Chinese boy . . . "

The majority of the interactions in the dreams are violent and aggressive and end in death. The dreams of the children of the Kalandia refugee camp indicate a hard and threatening reality, a fragile world with no defense. The typical "plot" of such a dream is played out in the camp: the boundaries of the dreamer's house are very permeable, nothing provides him with defense and security, strange people invade the house and attack the child. Frequently, they torture him to death. His parents are unable to protect him. One dream in particular caught my eye: "The Zionist Army surrounds our house and breaks in. My big brother is taken to prison and is tortured there. The soldiers continue to search the house. They throw everything around, but do not find the person they want [the dreamer himself]. They leave the house, but return, helped by a treacherous neighbor. This time they find me and my relatives, after we had all hidden in the closet in fright."

The Holocaust appears in many dreams of the Kiryat Arba children. An eleven-year-old girl writes: "My friend and I decided to go to Jericho. Suddenly we heard someone calling us from behind. They were my parents. They said that I have to take off the yellow star I was wearing. The star is a large

yellow piece of paper, showing that we support the partisans. The city, Jericho, was against the partisans. But it
turned out that my friend and I had taken off the star too late,
because suddenly someone came, took us to a grove of trees,
and ordered us to crawl on the ground along with many other
people. Crawling, we reached a tunnel, but only my father
was allowed to enter, and my mother and I had to continue to
the place for the women. Suddenly I saw something move: it
was an old woman starting out of her grave. Her face was covered with earth."

Guilt feelings appear only among the Jewish children.
So, for instance, in the dream of a twelve-year-old girl from
Kiryat Arba: " . . . suddenly someone grabs me, and I see
that it is happening in my house, but my family went away,
and Arab children are walking through our moms, and
their father holds me, he has a kaffiyeh and his face is cruel,
and I am not surprised that it is happening that these Arabs
now live in my house. I accept that as if that is the way it is
supposed to be."

It is a long and detailed study, but it seems to me that
these few examples are sufficient. The dreams offer neither escape nor relief. There are no moments of pity and
no friendly contact. Some of them are nightmares, difficult to read, and more difficult to realize the price being
paid by our children and the Arab children for living in
this conflict. This conflict, from which there is no escape
even in dreams.

The writer J. M. Coetzee, who also lives in a cruel
land, complex to the point of being almost insoluble,

recently received the Jerusalem Prize; in his speech he recalled the philosopher Nietzsche, who said: "We have art so that we shall not die of reality." "In South Africa," Coetzee said, "there is now too much truth for the art to hold. Truth that overwhelms and swamps every act of the imagination."

Among us, even dreams are crushed under the weight of reality.

One fact is particularly interesting, concerning what does *not* appear in this study: among some thousand dreams of Jewish and Arab children, there is not one which indicates a longing for peace.

And there are also refugees for whom a miracle happened and who were returned to their land.

Such an instance, of incomprehensible mercy, is that of those who reside in the village in Wadi Alfuqin: in 1948 they were uprooted from their village, and for twenty-four years they lived in a refugee camp, or with family members who took pity on them, or in rented houses, the houses of strangers, in Jericho and Deheisha and Husan and Amman, and suddenly, in 1972, some remote emperor lifted his little finger and gave the order: "Return them!" and they returned to the village from which they were exiled, and they, perhaps, are the only ones to have returned from refugee life to that of human beings, and they can testify to the differences, and can say something about the chances for reconciliation and forgiveness I went there.

Wadi Alfuqin is a fertile, watered valley. Springs flow,

the ground is productive and benevolent, and everyone has a storage pool for springwater, and kitchen gardens full of produce, and olive groves bordered by grapevines planted shoulder to shoulder. And at the top of the mountain which stands over the valley are the foundations of the ancient city of Beitar, and the new settlement Beitar Elit.

After the War of Independence, the valley was the focus of attacks on Israeli Army patrols passing nearby, along the border, and after the army took several retaliatory actions, the village was abandoned and its natives dispersed. Nearly all the houses in the village were demolished, and the ruins on the mountain slope are still bleached by the sun, and the remaining houses have become a training site for the army. On some of the ruins one can still make out the marks of the bullets fired by soldiers in the fifties.

Imtiyaz (the name means "excellence") had not yet been born when her parents fled from the village. They moved from place to place in the West Bank over the course of several years. When she was a baby, they came to the Deheisha refugee camp. She lived her entire childhood and youth in the camp, and a year ago she returned to Wadi Alfuqin: she married a man there. Her parents, who could not afford to build a house in the village, remained in Deheisha. She remembers the day, fifteen years ago, when the people of Alfuqin left the refugee camp and returned to their village. "Of course we were mad at them," she says. "We were angry that they were returning here to real life, and we remained there, in prison. They cried with happiness, and we cried out of jealousy and pain. There are still some there today who are angry with those who were able to return."

"They are mad at the ones who returned? 'What are they guilty of?"

"Whom should they be angry at?"

Whom, indeed? "The Jews threw us out of here, and the Jews brought us back." A wide-eyed old woman sighs as she listens to us from the roof of the house next door, between clumps of just-sheared sheep's wool hung out for air: the Jew taketh away and the Jew giveth.

It is a cool day in early spring. We are sheltered in a shady, broad yard, and the little valley lies at our feet, and the storage pools sparkle in the sun, and despite the Ramadan fast, my hosts bring me a glass of tea, and little by little people from every corner of the village gather around us, listening, nodding their heads, and telling their stories—but not freely. These are things people do not like to recall.

"Life in the camp is bad," one woman of about fifty says shyly. "You are always with your head down, waiting for the next blow. After a few years there you have nothing left but fear and poverty. You become like a dead person: you do not want anything and you do not hope. You wait for death. Even the children there are old. They are born with fear. Here, children are like children: they almost do not know what the army is. Only the *mustawtanin*, the settlers, are frightening."

Everyone glances upward, to the bauble of a settlement stuck into the mountain.

"When the families left Deheisha on their way back to the village and we stayed there," Imtiyaz relates, "I cried for nearly a week. They can return and we can't, because we didn't have the money to build a new house. I was small, and I didn't understand that. After all, we all lived like one big family, we shared everything, we suffered together for years, so why them and not us? After a while, when they began to come visit us in the camp, we would pelt them with questions. We wanted to know everything about the village: how the land was and the spring and the vegetables . . ."

"They would bring us vegetables in bags," remembers Hanan, a rounded young woman who knows a few words of Hebrew. "And we would kiss those vegetables. We would kiss each tomato a hundred times before we ate it there."

"But I actually like Deheisha and miss it," a woman says hotly. She has strong features and had come to sit across from me on a stool, her legs held apart, and had immediately begun vilifying our hosts for serving me a drink during Ramadan. "Even if your brother comes," she says to the taken-aback woman of the house, "do not give him anything to drink! Ah, when the Jordanians were here, they would shoot anyone who desecrated the fast. Since you came here, everything has changed. There is no respect for religion anymore."

You miss Deheisha?

Even the retarded woman, kneeling by the wall and hollowing out green squashes to be stuffed with rice and meat, stops to make a circular motion with her hand and looks at her in amazement.

"Yes. I miss it. I get goose bumps when I think of it," she says, and bares an arm to illustrate her meaning. "But there it's bad! Frightening!" Imtiyaz counters her, and she responds: "The fear is their doing"—indicating me with a movement of her head. "And I miss the people who were there. I miss my house. What, aren't they people, the ones there? Weren't we close to them? That's what I miss."

Apparently she is right, I think. A person can miss even a hard, bad place, if there were beautiful moments there, and if he has a memory of a single instance of grace, and maybe loved someone there or was loved. I thought of the army bases in the Sinai where I once served, jumbles of iron and cement thrown at random on a mountain, and how we made our lives there full, and how those neutral, dead places became dear to us.

Another woman joins the group, greeting us and sitting by us, and another young man, who brings us mandrake fruit to smell. Here it is called the "madman's apple," and it has a faint and wonderful aroma.

The name of the woman who just arrived is Wadha Isma'il, and she listens for a while to the stories of the others. Afterwards, she begins to speak, in a moderate tone, without any reproach in her voice, and tells me this: "After they expelled us from the village, we would come back to work our land. The Israeli Army pretended not to see us. They would have maneuvers up on the mountain, and we would work the land in the valley. We would come every day by donkey from Hebron in order to work our land. One day I came here with my father. I was young then, almost a girl. We worked a few hours, and we started on our way back home. Suddenly the Israeli soldiers surrounded us and separated me from my father. I saw that they blindfolded him with a rag and pushed him into some bushes. I remember that he still had a chance to turn to me once and call to me through the rag. Immediately afterwards I heard shots. Many shots. I began to cry. The soldiers who had stayed with me asked me: Who is that man to you? I said: He is my father. They said: Go to the garden down there, and you'll see that he is harvesting lettuce and eggplant. When I was some distance from them, I glanced back and I saw one of the soldiers aiming his rifle at me. I was frightened and bent over. His bullet hit my neck and came out on the other side."

I don't know what to say to her, and she interprets my silence, apparently, as disbelief. "Look," she says, and her work-hardened fingers undo her kerchief, and she smiles a sort of apology about having to bother me with her wound. I see an ugly scar in back, and another ugly scar in front. Young Hanan cries. It seems that Wadha is her mother. "Every time I hear that story, it is as if it were the first time," Hanan says.

Wadha lay among the bushes and played dead. The soldiers distanced themselves from her and then left the area. She rose, oozing blood, and bound her wounds with a handkerchief. Afterwards, she found her father on the ground, his hands tied behind his back, a large rock on his neck. There were thirty bullets in his body, the village elder, Abu Harb, told us later. Wadha, who is for a moment a girl once more, describes with movements of her body how she walked and tripped through the valley, at night, scared that the Israelis would shoot her from behind, or the Jordanians from in front. She concluded her story as she began it, quietly, with no tone of accusation, and her daughter Hanan stood and cried for all of us.

I pondered then about how much one must be suspicious of people who testify about themselves morning and night that they are merciful. They always taught us that we do not know how to be cruel or to hate our enemies, really hate. We are cleanhanded types. And despite that, every so often another ugly incident takes place, carried out by the merciful hands of people like us, people who never hate, and maybe the fact that we do not allow ourselves to hate actually testifies to the disparagement we feel toward the Arabs, since you do not hate a person whom you see as lower than you. It is hard for us, for instance, to hate children, because we sense that they are not our equals. In this context I recalled a story told me by a reserve soldier I met during the course of these seven weeks. It has no connection with Wadi Alfuqin, but it is very much connected to the entire matter.

"Once, when I was on reserve duty, there was a terrorist attack in the Old City in Jerusalem, near the Rockefeller Museum, and we set up a detainment area for Arab suspects in the courtyard of police headquarters. We picked up all the Arabs we caught. We brought entire truckloads.

How I beat them that night! There was another reservist, a young guy, with me, and I saw that every Arab he catches, he bites hard on the ear. Actually takes off a piece. I ask him why he did it, and he answered me: 'So that I'll know them next time we meet.'"

At the top of the village, in a small, dark house, next to the house of his extended family, the village elder lives. He is called Abu Harb, and he is eighty-five years old. He is, according to the residents, the village historian.

He sits on a colored reed mat, his shaking hand playing with a large, antiquated transistor radio. His eyes are much swollen, and his nose is oddly reddish. He remembers the Turks and the English and the Egyptians, who were here briefly, and the Jordanians he remembers, and now us. "In October 1948 we were exiled from here," he says (the only one in the village, he says, who knows the precise date), and for twenty-four years we were not here. We wandered from place to place for twenty-four years, and everywhere we went we would bury our dead, and afterwards we would wander onward, and for twenty-four years I did not sleep at night, I would lie awake and think, and the first night I returned to my village and slept in it was the happiest night of my life, because I slept on my own land."

In 1972 the people of the village received a notice from the military government that they could return to their village. They do not know who made the decision. They received a notice, and that same day the news spread to all the village's exiles, who had been dispersed to the four winds. When Abu Harb describes how they gathered and came here, I recall the book of Ezekiel, the vision of the dry bones which join together, cover themselves with flesh and sinew, and return to life.

"The military government gave us one month to return to the village," Abu Harb relates. "They told us that who-ever did not build a house within that month would not be allowed to return. We came that same night, from every place, and we set up booths and tents in the place that was once the village. Afterwards, we collected money and paved an asphalt road to bring construction materials in trucks. It was a harsh summer and we worked day and night, and we would sleep under the floor of the house we were building. Each one of us built a single room with a roof, and that was our claim."

He tells his story, and his wife, Ratiba, enters the room. She looks younger than he and her face is still smooth. Her face is dark, "but that is not my color from birth, it is only because of the damned sun of the camp, in Jericho," she explains. They have been married for sixty years, "and he never took another wife, other than me!" she boasts.

I asked them if they know why the Israeli authorities so suddenly allowed them to return to their village.

"We heard that the Israelis needed our place in Deheisha. They intended to bring to the camp a large group of Gazans whom they wanted to remove from the Gaza Strip. So they evacuated us."

"And did Gazans actually take your place there?"

"They came. But afterwards they stopped transferring people there from Gaza."

I do not know if that is the correct interpretation of this singular act of mercy. The fact is that it was all done in secrecy, under wraps. Maybe so as not to arouse demands from other exiles in the territories, or from Israeli Arabs who had been expelled from their villages. I tend to think that the explanation given by the people of Wadi Alfuqin, concerning their exchange for Gazans, is correct. In the twisted climate of the occupation, when one act of mercy is performed, it must almost of necessity be crooked and bent, and be nothing but another of the many faces of arbitrariness.

I ask my conversants how the return to their land affected them.

"Everything changed," Abu Harb says. "We now live here among real people. The people who stayed behind in Deheisha and in Jericho are miserable. They are going mad from sadness and longing for their land. They come and plead with us to give them a little garden plot. Just so they can regain a little self-respect. Something to live for. After all, it is not just land, it is everything. They are cut off from everything there. They have ceased to be people. We have been planted anew. Not only in the land. The land is the beginning: we are planted in life as a whole. In normal relations with other people. In tradition. In all the right things. We are no longer strangers in the world. We have the milk of our cows, the flour of our wheat. We are now complete people."

I have one more question. Maybe the most important question: The Israelis brought you back to your village. Do you hate them less now?

They exchange glances. The very old man, his wife, his daughter-in-law, his many grandchildren and great-grandchildren, all of whom have gathered in the room. The daughter-in-law speaks. She relates that her husband has been arrested on suspicion of taking part in terrorist acts. Immediately after his arrest, Israeli soldiers came and destroyed their house. It was a new house, just completed. The family was not given enough time to remove all its belongings. When it was destroyed, it collapsed on ten sacks of sugar and ten sacks of flour that had been bought at great cost and had been stored in the house for the house-warming celebration. The husband was released right afterwards without any charges having been brought against him. As she tells the story, her lips go white with fury and look like a whip scar on her face. Two other sons of Abu Harb are now under arrest in Israel. One is in prison and the other is awaiting trial. Abu Harb says: Both of them are innocent. And if they did something, they apparently had no choice. The injustice and bad effects of the situation are what turns normal people into criminals.

The mother, Ratiba, says: "The settlers come down from the mountain at night with dogs. They frighten us. They stole our spring, and call it sharing."

"The bus that takes their children to school," ten-year-old grandson Hazem says, "blocks the way for our bus every day, and we have to walk about a kilometer to school."

"They will expel us from here again," says another young man, about eighteen, and everyone nods in agreement.

"And then we will really go mad," says Grandmother Ratiba.

The old man, Abu Harb, sighs a long sigh, passes his hand over his face, and presses it against his eyes. The small children watch him. Returning home did not turn the heart of any one of them into one which loves us, the Israelis. Maybe it was foolish even to hope for that. Abu Harb rises to his feet with difficulty, and sees me to the door. We stand and look together over the beautiful and peaceful valley, and the smoke from the straw fires curls up into the air, and the thistles and wildflowers bloom as far as one can see. Now is the time of the yellow flowers. I tell Abu Harb that I called my book *The Yellow Time* in Hebrew, and he asks me if I have heard about the yellow wind. I say that I haven't, so he begins telling me about it, and about the yellow wind that will soon come, maybe even in his lifetime: the wind will come from the gate of Hell (from the gates of Paradise comes only a pleasant, cool wind)—*rih asfar*, it is called by the local Arabs, a hot and terrible east wind which comes once in a few generations, sets the world afire, and people seek shelter from its heat in the caves and caverns, but even there it finds those it seeks, those who have performed cruel and unjust deeds, and there, in the cracks in the boulders, it exterminates them, one by one. After that day, Abu Harb says, the land will be covered with bodies. The rocks will be white from the heat, and the mountains will crumble into a powder which will cover the land like yellow cotton.

DAVID HOROVITZ

A Little Too Close to God

O N THE WEDNESDAY, I ate a late lunch with Sharon and Alvin, two colleagues from work, at the Village Green, a vegetarian restaurant on Ben-Yehuda Street. We sat in the shade of a sun umbrella, munching our bean sprouts, gloomily comparing the sizes of our overdrafts.

By Thursday afternoon, the Village Green looked a little different. Its huge plate-glass storefront window had been shattered, its wooden chairs reduced to firewood. A young man in his early twenties, a Palestinian, had strolled along Ben-Yehuda at around three o'clock carrying a traveling bag, conversing easily with two of his friends. He had stopped outside

DAVID HOROVITZ, *a writer and English teacher, packed his bags and moved his family to Israel in 1983. His subsequent memoir,* A Little Too Close to God *(2000), is a sometimes humorous, sometimes tragic, always deeply personal account of day-to-day life in the midst of savage conflict.*

the Village Green; his friends had positioned themselves outside two other shops nearby. Then all three of them had pressed their buttons—three, so that their recruiters could emphasize how many were ready to die for the cause.

For hours afterward, rescue workers were mopping up their blood and scraping bits of their dismembered bodies off the walls and the tables and the chairs of the Village Green, off the fedoras and the trilbies in the display case at Fuerster's Hat Shop farther up the road, off the bridal gown hanging lopsidedly from the mutilated mannequin in the dress shop next door.

Their blood, and the blood of the five Israelis they had killed.

While hundreds of horrified, ghoulishly curious Jerusalmites were kept behind police barriers all along the street, I walked through the bomb zone with the devastation still fresh. Wonderful thing, a press card. It gets you access to places other folks just can't go near. I looked at a large chunk of a bomber's torso oozing blood from beneath a piece of white plastic sheeting. I heard one of the rescue workers call out from a café, as I scrunched past on the broken glass, "Aaron, there's a foot here." I smelled the faint but unmistakable odor of burned flesh—just like a summer barbecue, made revolting only by the context. And I saw the remains of that green sun umbrella we'd sat under twenty-four hours earlier at the Village Green. The cloth had been ripped away by the force of the blast, but the white metal frame was still there, spattered with blood. Chunks of human flesh were hanging from it, like scraps in a deranged butcher's display.

Almost everybody who has ever been to Israel has walked down Ben-Yehuda Street. My wife, Lisa, when we were at university, used to waitress at the Village Green; her roommate waitressed at the café across the street. Ben-Yehuda is where American seminary students hang out when ducking classes, where tourists shop for souvenirs, where locals grab a cheap falafel or shwarma lunch, where the tarot-card readers and the astrologers drink Turkish coffee during the long waits between gullible customers, where the disciples manning the outreach stand of the late Lubavitcher Rebbe attempt to persuade the secular male pedestrian traffic to don a skullcap, strap on tefillin (phylacteries), and say a prayer. And so, more than with any of the dozen-plus suicide bombings in the past few years, this Ben-Yehuda blast had everybody thinking, That could have been me.

But it really, *really* could have been me—and Sharon and Alvin. All we'd have had to do was eat lunch at the Village Green on Thursday instead of Wednesday.

My wife and I, naturally, discussed at length my closeish brush with death (as compared to the general, ongoing, slightly more distant brushes with death—the blasts in the vegetable markets where we sometimes shop, the late-night shooting on roads we've often used—to which all of us in Israel have tried to become accustomed over the years). But, you'll understand, we did not raise the matter of Daddy's lucky break with our eldest son, Josh, who was only five at the time. Still, the raw details of the bombing did not escape him, nor did we try to shield him from them completely. This is our reality, his reality, and he has to deal with it somehow, while his parents offer reassurance and try to explain the inexplicable. He watched news reports on television, overheard conversations, saw the newspaper photographs. His kindergarten teacher had the kids sit in a circle, their open, innocent faces turned anxiously toward her, to talk about the bomb, their fears, the dead people, the bad guys who had come to Jerusalem to kill.

And three days later, after Josh's five-year-old mind had done its best to grapple with the overload, as his mother and I and his younger brother and his baby sister drove home together from my office in late afternoon, he blurted out from the backseat: "If you *both* get killed, who's going to make our sandwiches?"

In a way, it is because of that question that I've written this book. Because my generous, sensitive eldest child, whom I've had the arrogance, or the stubbornness, or the blindness, or the faith, to try to bring up in Israel, is so attuned to the wicked violence of the world into which I've pitched him that he has already partly reconciled himself to the loss of either his mummy or his daddy and now is progressing toward preparing for the loss of us both. People are dying everywhere, he was saying, and I don't understand why. I'm scared one of you is going to die too, and that would be terrible. But what am I going to do, what is Adam going to do, what is Kayla going to do, if you both get killed? Who's going to wash us and dress us and read to us and hug us? And who's going to make our sandwiches for kindergarten?

I know that putting this down on paper isn't going to

alter anything dramatically. It won't stop the bombs or alleviate the hatreds. But it just might open some minds. And it might help me clarify my own thinking about living here: Whether I owe it to my family to keep doing what I came here for in the first place—playing a unique role, however small, in shaping the first Jewish state in two thousand years, completing a circle of history, bringing our modern Jewish family back to the land of its roots, to the city where my ancient royal namesake built his capital three thousand years ago, to be free, a majority, in our own country, to make our own decisions, and then live and die by them. Or whether Lisa and I ought to take the kids somewhere calmer and safer. I have the arrogance to worry about how growing up in a West Bank settlement may impact my sister's children, but what am I doing to my own, exposing them to all the anger and bloodshed? When you have children, you take more care crossing the road, you drive a touch more carefully. And, in my case, you start looking more deeply at how and where you're living, your reasons for being here, and whether they're still valid—whether what was right for a student, or a single man in his twenties, is right for a married man with three kids a decade later.

The theory, the way I absorbed it through years of largely mediocre Jewish education in London, was that this Israel was supposed to be the safe haven for the Jews, the refuge for the persecuted people, the democratic, free, independent homeland, awash in a sea of Arab hostility but holding its own and slowly rolling back the tide of hatred, gradually eliminating the existential threats, making its peace with its neighbors.

But it has not turned out that way—not completely, not yet. We have proved ourselves, gloriously, as a safe haven for Jewish people, a country that, had it existed at the time of the Holocaust, would have saved millions of lives. We have gathered hundreds of thousands of Jews over the decades from the countries of the Middle East, from North Africa, from all over Europe. In the past few years alone we have opened our doors to people from Syria and Yemen and Iran and Iraq, when Jewish life there became unlivable. While the combined might and resources of the Western world struggled to cope with the hundreds of thousands of ethnic Albanians made homeless in 1999 by the conflict in Kosovo, Israel, in the course of the 1990s, took in 800,000 Jews from the former Soviet Union—flew them here, housed them, gave them money to get on their feet, found jobs for them.

At the height of the Kosovo crisis, in May 1999, I flew on a Jewish Agency aid plane to Albania, carrying clothes and school supplies and toiletries, financed by private Israeli and American Jewish donations. We landed at Tirana Airport—a strip of tarmac in the countryside with rows of NATO helicopters lined up on either side—and were bused into the capital, where several thousand Kosovo Albanians were living in tents around the commandeered outdoor public swimming pool. The younger generation assured us that they would be going home soon; their parents and grandparents said far less, more conscious of the uncertainties that lay ahead. All of them were helpless, stranded, their lives in limbo. And then we flew on to Budapest, where 400 Jews from Belgrade were taking refuge in a Jewish-owned hotel while NATO bombed their capital. Most of them, too, assured us that they would be returning in a matter of days, but thirty of them—mainly in their late teens and early twenties—flew back with us to Israel, to try out life in the Jewish state. Another 150 had already made the journey. So while the world dithered about the ethnic Albanians, Israel was sending out its planes to collect the Jews, Jews who had never wanted Israel, who had assumed their country was stable and never dreamed they would need Israel. Israel helped pay for their hotel stay in Hungary. It paid for their flights to Tel Aviv. It lodged them in absorption centers, organized sightseeing tours and Hebrew classes, gave them pocket money, offered them automatic citizenship and every opportunity to stay. Many did. I felt proud to be flying back with them, proud of my country, proud that it was there for them.

But as for rolling back the tide of hatred and making our peace with the neighbors, here our record is less commendable. And while it would be comfortable and comforting to place all the blame for our woes on the other side, the Arabs, we have often been as pigheaded and racist and proprietary as they are, if not more so. For the three years that Benjamin Netanyahu misruled Israel, between 1996 and 1999, we made no real effort to reach peace with Syria, a peace that would also have put a halt to

our miniwar with Lebanon. Only with the election of
Ehud Barak as prime minister, in 1999, did that quest
resume in earnest. Jordan did make peace with us, in
1994, a warm peace that saw the late King Hussein pop-
ping over to Israel just to say hello, like any ordinary
neighbor. Netanyahu rewarded him, in the late summer of
1997, by sending a team of Mossad hit men to assassinate
one of his citizens, in broad daylight, on the streets of his
capital, using the kind of terrifying chemical agent that we
are so horrified to see Iraq and Iran developing. Our most
awkward enemies, the Palestinians, who unfortunately
happen to be living on much of the same land that we
covet for ourselves, claimed to have chosen the path of
coexistence a full decade ago, embracing the "two-state"
solution—each side settling for an equitable share of the
territory. When our prime minister of the day, Yitzhak
Rabin, attempted to negotiate the formal separation, one
of our own people, a purportedly Orthodox Jew, gunned
him down.

Of course, it is not all as simple as that. Not much is in
these parts. But, to some extent, we've spurned opportunities for peace because we've convinced ourselves that
the Arabs are lying, that they are tricking us about their
good intentions. Some of us seem to be waiting for every
single Palestinian and Jordanian and Syrian to declare
their love for us before we reconcile ourselves to them.
And some of us, I think, although few Israelis would admit
it, have even come to rather like being the big, bad guy on
the block, the uncompromising toughie whom everybody

would love to bring down but can't. The pre-state desire to build a tough Jewish nation, a self-sufficient people that nobody, not the Nazis, not the Arabs, could ever again render defenseless, has become embedded and sometimes exaggerated in our psyche. The power, our power, has gone to some of our heads.

In a recent Jewish New Year special issue, the Hebrew daily newspaper *Ma'ariv* published a commemorative magazine of photographs, landmark moments in our evolution. And there, in this slim volume of black-and-white images and short paragraphs of text, was encapsulated not only our awe-inspiring rebirth and rise to power, but also our fall from its graceful use. Israel has never been an easy place to live. It was born amid controversy, sanctioned by a world seeing to provide recompense to the Jews for the World War II extermination of their millions, but at no small cost to the hundreds of thousands of Arabs of Palestine. It was formally established, in May 1948, in the midst of hostilities intended by the Arab world to kill it before it could draw breath. And not a decade has since gone by without a major war and dozens of minor confrontations.

But the nature of those conflicts has changed as the years have passed, the relative moralities of the warring parties have shifted. And this matters. Because in the early pages of that *Ma'ariv* commemorative magazine, Israel is a gutsy young nation whose leadership and population cry out for peace but will struggle bravely through the wars imposed on them. Here is David Ben-Gurion, our first prime minister, reading out the "Declaration of Independence" in Tel Aviv in May 1948, with its call to the Arab peoples to make their peace with the new/old Jewish entity in their midst, a call issued even as the fighting gathers intensity. There, eight years later, is an anonymous kibbutz member turned soldier, easy but not arrogant with success at the culmination of the 1956 fighting in the Sinai. Then we see Rabin, the chief of staff in the 1967 Six-Day War caught unawares by the camera as he prepares to make his victory speech on Jerusalem's Mount Scopus, a speech in which he will talk, modestly, of a historic military achievement tinged with sadness for the fallen sons of Israel and the fallen Arab fighters.

Those were difficult days, but, at the risk of romanticizing a period long before my own time here, days apparently colored by generosity of spirit, by a national will for reconciliation; a belief that each war would be the last war or, if not, that it would be *one* of the last wars—that there would, someday soon, be a last war—and that Israel would finally find its quiet place in the region.

But our greatest military victory, that destruction of the Arab air forces at the start of the Six-Day War, the capture of the Sinai desert and the Gaza Strip and the Golan Heights and, especially, Jerusalem's Old City and the land on the West Bank of the Jordan River, turned out to be the start of our corruption. For somewhere in the national mentality, a latent messianism was reignited, an urge to call in an ancient debt: to reassert Jewish rule over all the territory of the God of Abraham and Moses willed us in the pages of the Bible. So now, in the *Ma'ariv* album, the photographs show the divine assurance in the arrogant posture of Rabbi Moshe Levinger, seated on the shoulders of his admiring supporters, defying the 1975 Rabin government by founding a Jewish settlement deep inside the captured West Bank. Flip the page and you face the last moments in the life of Emil Grunzweig, murdered by a right-wing Israeli during a left-wing protest against Israel's reckless invasion of Lebanon in 1982. We see the bitter yet confused features of an Israeli soldier in Gaza in the early days of the Palestinian Intifada in 1987, helmeted and kitted out with rifle and grenade launcher, yet helpless and uncertain in the midst of a milling swarm of Palestinian teenagers armed with only rocks and the frustrated recklessness born of twenty years of Israeli occupation. And finally, in October 1995, the camera immortalizes the venom in the eyes of a group of Jewish demonstrators, brandishing placards that denounce Rabin as a traitor for trying to make peace with the Palestinians, for daring to trade some of that God-given land—stigmatizing him with the perverted charge of treason that, a month later, would lead to his assassination in Tel Aviv.

It was a gradual descent from the moral high ground, so gradual that, even when we hit rock bottom with Rabin's assassination, we refused to acknowledge how low we had sunk. Four days after the prime minister was killed, the rabbinical leaders of the Orthodox community from which his assassin had emerged held a public meeting at Beit Agron, in central Jerusalem, at which one bearded sage after another rose to defend the values that Yigal Amir, the gunman, had absorbed, to argue in the face of all evidence that they bore no blame for the killing and the seething climate in which it had occurred, to castigate more moderate and secular Israelis—the hated "left"—for pointing the finger of blame in their direction. The one brave, foolhardy rabbi, Yoel Bin-Nun, who stood up to ridicule the delusionary effort at self-defense and who alleged that one or more unnamed rabbis had actually sanctioned the assassination, found himself threatened and ostracized by parts of his community.

In the murder of our military hero turned peacemaker, by one of his own Jewish people, we lost the last vestiges of our innocence.

At the end of the millennium, to live in Israel was to alternate between hope and despair, as the progress under Rabin gave way to the fatuous posturing of Netanyahu, replaced, in turn, by Rabin's would-be heir, Barak. Peace seemed close at hand, then receded, then came closer again. Our military superiority was challenged by Iran's drive to nuclear self-sufficiency and by the relentless attacks of the Hamas bombers and the Hizbollah gunmen on our northern border. Intifada violence flared intermittently. The spiritual father of the Hamas suicide bombers, Sheikh Ahmad Yassin, assured his extremist Islamic followers that Israel wouldn't be around much longer. And in the lower ebbs—especially when you read census figures predicting that the 1 million Palestinians of 1978, grown to 3 million today, would become 7.5 million by 2025, while we are 5 million Jews in 1999—it was hard to deride him.

Even more damagingly, we Israelis ourselves were disunited and bickering, grappling not only with internal rifts over the viability of making peace with our neighbors but with divides between the established Jews of European origin (the Ashkenazim) and those who came here, in poverty, from the Middle East and North Africa (the Sephardim), between Jews who cleave to the most zealous interpretations of God's law and those who seek a more pluralistic approach to their faith, and between our Jewish nation here in Israel and our fellow Jews who live overseas.

Barely fifty and heading into terminal decline? I hope not. I'd like to think of the late 1990s as our national coming-of-age, with the customary frustrations and growing pains, our maturity finally demonstrated in 1999 in our repudiation of the hate-mongering Netanyahu and our preference for a leader, Barak, seeking to achieve the near-impossible: leading us to peace and healing our internal divisions.

I want to believe that half a century from now, my children, grandchildren, and great-grandchildren will be celebrating the Israeli centenary and laughing gently at the concerns we are grappling with today, that we will have long since divided this land equitably with the Palestinians and the Syrians, and opened our borders to each other. I want to believe that Israelis up north won't be ducking into bomb shelters because of rocket fire from Lebanon, nor Israelis in Tel Aviv hiding underground to evade missiles from Iraq—that people, in short, won't be dying senseless, premature deaths; that the awful cycle of violence will have long since been broken.

I want to believe, moreover, that ours will be a Jewish country in the moral sense—a country admired for its ethical fiber, a genuine light unto the nations. I hope we will be a country, for example, ready not only to airlift Ethiopian Jews out of a life-threatening civil war—as we did in bringing 15,000 "home" to Israel on a single weekend in 1991—but to open our doors to other persecuted peoples as well. In the spring of 1999 we hardly excelled on that score: We rapidly repatriated to Egypt a few hundred Bedouin who had crossed the border to join relatives inside Israel and who claimed that a feud with another tribe was placing their lives in danger; and while we welcomed the Jews displaced by the Kosovo crisis, we found room for just 200 Albanians—plucked arbitrarily from among tens of thousands at a refugee camp on the Macedonian border—bringing the first group in on Holocaust Memorial Day, a coincidence that ought surely to have helped prompt a greater generosity of spirit. Netanyahu, milking their arrival for all it was worth on the tarmac at Ben-Gurion Airport, carelessly described this tiniest of gestures as the fulfillment of a "symbolic obligation"— "symbolic" being the operative word.

Israel, at once a moral Jewish state and a normal state— is it attainable? Well, that is the dream that sustains me here.

All the Jews of modern Israel are engaged in an ongoing experiment. And all of us, by being here, living the kinds of lives we do, and fighting for the causes we believe in, are determining how the experiment turns out. We have had our amazing successes: We have resuscitated a Jewish national entity on the very land where the Jewish people flourished thousands of years ago, its modern-day inhabitants able to gaze at the same golden landscape, climb the same gentle Jerusalem hills, bathe in the same Mediterranean waters. We have taken Hebrew out of the pages of our holy books and transformed it into a living, breathing language—the language my children speak as naturally as the native English of their parents. We have built a first-world economy and are on the cutting edge of science and technology. Rescuing those persecuted Jews from around the world, we have grown tenfold. And if we made a hash of the early absorption efforts in the 1940s and 1950s—brutally severing Sephardim from their traditions and trying to impose a secular, socialist lifestyle—we have tried to do better in the 1980s and 1990s, with some success with the Russians and rather less with the Ethiopians.

But many of the challenges are still ahead of us, and that is why, when things seem to be going backward, it gets so depressing here. Our democracy is not as stable as many of us would like to believe. We have killed one prime minister, and the potential for further political violence is undeniable. Death threats to politicians and judges are now routine. Our leaders move around in cordons of bodyguards.

There are powerful forces here for whom Orthodoxy is a priority and democracy an irritant. At precisely the same time the U.S. chief justice was presiding over the nonremoval of President Clinton from office in February

1999, and praising the robustness of American democracy and the high standard of the Senate hearings, our Supreme Court was coming under attack by our ultra-Orthodox politicians, its president derided by one legislator as a "Jew-hater" for having had the temerity to intervene in issues of birth, marriage, and burial that the ultra-Orthodox regard as their exclusive purview. The state's chief rabbis participated in a demonstration attended by hundreds of thousands of ultra-Orthodox Jews, called by the community's political leaders to challenge the Supreme Court's authority. Police were assigned to surround the Supreme Court complex itself for fear, unfounded this time, that the demonstrators would march on the building as they had two years before. We defenders of democracy were reduced to holding a counterdemonstration in the park below the Court, garnering a far smaller turnout, to chant our support for the embattled judges within. And none of our leading political figures, terrified of alienating ultra-Orthodox voters, chose to attend.

A few months later, when the Jerusalem District Court found Aryeh Deri, leader of the ultra-Orthodox Shas political party, guilty of bribe-taking, and sentenced him to four years in jail, Deri's rabbi simply rejected the court's ruling and declared that "Reb Aryeh is innocent." And again, terrified of the ultra-Orthodox influence at the ballot box, our mainstream political leaders failed to immediately break their ties with Deri, failed even to suspend him from the Knesset (parliament). In the elections of 1999, more than 400,000 Israelis voted for Deri's party, giving it seventeen of the 120 Knesset seats; they voted Shas even though the party was led by a convicted criminal, even though his campaign was essentially a rejection of the rule of law here, even though Shas would like to turn Israel into a theocracy. The Shas supporters, mainly working-class Sephardim, backed Deri not because he was challenging our democracy, but because that democracy had failed them because the state schools in their development towns are rundown and overcrowded, because job opportunities are scarce, because they live in poverty—and because he promised to use his influence to right those wrongs. If the government does not reach out to these people in the next few years, if it does not reallocate its funds to give them better schools, create jobs, and draw them into the mainstream, Shas and the other antidemocratic, ultra-Orthodox political movements, taking their adherents out of the workforce and into dependent, full-time Torah study, will flourish, and Israel will decline.

And yet, to look at the glass half-full, the Supreme Court remains independent, fights antidemocratic legislation, pushes for pluralism. Deri eventually had to resign his Knesset seat. And if his appeal is denied, he will go to jail. He and his supporters may hold his rabbi's word to be law, but the courts, for now, prevail.

We are still trying to find a middle ground on religion, to build a framework in which all our citizens can freely practice their own interpretation of their faith. The Orthodox-secular conflicts are vicious. And yet, in the last few years, small outreach groups have sprung up and flourished, ordinary people from different religious worlds sitting down to talk through their differences. And I have found, even in increasingly ultra-Orthodox Jerusalem, a framework for Judaism that is perfect for my family. I love the fact that my children are living in a Jewish environment, where it is the Hebrew date that gets written on the chalkboard in their classroom in the morning, where they learn about Jewish festivals in their regular curriculum, not at Sunday school, and where they experience those festivals with their entire nation. We can buy Chanukah doughnuts at every bakery in town. We see menorahs lighting tens of thousands of apartment windows. We shop in supermarkets bursting with matzos every Passover. We put up a sukkah each year, just like our ancient forebears did in the desert, and hear the same hammering all along our street. My blond, blue-eyed Adam, in one of the more innovative casting choices of our age, was dressed up in his kindergarten class last Pentecost in the white headdress and flowing robes of an Ethiopian Jew, to participate in a reenactment of that group's arrival in the Promised Land.

It is at once enchanting and terrifying living an experiment. We take everything to heart, see every shift as potentially decisive. It is profoundly unsettling—a roller-coaster ride. But it's addictive.

The harshest blow, the biggest threat so far to the success of our experiment, was the murder.

For three years and four months, beginning with the nail-biting election day of June 23, 1992, when Yitzhak

Rabin just squeezed into power, he gave many of us the delighted sense that Israel was settling into the Middle East. The years of Likud rule, of settlement-building and diplomatic stonewalling, when peace with Egypt had signally failed to yield peace with anybody else, were receding into the haze. Rabin was bringing Israel and himself full circle, the former army chief relinquishing the Arab territory he had captured, and winning normalized neighborly relations in turn.

That glorious delusion was blown apart by three bullets fired at almost point-blank range on the dark night of November 4, 1995. One of the bullets missed its mark and wounded a bodyguard. But the other two found their target—Rabin's unprotected back—and felled him. The assassin was not deranged. He was not poorly educated. He was no one's patsy. Amir was a former combat soldier, in his second year of law school at a Tel Aviv university. And he was a fixture at the university's "Kolel," the Jewish study center where the best and the brightest minds wrestled with the rabbinical arguments over all aspects of man's relationship with his fellow man and with his God, as conducted within the pages of the Mishneh, the Gemara, and other holy texts.

Amir acted alone that night. There was no one with hum in the bedroom of his Herzliyya home as he alternately loaded ordinary and hollowed-out bullets (for extra penetration) into the magazine of his pistol, tucked it into the waistband of his trousers, and walked off to catch a bus to the Tel Aviv square where the prime minister was speaking. But as Amir stepped out of the shadows and squeezed his trigger, he knew he was fulfilling the fervent wish of scores, maybe hundreds, of his fellow Israelis, and that thousands more would not be grieving for the soldier-statesman he was cutting down.

I'm not exaggerating. Nice, easygoing, normal Israelis, people I have worked with, had coffee with, played soccer with, told me right after the murder, while our nation was supposedly deep in shock, revulsion, and soul-searching, that, yes, maybe murder was a bit drastic, but Rabin did have to be stopped. "It's a shame it had to end this way," one of my soccer mates said with a kind of helpless shrug—a shrug that intimated that, while he wouldn't actually have loaded his own pistol and gone out stalking Rabin, he wouldn't have stood in Amir's way.

Amir gauged public sentiment shrewdly. As the student organizer of solidarity visits to the settlers of the occupied West Bank, panicked at the prospect of Arafat gaining control of their valleys and hilltops, Amir had heard the anti-Rabin vitriol, the charges that the government, resting as it did on the support of Arab members of Knesset, was "illegitimate," the assertion that the prime minister was abandoning the brave, selfless, pioneering West Bank Jews to be murdered by the vicious Arab masses who encircled them. Politically astute and involved, Amir had attended rallies organized by Netanyahu's right-wing opposition camp; heard the chants of "Rabin is a traitor," "Rabin is the son of a whore," "Rabin is a murderer"; listened as "respectable" politicians vilified the prime minister for leading his country "to the gates of Auschwitz" by making "a pact with the devil"—Arafat.

Amir told the policemen who grabbed him after the fatal shots had been fired that he had expected to die for the sake of his mission. But he survived. And now he sits in solitary confinement in a cell in the desert town of Beersheba, sustained by a flow of admiring letters, by the knowledge that Orthodox teenage girls tape his picture to their bedroom walls, by his mother's unflagging love—and by the confidence that the supporters who gather outside the jail to celebrate his birthdays will, sooner or later, muster the clout to have him released. He will be freed not for good behavior, he knows, nor on compassionate grounds in his frail old age. No, he will be freed as a hero, a savior, the only man in the country, as his sister once put it, who had the guts to demonstrate how deep was his love for his people.

Alongside the achievements of our young nation, the murder of Rabin—not by an Arab extremist but by one of his own countrymen—exposed our malaise. It underlined our polarizations, our political and religious divides. And if we cannot heal those rifts, they will grow to overshadow our successes. If we let them, our internal disputes, our anger, cynicism, mistrust, and intolerance, will destroy our society, ruin our relationship with Diaspora Jews, return us to our status of international pariah.

Under Rabin's predecessor, Yitzhak Shamir, I had been dismayed at the determination to spend most available resources on settlement expansion—complicating the prospects of an accord with the Palestinians—to the detriment of other pressing needs, notably building homes and creating jobs for the immigrants from the former Soviet Union. But I had somehow assumed that the wrongs would be put right, and Rabin's election appeared to confirm that. By the time Rabin was murdered, I had two children, and that meant my life had become much more deeply intertwined with that of the country. I could no longer afford to assume that the wrongs would be put right. For one thing, I began to doubt that they would; if they were not, I now had a family that was going to suffer—that I was putting at risk by living here. I had two boys who would one day be conscripted. Before Rabin was killed, I honestly never thought twice about whether I had done the right thing in moving here. Since November 4, 1995, not a week has gone by when I haven't agonized about the choice.

DEBORAH SONTAG

The Palestinian Conversation

I
T WAS CHRISTMAS in Gaza, where Christmas is irrelevant, yet the day felt somehow special. A brilliant sun glinted off metal debris in the dirt streets of the Rafah refugee camp and bathed that desperate place in an unusual glow. It was, in fact, downright tranquil inside the camp. The shebabs, the youths, who had spent much of the previous fifteen months hurling stones, were bent over books in a ramshackle library. Their leader, a grown-up named Abed al-Raouf Barbakh, had slicked his hair with pomade and donned a tie. "I dressed up for the cease-fire," he said, as he strode through the camp waving left and right, palming the heads of some boys and chasing others off with a hiss.

DEBORAH SONTAG, *Israeli Bureau Chief for the* New York Times, *writes on Israeli-Arab affairs for a variety of publications. Her interviews of Palestinians around Israel, entitled* A Palestinian Conversation, *first appeared in the* New Yorker.

Barbakh is a stocky, rough-edged street leader of Yasir Arafat's Fatah organization who, by his own account, is wanted by the Israelis for inciting the kids in Rafah to violence. During the bloody period that began in late September 2000, he indeed directed much of what he called the resistance effort inside the camp. On the day of my visit, however, he presented himself as a kind of youth counselor. His handgun tucked inside a pert black vest, he talked of planting a garden among the weeds and of setting up foreign exchange programs. He suggested that I consider sending my own children for a week in Rafah. "I promise I won't teach them to use weapons," he said.

After Arafat asked the Palestinians on December 16 to halt attacks on Israelis, he visited Barbakh's turf to beseech the residents of Rafah to honor his request. Barbakh boasted that he wagged his finger at Arafat and declared: "May the cease-fire go to hell. They are shooting at us. We can't offer them flowers." He said that Arafat waited him out. "Then he told me I was too agitated, and when the meeting ended, he ordered me arrested," Barbakh said.

Immediately, though, the loyal shebabs—my kids"— came to Barbakh's defense by burning the neighborhood police station. So a truce was reached; Palestinian police officers did not take Barbakh into custody, and he embraced the cease-fire in practice if not in principle. "We'll give Abu Amar a chance," he said, using Arafat's nom de guerre and speaking in his own way for a majority of Palestinians at that moment in time.

We sat in the camp's smoky cafe, which overlooks a
Bank of Amman branch set in a tableau of muddy depres-
sion near the Egyptian border. A blue-uniformed Palestinian police officer, a friend of Barbakh's, joined us silently.
We all sipped hot tea from glasses. And taking advantage of
the relative quiet, we talked and talked. It was one of
dozens of conversations that I had with Palestinians in the
West Bank and Gaza during that odd (and heartbreakingly
short-lived) moment that began just after Arafat, under
intense pressure from the international community,
ordered his own men to hold fire and forcefully persuaded
Islamic fundamentalist groups to halt suicide bombing
attacks inside Israel. The tit-for-tat violence had temporarily ceased.

For sixteen months, the downward spiral has been otherwise unrelenting. Since the failure of the Camp David
negotiations in the summer of 2000, there has been one
provocation after another. Ariel Sharon made his heavily
guarded visit to the plaza outside Al Aksa Mosque to
demonstrate Jewish sovereignty over the Temple Mount,
the Palestinian street exploded, the Israelis quelled volatile
demonstrations with deadly fire, the Palestinians moved
from stones to guns to bombs, the Israelis began assassinat-
ing suspected militants and the momentum of attacks, and
counterattacks took on a bloody life of its own.

It has been a devastating period for everyone, and the
Palestinians know what it has cost them. The Aksa intifada,
as it has come to be known, has resulted in about 800 Palestinian deaths, thousands of injuries, a crippled economy and

an infrastructure devastated by bombardment and bulldozer. Suicide bombings have weakened international support for the Palestinian nationalist cause. Arafat, once a frequent flier to the Clinton White House, is stuck in Ramallah with Israeli tanks hemming his compound. Most Palestinians are under a kind of lock-down inside their towns, "220 discontinuous little ghettos," Edward W. Said, the Palestinian-American intellectual, has called them. The checkpoints have become more backlogged and humiliating than ever: as if time were going backward, many Palestinians have returned to riding donkeys on dirt roads to circumvent them. And Arafat's crackdown on militant Islamic groups—Hamas and Islamic Jihad—has provoked turbulent divisions inside Palestinian society itself.

Yet for a moment there was this lull. Granted, it felt more like a standoff as the Palestinians waited to see whether Israel would either reciprocate by loosening restrictions on their movement or nudge Palestinian fighters back into action with another assassination. But even the standoff gave people the time and the mental space to think with cooler heads about their situation, and I felt as if I was tapping into a vibrant communal conversation that revealed both deep disagreements within Palestinian society and a startling, defiant optimism about the future—if not the near future.

And so it was that in our conversation, even someone like Barbakh, a human powder keg, could allow himself to entertain the idea of peace. When we spoke, he made his intifada credentials perfectly clear—shot eleven times during the first

Palestinian uprising, wanted by the Israelis during the second. But he also mentioned a few pacific credentials, like some coexistence programs in which he had once participated. And whether or not he was sincere, he sensed that it would be politic to ask me to send the world a message that even he, a fighter, really wanted quiet. "We are tired and fed up with all the fighting," he said. "We want all the blood that has been shed to be enough. Give us our small, little country, our West Bank and Gaza, and then it will all end. Israel can keep Israel and leave us the hell alone."

Before I traveled to Jerusalem, which I left in August after three years there as a reporter, I e-mailed friends to commiserate about how things had gone from horrible to worse over the fall. My Israeli pen pals sounded pretty despairing, but the Palestinians didn't. It wasn't as if they saw a rainbow on the horizon, but they seemed to have reset their clocks, accepting the idea that their struggle for independence might take a good deal longer.

My Palestinian e-mail correspondents reminded me never to underestimate, as one put it, "the capacity of the Palestinians to withstand sufferness." That is the term that many Palestinians use in English; it sounds more eternal than suffering. Its linguistic companion is steadfastness. Sufferness and steadfastness. My Palestinian correspondents told me that I was looking at the situation like an American, a Westerner, with a terrible impatience for the conflict to be resolved. "Of course, we can't tolerate it," David Khoury, a Palestinian-American businessman, later told me. "But we have to, so we have extended the limits of our tolerance."

The Khoury clan lives in Taybeh, a charming village near Ramallah, which is the center of cultural and commercial life in the West Bank. Arriving at the family's house, I came upon a slightly surreal image. David's twelve-year-old son, Constantine, was Rollerblading in circles in the garage, a floppy felt Santa hat on his head and a GameBoy under his nose. "Our kids are going stir-crazy because of the closure," David said. "They haven't had school for three weeks."

The Khourys are not typical Palestinians. They are Christian and affluent, and in a land of few drinkers they produce what has become the Palestinian national beer, Taybeh. But they nonetheless represent an important group of Palestinians, who returned from abroad after the Oslo peace declarations of 1993 to wager on a future. Oslo created a framework in which Israel would transfer territory in the West Bank and Gaza to a newly created Palestinian Authority that would guarantee Israel's security. During a five-year interim period, Israel and the Palestinian Authority would negotiate the thorny final issues—including the status of Jerusalem and the Palestinian refugees—and establish a permanent peace accord. Implicit in Oslo was a two-state solution whereby Israel and Palestine would coexist.

Like many Palestinians, the Khourys embraced what they saw as the compromise in Oslo—that the Palestinians would recognize Israel, renounce their claim to all of what they called historic Palestine, and settle for 22 percent of the land; that is, the West Bank and Gaza. They embraced it with such enthusiasm that David and his younger brother, Nadim, flew from the United States to

Tunis before Arafat returned from exile to secure his permission for, of all things, a brewery in the West Bank. A photograph of them with Arafat in Tunis hangs near their tanks and fermenters, next to St. George, the patron saint of Taybeh, slaying a dragon.

We were chatting beneath these incongruous images in the dim, unheated microbrewery next door to their home. David wore a short-sleeved polo shirt, while his silver-haired father, Canaan, was wrapped tightly in a wool overcoat and cashmere scarf. Dressed in a smart pantsuit, David's wife, Maria, looked nothing like a typical villager; she is Greek-American, although an extremely articulate advocate of the Palestinian cause.

In the late 1970s, the Khoury brothers went off to Massachusetts to attend college and ended up working at a liquor store after classes. Eventually, they bought Foley's Liquors in Brookline, kept its good Irish name, married and produced American children, and became naturalized citizens. Still, something was missing from their lives. So after Oslo, they were thrilled to extract their children from their American lifestyle and take them home. "We felt this was a good, innocent upbringing until the Palestinian uprising started, you know, with the shooting and the bombing," Maria said.

Before the uprising began, the Khoury brothers had been made uneasy by all the potholes along what they had assumed would be a one-way road to peace. They saw Ofra, the settlement next door, grow with every passing year and other new settlements plant themselves in what was supposed to become Palestine. They saw May 1999 pass ominously without the resolution of the Israeli-Palestinian conflict foreseen in Oslo.

But they lived on hope, choosing to believe that the Israeli and Palestinian people were moving toward peace even if their leaders were dueling over borders. They themselves were building business relationships with Israeli winemakers and playing host to Israeli tour groups. A rabbi from Ofra kosherized their fresh-tasting light beer, which found a clientele in Israel. So optimistic were they that they sank a foundation for their new lives and built atop it a white stone mansion.

Then everything unraveled, and the Taybeh Brewing Company was devastated along with the rest of Palestinian civil and commercial life. Taybeh, which had been turning out 6,000 cases a month in the summer of 2000, suffered a 75 percent decline in business the following year. Travel restrictions prevented it from importing ingredients and transporting its product in a timely fashion. It essentially lost its markets in Jordan, Israel, and Bethlehem. Even Ramallah, theoretically ten minutes away, became a circuitous, sometimes day-long haul for its trucks. So the Khourys all but halted production. "We are idling," David said. "All of Palestine is idling."

David told me about a recent phone conversation with an Israeli commerce official who was trying to determine how much in taxes to collect from him. David told him that he was barely producing beer. The official then said: "You're American. The best thing for you and your father and your brother would be to go back." David responded: "And leave the land here for you? In your dreams."

During their summer vacation in the States, Maria did propose that they remain rather than face another academic year of roadblocks on the way to school. But Elena, sixteen, had a breathtaking answer for her mother: "That's my legacy as a Palestinian—I have to suffer."

While we talked, David, his craggy face betraying little emotion, declared, "I am for this uprising." He described himself as a man of peace, but he said: "If we sit still, Palestine will never be ours again. Algeria had one million martyrs before they had their independence."

A Palestinian poll, published at the end of December, seemed to speak for David Khoury. It showed that a strong majority of Palestinians supported an immediate cease-fire and a return to peace negotiations. But the poll also reflected a second sentiment: nine out of ten Palestinians hypothetically—that is, if the cease-fire failed, which they presumed it would—supported armed attacks on Israeli soldiers and settlers in the occupied territories as a form of self-defense and as a tactic to pressure the Israelis to withdraw. "This is our right, to resist the occupation," David said. "The Israelis defend themselves, and we defend ourselves."

Toward the end of our conversation, David ruminated a bit on the suicide bombers. He and his wife condemned the bombings because "we don't want innocent civilians to die." But Maria said that the bombers themselves had to be understood as products of desperate circumstances, and David effectively said that he was impressed by their self-sacrifice. "Theirs is real faith," he said.

This appeared to be a bit much for his father to handle. He sputtered: "Excuse me, David, but what did they do, these noble creatures? Blow themselves up? They blew themselves up and blew us up with them. To hell with them. What is the result of their self-sacrifice? Now America is saying Arafat is bin Laden? Bravo for Hamas."

David changed the subject. "Are you sure we can't get you a beer?" he asked me.

From hilltop mansions in the West Bank to seaside shanties in Gaza, almost every Palestinian has been shaken economically by the last sixteen months. According to the most recent United Nations estimates, the Palestinian economy lost as much as $3.2 billion by the end of September 2001, one year after the intifada began. For someone like Khoury, that meant deferred earnings. For someone like Saeda al Ghandar, the wife of a street vendor in Gaza, that meant deferred meals. Almost half the Palestinian population is getting by on less than $2 a day now—more than double the poverty rate before the intifada began.

When I knocked on Ghandar's door in a fetid alleyway of the Jabaliya refugee camp, I interrupted her packing. Ghandar, twenty-five, was anxiously stuffing clothes into a plastic bag to move her four young children to her sister's apartment for the night. Israeli warplanes had been buzzing the skies all day, and she feared that the evening would bring another bombardment. Since she barely has a roof over her head, she felt particularly exposed.

We sat in the family's outer room, a cement cube with a missing top. Her laundry hung between us, dancing in the wind, and a gingham curtain hid the hole in the ground that serves as her family's toilet. The bedroom, where all six of them sleep in one bed, had a tin roof that just barely fit.

Ghandar rested for a few minutes, leaning her pregnant body on a stool as her children—all under the age of five—whizzed around her. The oldest boy, his bare feet dirty and his nose running, was lost in make-believe. With a rag on his head, he was hawking invisible goods. "Fish here!" he cried like his father, who sells bream in the streets.

"All the time, we have to leave our house," Ghandar said. "When I hear the planes, I leave. When I hear about a suicide bombing in Israel, I leave. It's not good, these attacks that the Palestinians are doing. It only brings Israeli retaliation. We were really very happy before this intifada, but the shelling, it makes us very scared."

Was Ghandar really very happy before this intifada? Her family was poor then too, she readily admitted, but now they are dirt poor; the Israelis, citing security concerns, have intermittently prevented fishing off the Gaza coast, and her husband has little to hawk. Ghandar said she has sold all her possessions except a gilded bangle and one pair of dangly earrings. What she really misses, though, is not her jewelry or even the security of knowing that she will have food to put on the table. She misses the quiet.

I asked Ghandar if she aspired to anything more than quiet. She said, sure, a Palestinian state, but she said it as if it were as likely as her getting wall-to-wall carpeting. I asked if she held Arafat responsible for the mess she is in. "What more could he do than he is already doing?" she said. "If he could do more, he would. He spent all his life working for us." Besides, she contested my assertion that her situation was a mess.

"All my days are beautiful," she said. "If we let ourselves be depressed, we would die. God won't forget us. God doesn't forget anything he creates, even in Gaza."

If only Hussam Khader could have such faith. Khader, a maverick Palestinian legislator, is as hypercritical of God and of Arafat as Ghandar is a believer. Khader once took the podium in the Legislature to sarcastically propose a new law: that Yasir Arafat, once and for all, be declared the god of Palestine.

I was thinking about that little bit of theater as I sat waiting to see Khader in his modest office in the Balata refugee camp, a hardscrabble shantytown on the edge of Nablus in the West Bank. Khader grew up in Balata, and he cut his teeth politically in the first intifada, during which he found himself on the first helicopter of Palestinians deported by Israel to Lebanon. Khader was Fatah through and through—Arafat's Fatah was and remains the dominant political organization—and he revered Arafat until the Palestinian leader returned from exile and began running the Palestinian Authority with the associates he had brought home with him from Tunis. Khader was one of the first Palestinians to suggest that the Tunisian returnees were setting up an economy that might benefit them at the expense of the people. He warned against corruption and called for transparency in government. During the 1996 elections for the Palestinian Legislative Council, which was created by Oslo, Khader snubbed Fatah and won as an independent.

A few days before my visit to Nablus, Palestinian police officers killed six Palestinians in Gaza who were rioting against Arafat's crackdown on Islamic groups. After resisting Israeli and American pressure to jail Islamic militants, Arafat was finally doing so because he was finding himself increasingly isolated internationally.

That was the subject of discussion in the antechamber of Khader's office, with Khader's assistant vehemently proclaiming, "Arafat is a dictator," and then nervously insisting that I not use his name in this article. Khader had no such compunctions. A gregarious, mustachioed character, he expresses himself pungently, punctuating his words with hoarse laughter.

Some fellow Fatah members paid a call on Khader while I was there. With slaps on the back, they tried to persuade him to participate in a march in Nablus the following day to rally support for Arafat after the bloody showdown in Gaza. All the local schoolchildren would be going and government employees and, of course, le tout Fatah.

"Forget about it," Khader said. "These marches will not change the fact that with time our Monsieur Arafat is losing his power as the symbol of our national struggle. All the Viagra in the world will not give him back his potency. After the Israelis bombed his helicopter, you might have persuaded me to get out on the streets in solidarity with Abu Amar. But not at the end of a week in which Palestinian security forces shot dead their fellow Palestinians."

Khader laughed at the banners for the march that proclaimed Arafat "the hero of the legendary steadfastness in the Camp David negotiations." But understanding those banners is crucial. Although many Israelis and Americans believe that Arafat's "steadfastness" at Camp David was deadly for the Palestinian cause, this is not one of the many things that Palestinians debate. Palestinians, Khader included, universally believe that Camp David offered nothing more than a half-baked, hurried ultimatum of a deal. They had grown discouraged with the protracted peace process over the seven years that followed Oslo's promises, and many Palestinians had lost faith in Arafat's ability to deliver what he had promised: a Palestinian state in all of the West Bank and Gaza with East Jerusalem as its capital. So when he walked away from Camp David empty-handed, they applauded him. Better to wait another generation, they said, than to accept an unjust peace after a half-century of struggle.

In Israeli eyes, Arafat walked away from the most generous offer he will ever get from an Israeli prime minister. In Palestinian eyes, however, the outline of an offer put on the table by Ehud Barak "fell far short of minimum requirements for a viable, independent Palestinian state," as a senior Palestinian negotiator wrote in a letter to members of the United States Congress. Barak was offering nothing more than "three noncontiguous cantons" surrounded by

Israeli-controlled territory in the West Bank, the letter continued, concluding, it "would have made Palestine nothing more than Arab 'Bantustans' perpetually at the mercy of Israeli economic and military closures."

Khader, who agrees with this assessment, rose to take me down the stairs and past the giant spools of wire crowding the sidewalk beneath his office. He wanted to show me a wall. In May 2000, four Israeli artists came to Balata and worked with local youths to paint a brilliant ode to peace on that wall. In rainbow colors, they splashed, "A Future Without Fear," in Arabic and in Hebrew. But in October 2000, after the intifada began quite raucously in Nablus, residents of the camp tore down the wall and then rebuilt it with a new slogan, "One Choice—to Return or to Die," referring to the refugees' desire to return to their homes in what is now Israel.

Khader told me that he had given his all to the peace process. "I went to the Knesset, and they introduced me as a man of peace," he said. "I went to Neve Shalom and preached coexistence. I went to Cairo and preached normalization. But now I am just another number in the Israelis' computer. There is nothing in my file that says, 'He was a peace partner.' Now I am another Palestinian face into which the soldiers can shine their flashlights."

When the Palestinian uprising began in 2000, Khader, like others, saw it as an explosion of frustration—frustration with the peace effort and with the Palestinian Authority itself. He says that the intifada has succeeded on a military level and explained this coldbloodedly: "There was one Israeli killed for every three Palestinians killed, and this is the first time we reached such a ratio. This created a balance of fear between the two sides. And Israel's fear will give us leverage. That can be seen by what happened to Barak's offer between Camp David and Taba." Even while the intifada was raging, Israeli and Palestinian negotiators met in Taba, Egypt, in January 2001, and the Israelis significantly improved on their offer to the Palestinians. But the negotiations ended inconclusively, postponed until after the election that Barak lost to Sharon in February 2001, and there have been no peace talks since.

Khader, however, thinks that the intifada has degenerated into an orgy of revenge and should be terminated. He thinks that Arafat should do everything in his power to push the Israelis back to the negotiating table, which he assumes means helping to engineer the collapse of Sharon's government. But he is deeply disappointed that the Palestinian government succeeded in channeling all the Palestinian rage at the Israelis and that there was no real uprising against the authority itself. He tried to plant the seeds. He publicly criticized high officials of the Palestinian Authority for sending their families abroad after the intifada began. But his criticism did little more than create a stir.

Which means that if negotiations start again, "it will be the same corrupt people representing us," Khader said. "I pray to God that I wake up one morning and discover that these people have fled to Europe with their money and their children. If I were Yasir Arafat, I'd start to clean house. If he wants to end his life as a hero, he will do this.

Otherwise, Arafat will not be remembered by history. I am told that there is a saying in the Torah that many who are now in their graves believed that life would not continue without them. But it did."

A truck driver for an Israeli company, Abu Salem was shot in November 2000 when he turned into the midst of an exchange of fire between Palestinian gunmen and Israeli settlers and soldiers. He heard "Arab, Arab," in Hebrew, and he accelerated. The cab of his truck had no door; he took several high-velocity bullets in his left leg, which erupted. That was thirteen months and eleven operations before we spoke on Christmas Eve.

"My injury is for nothing," he said. "I was just in the wrong place at the wrong time. I should not be celebrated as a martyr. I wasn't even resisting. I don't believe in throwing stones. You throw a stone; they bring a tank. It's not my nature to get involved in politics. My reality was that I had a good job and I worked with Israelis. It was a natural thing for us to coexist. Actually, after this happened, my Israeli bosses used to call me. Then it fell off; they are busy in their work and they don't think of you anymore."

We had moved to the hospital cafeteria so that he could eat his supper, a concoction featuring diced hot dogs. He was busy hobbling on crutches to a pay phone, searching for a ride to the evening's festivities in Bethlehem. The Israelis had forbidden Arafat to attend the Christmas Eve ceremony. "But they can't stop me, can they?" Abu Salem, who is Muslim, said. "When they humiliate Yasir Arafat, they humiliate all of us. It is my duty to go in his place."

I asked Abu Salem if he had any advice for Arafat. "My advice is for the Palestinian people," he said. "I think it's in the interest of the people to calm things down because we are the ones who are paying a heavy price. I feel bad that the Israelis have lost innocent civilians. But we have lost more. We are under siege. We are hungry. We are unemployed. We are—I am—crippled."

Abu Salem shook my hand. "Thank you for paying attention to me," he said and hopped away.

When I visited Abdel Kareem Eid in his Gaza City home, he was reclining on embroidered cushions on his living room floor, overseeing an intifada soap opera starring members of his own sizable family. The seventy-four-year-old patriarch, a retired truck driver, wore a flowing pinstriped caftan. And moving his hands like a traffic cop, he tried to direct the flow of heated conversation between the half of his family that is Fatah and the half that is Hamas. Adding extra zip to the raucousness, almost all the men were packing.

To his left sat wife No. 1, to his right wife No. 2, and gathered around them in concentric circles were dozens of children and grandchildren. As best as Kareem Eid could count, he has twenty children and eighty-seven grandchildren, some black (like wife No. 1), some light (like wife No. 2). Five are Palestinian security officers, members of Fatah. At least five others are Hamasniks, and an eleventh son identified himself as a fan of Saddam Hussein.

While one grandmother knitted, one mother breastfed, and the teenage girls giggled, a well-groomed police officer son declared: "We have one authority, one leadership, one book of law, and we have to abide by it. If my brother breaks the law, I will put him in jail."

A Hamas brother who was wearing a New York Giants ski cap scowled: "You better put on a mask so I don't recognize you! Why should I go to jail? You think you're better than me because you're with the authority. The authority changes its policies every day. Today cease-fire, tomorrow fire. You pretend you have the rule of law. But you're really no different from us."

Another Hamas brother, also wearing a Giants cap, interjected, "You're a Muslim just like us, and your constitution should be the Koran."

The oldest Fatah brother, joking around, took off his jacket as if he were preparing for a fight on the Jerry Springer show. "Seriously," he said, "Hamas thinks we wimped out on the struggle, that we don't care anymore. But there's struggle their way and there's struggle our way, and sometimes those ways overlap."

Kareem Eid said: "If the Israelis attack us, we should attack back. If they give their hand in peace, we should give ours." One of his Hamas sons spat: "There will be no peace. It's us or them."

I asked the Hamasniks if they were Giants fans. "It's just for warmth," one said, squirming and folding under the logo on the knitted hat. The other barked out, "I like New York because of what happened to it in September."

A Palestinian police officer brother jumped to his feet: "I condemn that remark. Eat it! Eat it!" The Hamasnik snickered, "Or what, you'll arrest me?"

The patriarch laughed throughout the conversation. "This is normal for Gaza," he said. "You find a father who's Hamas, his son may be Fatah or vice versa. It's like you find a father who sells stuff on a donkey, his son may be a doctor. Do you like grilled meat? I like boiled meat. You like falafel? I like salad."

Wife No. 1 interrupted: "What nonsense are you spouting?" And the patriarch answered, "You are my moon," and to the other wife, "You are my star."

The lights blinked out, a routine electricity break. All that could be seen in the darkness was the glow of a dozen cigarettes. When the lights came back on, the patriarch and his sons invited me into the old man's bedroom to see something special: a stuffed white kitten. It was not just any stuffed white kitten, though. The Hamas brothers demonstrated. They clapped their hands, and the cat meowed. Other brothers, police officers, joined them. They all laughed and clapped, and the cat kept up its mechanical purring.

The father said: "You see, there will never be a civil war in Gaza. We are all brothers."

The morgue in Gaza City was empty of the victims of the fratricide that had taken place just days before when the Palestinian police officers killed the Islamic militants. The cold steel tables were empty of any trace of the Israeli-Palestinian conflict, too. So were the freezer boxes where

Dr. Abdel Razik el-Masri stores the bodies before he autopsies them.

So we sipped tiny cups of coffee in a sanitized house of horrors. In the previous fifteen months, Masri said, nibbling a cookie, he had dissected hundreds of bodies, many belonging to children. Would I like to see the CD-ROM's? he asked. I declined. He told me that I was better off because the Israelis "killed without any respect for humanity." (That is what the Israelis say about the Palestinians, too, each believing the other is killing with particular viciousness.)

"If there existed other forensic specialists in Gaza, we would have left our work after two or three months," Masri said. "But there was no one else, so we tolerated what Allah wanted us to tolerate. We didn't get tired so others wouldn't get tired. We didn't weep so others wouldn't weep."

I asked Masri how his work had affected his outlook on the conflict. He had sounded so embittered that I did not expect his answer to start with a reference to an Israeli coastal town.

"I miss Netanya," he said. "I used to go to ulpan there in the summer, and my Hebrew was really getting somewhere. I'd like to go back to Netanya. I'd like to go again to Tel Aviv. We used to spend the night there without any fear. I'd like to live together again with the Israelis as neighboring peoples. We can visit them, they can visit us. We can live with them, sleep with them, and they can live with us, sleep with us. But they need to change their way of believing. They need to put their hand in the hand of our president, and we will all have success and a civilized life."

It would be only a couple of weeks before the good doctor, like his Israeli colleagues, would start to get busy again and his brief honeyed reverie would be shattered by death, death, and more death. Nonetheless, the doctor would cling to his hopes even as he extracted more bullets from more bodies. The doctor, like most of those with whom I spoke, chose to defy the depressing reality by stubbornly—steadfastly—believing that an equitable resolution of the Israeli-Palestinian conflict is not only possible but inevitable. "It is just and right, and therefore it shall be," he said. The doctor was fuzzy about how it would happen; almost everybody was fuzzy about the means to the end. But the end—well, the doctor told me, even if it takes another generation or two, eventually there will be a Palestinian state alongside Israel that will make all the sufferness worthwhile.

ADINA HOFFMAN

House of Windows

I T WAS FRIDAY, half an hour before the pre-Sab-
bath siren wail, when I realized we had no olive oil.
We had drained our last bottle down to the murky
dregs and all the stores were closed.

Maybe Benny would sell us some from his
stash. This stocky little jester of a Scottish antiquities dealer
lived downstairs from Mazal, on the chilly ground floor of a
grand house whose lintel was marked

1896
١٨٩٧

In addition to the several
Near Eastern languages that our
neighbor the Glasgow native had
acquired over the years, he had
adopted the local tribal custom of
leaving his wife at home to handle
the children while he wandered

ADINA HOFFMAN
*has lived in Jerusalem
for the past nine years.
In this piece excerpted
from her book* House
of Windows *(2000),
she writes about the
everyday lives of her
friends and neighbors—
ordinary people trying to
live normal lives in a
city often overshadowed
by rampant violence
and turmoil.*

elsewhere—to our house, for instance—where he would stride, often barefoot, onto our porch, smile rakishly at me, then greet my husband through a toothy grin in gutter Arabic and offer up a duty-free cigar, brought back from one of his frequent trips to visit a Swiss collector or German curator. A sly wit, with a disconcerting knack for shifting from broad teasing to utter seriousness in a flash (his brooding deadpan made it hard to distinguish the two), Benny made jokes that were swift and clever, spiked with salty entendre. His elastic English came as a tremendous relief after the thin, even broken, idiom that one heard from the mouths of so many native English speakers who had lived in Israel for years and lazily let their own language slip. Being in this place for an extended period, I had begun to doubt the sharpness of my mother tongue (prepositions were the first thing to go, with practical nouns close behind), and I liked talking with Benny, as a way of keeping linguistically fit. He was also quite knowledgeable—an expert on ancient seals, he wrote articles for museum catalogues and helped to assemble important exhibits—yet with his ruddy coloring, leathery hands, worn T-shirt, and unceremonious air, he could have passed for a day laborer.

In addition to his messy but priceless basement cache of dainty, dotted Phoenician pots, almond-eyed ancient Egyptian death masks, and jumbled piles upon piles of Ottoman seals, Roman coins, and early Christian signet rings (all of which he handled as carefully as he might a heap of mismatched Tupperware or pocket of spare change), I knew Benny had a jerry can of especially pungent olive oil that he'd picked up on one of his drives to Jericho. He would go there to sit, drink thick coffee, and swap dirty jokes in his broguish Palestinian dialect with his colleagues and clients, "gentlemen of the Oriental persuasion" as he called them. This was how he operated, bringing back from these West Bank sojourns either bids to do business of some obscure (to me) buying-selling-middleman-playing type or—what mattered more on this particular day—large plastic vats of hand-ground *tehina* and full tanks of green oil, collected as edible down payment or in place of change.

Peter, meanwhile, had spent the past hour watering and tending the garden across the street in a final weedy rush before the horn sounded and such work became taboo in the neighbors' yard. By now I was a bit desperate: Could he please go ask Benny if we could buy some oil? This was still early in our friendship with Benny, when our neighbor would address himself in a raucous, man-to-man way to Peter, and turn to me in a more restrained, even chivalrous, manner. Since then, he had relaxed in my presence, but at that point I didn't feel I could ask for the oil myself.

"Not now," Peter yawned, stretching out across the couch in end-of-the-week exhaustion.

"I can't make dinner otherwise—" I started to whine, but he had already dwindled off into his catnap and I was left alone with the impending darkness and my empty oil bottle.

Of course there was still the most obvious solution—at once the simplest (physically) and most complicated (emotionally). I put on a sweater, collected my keys, and left the apartment as quietly as I could, turning downhill at the doorstep, away from town, and past the so-called House of Windows. This elusive structure sat at the foot of our street, its rear facade studded with no less than three dozen irregularly sized and staggered openings, each commanding what I imagined must be its own singular view, or views. Part of the odd demeanor of this hundred-year-old apartment building, though, came from the apparent absence, behind those panes, of peering eyes. No matter how many trips I made past the wall of windows, I never once glimpsed anyone looking out, or caught the back of a head turning away. At the same time, I had the definite sense as I moved by those stone arches, like thirty-six raised eyebrows, that *the house itself was staring,* keeping a steady, unblinking watch over the scene below and all those who came and went with the years. No one knew exactly why the building looked this way—if the (anonymous) architect had meant these apertures as quirky, light-giving ornament, or if he had intended for the windows to serve some other, now-forgotten function. One friend speculated that the place had been fashioned as a monastery and that each window belonged to a separate cell. His guess was reasonable (it was right next door to the Silesian Sisters' convent and day school) but incorrect, so far as I knew. The rather ordinary domestic floor plan of the house appeared in most books about Jerusalem architecture; according to the vague characterizations in these guides, the shape and placement of the windows on the rear facade were of "particular interest," but that was all . . . there were no cells or other obvious clues to the logic of its design. Rather, at the front, an outdoor staircase led up to a landing that branched into corridors on the right and left, off which sat several spacious, symmetrical rooms. (Facing the house from that graceful but more ordinary angle, one would never know of its peculiar backside.) Windows there were aplenty, but no building nearby was more opaque.

The dimming light would soon melt into dark. Walking faster now, I proceeded a few short streets east, past the old men shuffling to synagogue and their grandchildren playing in the road, toward the highway that marked the unofficial but very real border between the two halves of the city, Jewish and Arab. The stoplight there brought an end to Musrara, our neighborhood, and a start to Musrara, the mirror neighborhood on the other side.

Before this road existed, the space between Musrara and Musrara was no-man's-land, separating Israel from Jordan, and though the sandbags and soldiers had been gone for exactly the length of my lifetime, I still felt I was crossing a border—one that was, in its very nebulousness, trickier to navigate than an official checkpoint like that at Beit She'an. One passed over, without documents, as through Alice's looking glass.

The two neighborhoods went by the same name, and at this hour the swifts darted indiscriminately over both. But one was here and one was there, and despite the politicians' rhetoric that pretended this city was "united," when I stood waiting to cross the six-lane swath of asphalt that ran between the East and the West it was plain to me as the giddy gold of the mosque's dome that I was posed to leave

one universe and enter into another. In an exaggerated version of the process that took place every time I passed over
the threshold of my own house and out into the world, I was
entering someone else's city now, in this case, a place at once
next door and galaxies away. (Some of what I describe is sub-
jective, some not: When, in early September, the clocks are
moved back an hour in Israel to mark the start of "winter
time" they aren't yet changed over there, in the East, so that
for a few absurdist weeks one can literally cross the street
and find oneself in another time zone, in effect another season, where summer evenings linger on in the light.) Unlike
most of our Israeli friends who hadn't ventured east since the
intifada started in 1987, I wasn't scared there—and we
would go often, to eat hummus, to wander and buy vegetables or olive oil, as I was about to do now—but I was aware,
too, and not especially eager to rid myself of the sense, that
the East would always remain for me a little strange, necessarily foreign. As I walked there I carried myself differently,
with the light step and quiet tones of a trespasser, an inter-
loper with the good fortune and means to travel abroad just
to buy olive oil to dress her weekend salad.

Half a century before, the east and west of Musrara had
been a single neighborhood. There were stories I'd heard
about how, in 1948, in the days just after the Palestinian residents of the houses on what was soon to be the Israeli side
had fled in fear for their lives—some left beds unmade and
food on the table or even cooking on the stove where it
burned to black—a few had tried to sneak back across the
border at night to collect their belongings. There were also

apocryphal tales of fortunes buried beneath the colorful
floor tiles, and more plausible mention of Jewish treasure
hunters who had looted drawers, taken paintings and pianos,
and even dug up those tiles, in search of the riches they imagined were hidden underfoot.

One personal history I read described the anguish of a
well-known Palestinian doctor and his German wife who
were forced to abandon the house they had built in Musrara
some thirty-five years before. Their children were all safe,
studying in Europe and Beirut, but after the third floor of
their home was demolished by a direct mortar hit, they had no
choice but to pack a bag each and go. That this man was at the
time also the foremost scholar of Palestinian folk amulets
seems especially ironic. Realizing that war was inevitable, he
had managed to box and transport to safety his substantial collection of brass and silver talismans, wolf's-tooth pendants,
paper charms, glass beads, gilded garlic, tortoiseshell and
hedgehog-fur cradle ornaments, dried cow's eyes, and "fear
cups," the magical bowls believed to heal—though not even
his possession of some 1400 lucky pieces could hold the evil
eye at bay: Every day after they fled to the small room the
Greek Orthodox Patriarch provided them in the Old City
(where the doctor lived with his wife, sister, and sister-in-law,
and from which he continued to operate his clinic), the couple
would climb to the top of the ramparts and look across at the
sight of their private library being ransacked, their Bieder-
meier furniture loaded into trucks and taken away. From this
helpless vantage point the couple also watched as their house
was torched and burned to the ground.

According to other accounts from the period, the Jewish immigrants who were sent by the Israeli government to occupy these badly damaged houses in the months after the Arab exodus ended and the wartime shelling stopped often slept on the mattresses and kept their clothes in the standing closets left behind by the refugees. Our house was one of these houses, and these immigrants were our neighbors. And although our furniture was all our own, and the apartment's mortgage was listed in our name, I knew our house had other owners, somewhere in the world. Who? Where? Meeting Samira and Mahmud had made tangible for me the unsettling fact that I'd known before but had kept until that time conveniently general: *Somewhere*—they could be abroad or even just a few blocks away, exiled to the other Musrara—there probably lived a family who carried the memory of our house with them always, like one of the doctor's talismans. Or was it a constant, aching regret, like the long-ago loss of a newborn child? What, I wondered, had become of the people who had eaten meals and laughed and argued and powdered their noses in these rooms, who'd awakened facing these ceilings? Had they left in a rush or did they pack and go earlier, taking their trunks and valuables with them, as if for a long vacation?

Our neighbor Rafi still paid key money, a Levantine sort of lifelong maintenance fee, to an eighty-five-year-old Armenian lawyer who represented his building's original Greek Cypriot landlords (unlike the Arabs, the Greeks who had fled were not considered "enemies" by the state, so families like this one had been allowed to maintain pre-1948 ownership of their houses in West Jerusalem), and on the day when I summoned the nerve to approach City Hall and request information about our house's former owners. Rafi also appeared on the second floor, limping more severely than usual, took a number, and sat down for the long wait. Sweating and shifting his gaze anxiously, he explained that since his mother's death a few months earlier, her part of their shared apartment had come under dispute. The same Greeks owned these rooms, including the kitchen, with its Old World pantry and painted wooden cabinets, and though Rafi wanted to pay extra to keep the place to himself, there seemed to be a problem. He had come to find certain documents that might bolster his claims to the property. "And what are *you* doing here?" he asked, in his clipped but able English with which he liked to address me when I brought him a day-old *Jerusalem Post* so that he could practice reading from left to right. I answered that I was curious about our house's history. My curiosity, though, got little more than a blank look from Rafi, who steered the conversation distractedly back to Hebrew and his own troubles: Since his mother died, it was hard for him to get by, he said. He ordered food from a caterer, had a cleaning woman come twice a week, and managed to do his own laundry, but things were hard, very hard for a man without a wife. I listened and nodded as Rafi went on with his monologue, a more emotional version of which Peter had already heard from Rafi and recounted for me. When the older man talked to Peter in private he admitted he would like to marry but "wasn't in demand" and, turning the subject back to his late mother, began very softly to weep.

After I sat for forty-five minutes with Rafi, my nerves rubbed thin by the harsh fluorescent light and synthetic chill of the air conditioning, one of the blue-jeans-and-sandals-wearing bureaucrats wandered from the room to which we and the small crowd around us were awaiting entry, and mumbled with an indifferent clerical shrug that the workers were on strike. We should come back some other time. . . .

In truth I knew my answer might lie much closer in Istanbul—just across the highway. Realizing that the *Through the Looking Glass* principle was also in effect here, I decided to walk to the East, to Orient House, the officially unofficial Palestinian city hall or foreign ministry, where according to various newspaper accounts documents had been gathered in preparation for the rather ominously dubbed Final Status stage of the peace talks, to prove pre-1948 Palestinian ownership of houses in neighborhoods like our own. No doubt the records there would stand in direct, contentious contrast to those in the West, with building and ownership form Ottoman times and through the Mandate charted, the books thinning out at about the time the records at the West Jerusalem archive thickened. . . .

Like most Israelis, my contact with Palestinians was limited almost entirely to the impersonal, extremely unbalanced realm of fleeting dealings with construction workers, waiters, janitors, and shopkeepers' assistants. We'd attended a few peace group meetings with Palestinian activists, though the willed, ambassadorial nature of these occasions, I found, precluded real closeness. First names, baklava, and sweet cardamom coffee were invariably passed around the room, and it rarely went beyond that. More recently, Peter's various Arabic teachers had widened the circle of our cross-cultural interactions in a small though meaningful way. For the first time ever, we had a few Palestinian friends. But instead of taking the edge off my curiosity, these new relationships only made me eager to push further into that other close-but-distant world, to make the abstractions concrete. And while I realized that my research project was a paltry gesture, no real weapon against the larger, darker, more general forces at work all around me, and one unlikely to matter in the slightest to the particular family of Palestinians concerned (their own relation to the house would not be affected by my discovery of their surname; I had no plans to turn over the deed to our home), it still seemed to me imperative to try to learn who they were—for my own sake. And even if I could do nothing practical with this knowledge, I could not agree to pretend not to care.

Ignoring the situation, meanwhile, is a luxury most Palestinians do not have, and when I passed by on my way to Orient House that scorching morning, around eight-thirty, the throng outside the Ministry of the Interior was already enormous and desperate looking in a muted though palpable way. Young boys with old men's faces wandered through and hawked ice cream from wooden boxes slung over their shoulders. Women in long dresses and head scarves held umbrellas high above the pushing crowd, in what appeared a futile attempt to keep cool. And on the sidewalk opposite, the usual fleet of self-employed scribes stood before their collapsible card tables, each armed with a manual typewriter and pad of forms, taking dictation and translating for those who could not write or answer the Hebrew questions alone. Aside from a jeep filled with helmet-and-nightstick-toting border policemen, I was the only Jew in sight, and a small path cleared before me as I passed through the crowd and alongside the High Life grocery store, a little treasure chest of a market run by Palestinians who had apparently spent time in the United States and whose English flowed, quick and colloquial. The store's shelves were filled with exotic European, Asian, and American items that never surfaced in Israel proper—Indian fish spices, tinned French chestnuts, blue-corn nacho chips, obscure Dutch beers, and the like. Though we often shopped there on Saturdays or in the late afternoon, when the ministry was closed and the street outside quiet, the place seemed different, more decadent on a weekday morning, with these weary, pushing crowds out front and its jolly name reduced to a stinging irony. The high life indeed!

Similar crowds usually spilled from the sidewalks before the American consulate, one street over, though the first time I went there, in search of an absentee ballot for a U.S. presidential election, I stood at length on the wrong line. Without thinking, I'd surveyed the two groups of people awaiting entry—one Israeli, one Palestinian—and gone automatically to take my place with the Israelis. Only after waiting patiently and for some time did it occur to me that the people around me, my ostensible countrymen, were filling out request forms for American tourist visas: They were planning to go to the country of my birth for vacation, or a few years of study. Meanwhile, the other line was not meant for Palestinians per se, but for American citizens, all of whom, in this particular instance, were Arabs, people whose country of birth was probably right here, but who held citizenship elsewhere—in Dubuque? Embarrassed, I switched lines and awaited my turn to enter.

Now, as I walked toward Orient House, I found myself metamorphosing, for convenience' sake, into an American, plain and simple—that is, more of an American than I'd ever felt myself when I lived in the United Stares, where I considered myself first of all a Jew. Several times I stopped to ask directions in English, and found I was inadvertently acting a chipper part, full of bright thanks and smiles.

By the time I got to Orient House, a quirky two-tiered structure whose slightly quaint, jewel-box design belies its serious function as the center of Palestinian political activity in Jerusalem, I had evolved completely, not just into a flag-saluting, milk-fed prairie dweller but an American Journalist. Perhaps my use of the disguise was hypocritical; as I moved toward the security booth, though, I chose to eat all the disparaging thoughts I'd had about journalists over the years and take advantage of the path the word would clear before me . . . and sure enough, when I announced myself a Reporter, I was waved inside the fancy wrought-iron gates by the rather baffled-looking guard who seemed brand new to the job and simply shrugged me through. And so I moved up the steps and across the black-and-white tiles of the checkered patio, passing the clusters of brawny young men with dark glasses and cell phones who dawdled on the stairs, chain-smoking and talking. Were they Palestinian police? According to the Oslo accords, their presence wasn't allowed in Jerusalem, though I was fairly certain that this was the tacit job description of most of the large, thuggy crew. They carried themselves in the officious manner of proud recruits who'd been vested with titles, equipment, and a certain cachet, but scant actual power, and when I entered the foyer and stood trying to figure out which hallway I should follow, several of them rushed to help. "Welcome? Welcome?" they chimed, and proceeded to lead me en masse to the appropriate door in broken English and with timid, almost girlish smiles. (This overenthusiastic reception stood in laughable contrast to the oblivious, take-a-number-and-rot situation at the busy West Jerusalem City Hall.) I had a sense that they'd been sitting idly for days on end and were thrilled at the chance to do something, anything to make themselves useful. The whole building seemed suspended in lacy limbo—clerks sat drowsily at their desks, sipping coffee, few ordinary citizens wandered the halls, and the air itself scarcely seemed to move—though in addition to the typical Middle Eastern slackening of bureaucratic pace that their inertia implied, I realized that this might be a charade orchestrated with skill for outsider eyes like my own. Technically, Orient House was not supposed to operate in an official capacity, so that the *appearance* of inactivity was probably carefully cultivated, while real business went on behind closed doors. I approached one of the secretaries and roused her from her trance.

Walid, she explained, was the man I needed to see,

though "Walid will not come here today." As she spoke, the pretty young woman with the knot of gold chains at her throat and thick, liver-colored lipstick eyed me warily from behind her computer screen. An older man, a clerk or official in a tie and cardigan, despite the heat, stood alongside her, also staring skeptically at me as I spoke. I should come back tomorrow, she said. In the morning. At nine o'clock. "You would care," she ordered me with a question, "to leave your name and reason?" In blocky letters I inscribed the point of my visit on the pink slip of paper she provided, taking pains to sound as dispassionate as possible. (I did not refer to "my" house.) Skimming what I'd written, she now questioned with an assertion, apparently as impatient as the policemen who loitered outside to be of some active help. "It is the West Bank you are interested in," she offered. "Settlements."

"Actually, it's West Jerusalem, one neighborhood there—"

She looked wary, and the man beside her continued to peer grimly at me. "Yes. Walid will know of this."

"Great!" I heard myself saying, again in too chipper a tone. "Great! I'll be back tomorrow." I gulped, smiled at both of them, turned to go, and felt their eyes following me in suspicious silence as I moved down the empty corridor.

Walid, it turned out, was a bearish man with crisp, slightly formal English, a shock of prematurely graying hair, a gold wedding band, and firm handshake. He welcomed me into his cluttered office where a fan whirled near the window and asked, in the friendliest and most businesslike tones I had heard anyone use since I'd entered Orient House, what he could do for me.

Almost before I had finished explaining that I was researching the history of Musrara, the history of several particular houses there, in fact, and I wanted to know if perhaps there might be records available, concerning home ownership or—Walid understood and had pulled a chair beside the metal bookcases that lined one whole wall, stood on tiptoe, and reached for a binder. "Here. . . ."

Now the details came flooding, more details than I could have hoped: A footnote in [a] book sent me to the reading room of the National Library, where a journal article related with pointillistic care the exact make of the cameras that Jewish photographer Yosef Schweig and his assistants, both Arab and Jewish, used to carry out orders (a small Leica and three microphotography machines flown in specially for the RAF). And now I knew that as of November 17, 1947, there existed in Palestine 884 Ottoman Registers; 2,192 Registers of Deeds; 1,424 Registers of Title; 47 Registers of Writs and Orders; 690 Deeds Books; 1,906 compendiums of documents; and 247,600 files of unsettled lands. (Surely our house must be listed there, somewhere?) So, too, I read of the long, tedious, and physically elaborate process of photographing these heavy bound books and loose-leaf pages day after day at the besieged Public Information Office in the Palace Hotel, and of the trail the documents had followed afterward. The original books were eventually handed over to the

Emergency Committee, a Jewish body organized to assume command over the various British offices as they shut down or ceased to function, although once the committee had taken physical control of the books, they found themselves stumped as to how to preserve this library of heavy volumes in the midst of a war. "Please lend a hand," wrote one desperate committee member to the Israeli Ministry of justice, "to save the land books from the Jews." Meanwhile the backup microfilm was shipped, undeveloped, to London, where it was stored and then, starting in 1949, returned to Israel incrementally in the form of printed enlargements. By then the Jewish state had been declared—and with it a customs office, whose functionaries didn't hesitate to tax the shipments of local property records when they returned, carefully marked by English officials "Cinema Films." Finally, the article recounted that in February 1953, the remaining fourteen hundred rolls of film were returned to the director of land registration and land settlement at the Israeli Ministry of justice, where the books themselves had also come to rest.

So that was it, the address to which I should have turned in the very first place, before Scotland, before the Little J____, the busy journalist, Walid and his skeptical secretary, before the photo shop, the map room, Ophir, Yehezkel, the archive librarian and the striking workers on the second floor of West Jerusalem's City Hall. I picked up a phone book, found the ministry's downtown address, and walked in five minutes to the office, which turned out to be located in an ugly firetrap of a skyscraper smack-dab at the center of town, one floor up from the salon of the gregarious former Bostonian who sometimes cut my hair.

Five minutes and fifty shekels later, I had before me a document, stamped with an official Department of Justice purple seal, that listed—on the basis of the block and plot numbers I had provided—the owners' names, dates of transactions, métrage, property divisions, and boundaries as of March 31, 1945, when the last official activity was noted, as well as the book (#1015) and page numbers (p. 8123) of the volumes Spry had rescued. The British data had been translated into Hebrew and computerized since then, and in this process a few typos seemed to have been tossed into the already-dizzying brew. In the earliest notation there, the owner had for some reason transferred information about the house from one Ottoman registry book to another. This must have occurred on July 1, 1917, but it was listed as 1317, an obvious impossibility since the Turks did not arrive in Palestine for another two hundred years and, anyhow, the land that would one day be Musrara was at the time, and until 1870— when a few intrepid families swallowed their fear of roving bandits and lions and began to venture out beyond the crowded confines of the Old City walls—nothing but an empty stretch of rocks. Then again, maybe this wasn't a typist's mistake at all. Could it be that the record mixed Gregorian dates with Muslim, lunar ones, and that 01/07/1317 was not July 1, 1317, at all, but the first day of the month of Rajab in the 1,317th year of the Hejira—that is, 1901 on the calendar the British authorities would have recognized?

What, though, beyond the dates and names, did these

notations mean? I could not decipher all the codes myself, and so brought them to a lawyer, R., a close friend's new boyfriend, who worked at a research institute in a stone mansion in a quiet, ritzy part of town. This house, too, he told me, had its history: built by "Jewish Arabs," members of Jerusalem's long-standing community of Sephardic aristocrats at the turn of the century. In one apartment downstairs—R. hadn't seen it himself, though he'd heard—the original bathroom still stood, with its sunken marble tub and elegant old brass fixtures.

He surveyed the papers I placed before him and tried, piece by piece, to understand and explain them. It was, he admitted, difficult, even impossible on the basis of this particular document to say anything for certain: The records were impartial, filled with odd holes and gray patches, with some crucial information missing entirely. (The Ministry of Justice had itself added a disclaimer, declaring the registration of the property in question "NOT IN ORDER.") One man, Hajj Hassan Ben Halil Al ____, was listed as an owner as far back as that 1917/1317/1901 date, though his portion of the property only constituted two-thirds of the whole. To whom had the rest belonged? And where, too, were the lines drawn within the house? Were the rooms that would one day make up our apartment a part of Hajj Hassan's quarters at all, or did they belong to that other, shadow figure? What was the nature of the transaction that took place in March 1945, when three men with the same (Muslim) last name acquired equal parts of the house? It looked, on the face of it, like an inheritance, though the word *sale* appeared here, without further explanation. Who were these men? From whom had they purchased their share of the house? Collectively, their portion amounted to that earlier, missing third: Did Hajj Hassan still hold the rights to the rest, alongside them, or had he sold them a segment of what he owned? If so, who held the deed to the rest of the house?

Were these men brothers going in on a joint business venture? A father and his two sons? And what had happened three years later, after the departure of the British and the war, when the cease-fire line had been drawn just two streets away and this house come under Israeli control? Where were the three men then? According to the law, if they were not physically present in the house on September 1, 1948, the place could automatically be seized by the so-called Custodian of Absentee Properties. I had read accounts of how, by the end of May 1949, the neighborhood had already been settled by new immigrants. Still, even if the houses had become the de facto homes of Jewish families, why hadn't de jure measures been taken to mark this change in the books?

"This is just the tip of the iceberg," announced R., who had cheerfully begun to draw up a list for me of possible sources for further information. There were, he said, ways to fill in at least some of these blanks. I'd need to look in certain files, which meant I would first have to get power of attorney from X, and then I could also consult with Y, who might be able to provide more precise material, which would in turn lead me to Z. He was being kind and lawyerly, as I had hoped that he would be, but even as he spoke, I could feel my grip on the hard facts I'd been so eager to locate slipping, giving way to another state of mind altogether, and one I couldn't very well admit to R., who had after all just Xeroxed my documents and offered to consult with the institute's expert on such matters, and to look for an article he knew of, that might provide historical data on the process of land expropriation, and . . .

I was swept suddenly by a longing to be done forever with this wild goose chase. This feeling was born in part of fatigue—what I'd thought was the end of a long and complicated search was in truth just a beginning—as well as a plainer recognition of the self-serving and potentially cruel nature of the task I had set myself, and by inadvertent extension the Palestinians who had once lived in the house. It was not that I wasn't curious to learn more, just that in discovering the identity of our apartment's former owners, I still hadn't come close to *knowing* anything at all. And to know, in the tactile (not the legal) terms that would matter to me, would mean to track down these people or their descendants and pry, ask them dozens of questions about their memories of life in the house. Meanwhile, the cost of exacting such information, about their furniture, food, neighbors, musical tastes, might well exceed the value of my quest. Who did I think I was? Why did I think they should want to reveal these particulars to me? What three-thousand-year-old mess was I getting myself into? Though of course by merely coming to live here I was already involved. . . . "Very deep is the well of the past." Thomas Mann got it right: "Should we not call it bottomless?"

With my earlier doubts only magnified and my findings

officially "NOT IN ORDER," I decided to stop. There were, I saw now, details better left vague or buried, their sharp, bony edges allowed to dull with the years—to rest in peace, as it were. Peace might come, and with it an over-arching resolution coat least some of this conflict—but my digging wasn't going to help it along.

Olive oil was hard to come by that season. Because of the hot summer, I'd been told, the olive harvest was tiny. Families were keeping and pressing or curing what they'd gathered for themselves.

"Zeit?" It was one of my only Arabic words, from *zeitun,* "olives," *zeitim* in Hebrew, and I uttered it now, after crossing the highway and passing the 4 Eyes optical clinic, the Al Amin and Mussrarah bakeries, with their heaps of sesame-covered cookies, meat pies, and pastel-frosted cakes on display. "Oil?" the old man in the grocery store squinted at me, sizing me up in the Friday-evening half dark, and reached behind him for the pale unctuous stuff my foreign demeanor must have suggested, a large plastic bottle of synthetic-looking, yellowish sunflower essence. *"La,"* I tried. "No. *Zeit Zeitun."* It seemed redundant, but was apparently necessary to explain I meant olive oil. In Arabic, as in English (whose oil comes from the Greek *elaia,* "olive"), the root of the word had by now been watered down and had floated away on a generic, mass-produced slick of soy and corn.

"La," he bounced back at me in Arabic then finished in Hebrew, as he turned away. "I have none."

At the next stand, with its mishmash of traditional and

newfangled goods—the shelves of *tehina*, rose and orange blossom water, open sacks of rice, beans, birdseed, and dried-yogurt balls alongside the economy-sized Pampers packages, sliced white bread, potato chips, and piles of soda and sugar syrup bottles whose contents came in the craziest make-believe colors—turquoise, bright orange, and lollipop red—I asked again *"Zeit zeitun?"* and the man shook his head no without saying a word.

But at the last shop along this stretch, whose merchandise consisted of another crowded patchwork array of old-styled and new goods, wares both organic and completely artificial, a young man with serious spectacles nodded at my request, waved me inside, and called out something in Arabic to his father or uncle, behind the counter. The older man gave me the same thoughtful nod, then disappeared behind a wall of high-stacked cans, finally producing a single, tall, shapely plastic Coca-Cola bottle, its label still intact, cleaned and filled to the top with the grassy green oil I'd been searching for, a kind of liquid treasure. Feeling lucky, I paid, thanked them both and, clutching my prize, turned and ambled westward. Night was falling fast as I passed back out of that other city, across the highway, over one street, and up one more, alongside the ever staring wall of windows.

On a Kibbutz

LUCKY IS NOLA'S DOG. John's dog is Mississippi. But John loves Lucky too, and Nola dotes on Mississippi. And then there are the children—one daughter in the army, and a younger child who still sleeps in the kibbutz dormitory. Lucky is a woolly brown dog, old and nervous. His master was killed in the Golan. When there is a sonic boom over the kibbutz, the dog rushes out, growling. He seems to remember the falling bombs. He is too feeble to bark, too old to run, his teeth are bad, his eyes under the brown fringe are dull, and he is clotted under the tail. Mississippi is a big, long-legged, short-haired, brown-and-white, clever, lively, affectionate, and greedy animal. She

SAUL BELLOW *is a Nobel and Pulitzer Prize-winning author. This piece is excerpted from* To Jerusalem and Back, *written more than twenty-five years ago. It chronicles his experience of life on a kibbutz in a city struggling to find peace but which remains as embattled now as it was then.*

is a "child dog"—sits in your lap, puts a paw on your arm
when you reach for a tidbit to get it for herself. Since she
weighs fifty pounds or more she is not welcome in my lap,
but she sits on John and Nola and on the guests—those
who permit it. She is winsome but also flatulent. She eats
too many sweets but is good company, a wonderful listener
and conversationalist; she growls and snuffles when you
speak directly to her. She "sings" along with the record
player. The Auerbachs are proud of this musical yelping.

In the morning we hear the news in Hebrew and then
again on the BBC. We eat an Israeli breakfast of fried
eggs, sliced cheese, cucumbers, olives, green onions,
tomatoes, and little salt fish. Bread is toasted on the coal-
oil heater. The dogs have learned the trick of the door and
bang in and out. Between the rows of small kibbutz
dwellings the lawn are ragged but very green. Light and
warmth come from the sea. Under the kibbutz lie the ruins
of Herod's Caesarea. There are Roman fragments everywhere. Marble columns in the grasses. Fallen capitals
make garden seats. You only have to prod the ground to
find fragments of pottery, bits of statuary, a pair of dancing satyr legs. John's tightly packed bookshelves are
fringed with such relics. On the crowded desk stands a
framed photograph of the dead son, with a small beard like
John's, smiling with John's own warmth.

We walk in the citrus groves after breakfast, taking
Mississippi with us (John is seldom without her); the soil is
kept loose and soft among the trees, the leaves are glossy,
the ground itself is fragrant. Many of the trees are still

unharvested and bending, tangerines and lemons as dense as stars. "Oh that I were an orange tree/That busie plant!" wrote George Herbert. To put forth such leaves, to be hung with oranges, to be a blessing—one feels the temptation of this on such a morning, and I even feel a fibrous woodiness entering my arms as I consider it. You want to take root and stay forever in the most temperate and blue of temperate places. John mourns his son, he always mourns his son, but he is also smiling in the sunlight.

In the exporting of oranges there is competition from the North African countries and from Spain. "We are very idealistic here, but when we read about frosts in Spain we're glad as hell," John says.

All this was once dune land. Soil had to be carted in and mixed with the sand. Many years of digging and tending made these orchards. Relaxing, breathing freely, you feel what a wonderful place has been created here, a homeplace for body and soul; then you remember that on the beaches there are armed patrols. It is always possible that terrorists may come in rubber dinghies that cannot be detected by radar. They entered Tel Aviv itself in March 1975 and seized a hotel at the seashore. People were murdered. John keeps an Uzi in his bedroom cupboard. Nola scoffs at this. "We'd both be dead before you could reach your gun," she says. Cheerful Nola laughs. An expressive woman—she uses her forearm to wave away John's preparations. "Sometimes he does the drill and I have to time him to see how long it takes to jump out of bed, open the cupboard, get the gun, put in the clip, and turn around.

They'd mow us down before he could get a foot on the floor."

Mississippi is part of the alarm system. "She'd bark," says John.

Just now Mississippi is racing through the orchards, nose to the ground. The air is sweet, and the sun like a mild alcohol makes you yearn for good things. You rest under a tree and eat tangerines, only slightly heavyhearted.

From the oranges we go to the banana groves. The green bananas are tied up in plastic tunics. The great banana flower hangs groundward like the sexual organ of a stallion. The long leaves resemble manes. After two years the ground has to be plowed up and lie fallow. Groves are planted elsewhere—more hard labor. "You noticed before," says John, "that some of the orange trees were withered. Their roots get into Roman ruins and they die. Some years ago, while we were plowing, we turned up an entire Roman street."

He takes me to the Herodian Hippodrome. American archeologists have dug out some of the old walls. We look down into the diggings, where labels flutter from every stratum. There are more potsherds than soil in these bluffs—the broken jugs of slaves who raised the walls two thousand years ago. At the center of the Hippodrome, a long graceful ellipse, is a fallen monolith weighing many tons. We sit under fig trees on the slope while Mississippi runs through the high smooth grass. The wind is soft and works the grass gracefully. It makes white air courses in the green.

Whenever John ships out he takes the dog for company. He had enough of solitude when he sailed on German ships under forged papers. He does not like to be alone. Now and again he was under suspicion. A German officer who sensed that he was Jewish threatened to turn him in, but one night when the ship was only hours out of Danzig she struck a mine and went down, the officer with her. John himself was pulled from the sea by his mates. Once he waited in a line of nude men whom a German doctor, a woman, was examining for venereal disease. In that lineup he alone was circumcised. He came before the woman and was examined; she looked into his face and she let him live.

John and I go back through the orange groves. There are large weasels living in the bushy growth along the pipeline. We see a pair of them at a distance in the road. They could easily do for Mississippi. She is luckily far off. We sit under a pine on the hilltop and look out to sea where a freighter moves slowly toward Ashkelon. Nearer to shore, a trawler chuffs. The kibbutz does little fishing now. Off the Egyptian coast, John has been shot at, and not long ago several members of the kibbutz were thrown illegally into jail by the Turks, accused of fishing in Turkish waters. Twenty people gave false testimony. They could have had a thousand witnesses. It took three months to get these men released. A lawyer was found who knew the judge. His itemized bill came to ten thousand dollars— five for the judge, five for himself.

Enough of this sweet sun and the transparent blue-green. We turn our backs on it to have a drink before lunch. Kibbutzniks ride by on clumsy old bikes. They wear cloth caps and pedal slowly; their day starts at six. Plain-looking working people from the tile factory and from the barn steer toward the dining hall. The kibbutzniks are a mixed group. There is one lone Orthodox Jew, who has no congregation to pray with. There are several older gentiles, one a Spaniard, one a Scandinavian, who married Jewish women and settled here. The Spaniard, an anarchist, plans to return to Spain now that Franco has died. One member of the kibbutz is a financial wizard, another was a high-ranking army officer who for obscure reasons fell into disgrace. The dusty tarmac path we follow winds through the settlement. Beside the undistinguished houses stand red poinsettias. Here, too, lie Roman relics. Then we come upon a basketball court, and then the rusty tracks of a children's choo-choo, and then the separate quarters for young women of eighteen, and a museum of antiquities, and a recreation hall. A strong odor of cattle comes from the feeding lot. I tell John that Gurdjiev had Katherine Mansfield resting in the stable at Fontainebleau, claiming that the cows' breath would cure her tuberculosis. John loves to hear such bits of literary history. We go into his house and Mississippi climbs into his lap while we drink Russian vodka. "We could live with those bastards if they limited themselves to making this Stolichnaya. . . ."

When I was a graduate student in anthropology, it was my immature ambition to investigate bands of Eskimos who were reported to have chosen to starve rather than eat foods that were abundant but under taboo. How much, I asked myself, did people yield to culture or to their life-long preoccupations, and at what point would the animal need to survive break through the restraints of custom and belief? I suspected then that among primitive peoples the objective facts counted for less. But I'm not at all certain now that civilized minds are more flexible and capable of grasping reality, or that they have livelier, more intelligent reactions to the threat of extinction. I grant that as an American I am more subject to illusion than my cousins. But will the Israeli veterans of hardships, massacres, and wars know how to save themselves? Has the experience of crisis taught them what to do? I have read writers on the Holocaust who made the most grave criticisms of Euro-pean Jewry, arguing that they doomed themselves by their unwillingness to surrender their comfortable ways, their property, their passive habits, their acceptance of bureau-cracy, and were led to slaughter unresisting. I do not see the point of scolding the dead. But if history is indeed a nightmare, as Karl Marx and James Joyce said, it is time for the Jews, a historical people, to rouse themselves, to burst from historical sleep. And Israel's political leaders do not seem to me to be awake. I sometimes think there are two Israelis. The real one is territorially insignificant. The other, the mental Israel, is immense, a country ines-timably important, playing a major role in the world, as broad as all history—and perhaps as deep as sleep. . . .

Israel's leaders are plainly still capable of pulling

themselves together. Perhaps the slaughter to the north (to call it mass murder is no exaggeration) has sobered them.

No one can know what the Lebanese casualty figures are. And what if we did know? Would 40,000 dead appall us more than 30,000? One can only wonder how all this killing is registered in the mind and spirit of the race. It has been estimated that the Khmer Rouge has destroyed a million and a half Cambodians, apparently as part of a design for improvement and renewal. What is the meaning of such corpse-making? In ancient times the walls of captured cities in the Middle East were sometimes hung with the skins of the vanquished. That custom has died out. But the eagerness to kill for political ends—or to justify killing by such ends—is as keen now as it ever was.

P . J .   O ' R O U R K E

Zion's Vital Signs

PASSOVER IS MY IDEA of a perfect holiday. Dear God, when you're handing out plagues of darkness, locusts, hail, boils, flies, lice, frogs, and cattle murrain, and turning the Nile to blood and smiting the firstborn, give me a pass. And tell me when it's over.

The Lord did well by me this Passover—brilliant sunshine on the beaches of Tel Aviv, pellucid waters, no flies in my room at the Hilton, and certainly no lice. I am a first—born myself, but I was not the least smitten, not even by the cute waitress at the Hilton's kosher sushi restaurant. I am a happily married man. And by the way, Leviticus 11:10 says, "Of any living thing which is in the waters, they shall be an abomi-

P. J. O'ROURKE
*is the author of
numerous books and
a frequent contributor
to magazines such
as* Rolling Stone,
the Atlantic, *and*
the New Yorker.
*In "Zion's Vital
Signs" (which originally
appeared in the*
Atlantic) *O'Rourke
makes light-hearted sense
of daily life in Israel.*

nation unto you"—an apt description of sushi as far as I'm concerned. But gentiles aren't expected to understand the intricacies of dietary law, although extra complications thereof lead to Passover's main drawback: food and—more important to gentiles—drink.

"I'll have a Scotch," I said to the Hilton's bar-tender.

"Scotch isn't kosher," he said. "It's made with leaven."

"Gin and tonic," I said.

"Gin isn't kosher."

"What can I have?"

"You can have a screwdriver—Israeli vodka and orange juice."

"What's Israeli vodka like?" I asked.

"The orange juice is very good"

There was no plague of tourists in Israel. It should have been a period of hectic visitation, with Passover beginning April 7 and the Eastern Orthodox and Western Easters coinciding a week later. But Israel's income from tourism dropped by 58 percent in the last quarter of 2000, and to judge by the queue-less ticket counters at Ben-Gurion Airport and the empty-seated aisles of El Al, the drop had continued. The marble lobby of the Hilton echoed, when at all, with the chatter of idle desk clerks and bellhops. The din of strife had rendered Israel quiet.

Quiet without portentous hush-traffic hum, air-conditioning buzz, and cell-phone beeps indicated ordinary life in an ordinary place. Tourism wasn't the only thing there was no sign of in Israel. No demonstrations blocked intersections; public-address systems failed to crackle with imperatives; exigent posters weren't stuck to walls except to advertise raves. There was no sign of crisis, international or bilateral or domestic political, although all news reports agreed that a crisis raged here, and an economic crisis besides. A 12 percent quarterly decline in gross domestic product was unevident in boarded-up shops and empty cafés, which didn't exist, and beggars and the homeless, who weren't on the streets.

There was no sign of terrorism's effects. The Carmel Market was crowded with people either wholly unafraid or indifferent to whether they were blown up singly or in bunches. If police security was pervasive, it was invisible. Israel, I've heard, is hated fanatically by millions of Muslims around the world, whereas Congress is loathed only by a small number of well-informed people who follow politics closely. But a walk around anything in Israel is less impeded by barriers and armed guards than a walk around the Capitol building in Washington.

There was no sign of war. Plenty of soldiers were to be seen, carrying their weapons, but this is no shock to the frequent traveler. For all that the world looks askance at America's lack of gun control, foreigners love to wave guns around. Nothing about the Israeli Defense Forces is as odd as Italian carabinieri brandishing their machine pistols while grimly patrolling that flash-point Venice.

There was, in fact, no sign of anything in Tel Aviv. In particular there was no sign of Israel's vital strategic importance to world peace—except, of course, those signs of

vital strategic importance to world peace one sees everywhere, the lettering here in Hebrew but the trademark
logos recognizable enough.

Tel Aviv is new, built on the sand dunes north of Jaffa in
the 1890s, about the same time Miami was founded. The
cities bear a resemblance in size, site, climate, and architecture, which ranges from the bland to the fancifully bland. In
Miami the striving, somewhat troublesome immigrant population is the result of Russia's meddling with Cuba. In Tel
Aviv the striving, somewhat troublesome immigrant population is the result of Russia's meddling with itself. I found a
Russian restaurant where they couldn't have cared less
what was made with leaven, where they had Scotch, and
where, over one Scotch too many, I contemplated the
absurdity of Israel's being an ordinary place.

What if people who had been away for ages, out and on
their own, suddenly showed up at their old home and decided to move back in? My friends with grown-up children tell
me this happens all the time. What if the countless ancient
tribal groups that are now defeated, dispersed, and stateless
contrived to re-establish themselves in their ancestral lands
in such a way as to dominate everyone around them? The
Mashantucket Pequots are doing so this minute at their Fox-
woods casino, in southeastern Connecticut. What if a religious group sought a homeland never minding how multi-
farious its religion had become or how divergent its adherents were in principles and practices? A homeland for
Protestants would have to satisfy the aspirations of born-
again literalists holding forth about creationism in their

concrete-block tabernacles and also to fulfill the hopes and
dreams of vaguely churched latitudinarians praising God's
creation by boating on Sundays. Protestant Zion would
need to be perfect both for sniping at abortion doctors in
North Carolina and for marrying lesbians in Vermont. As
an American, I already live in that country.

Maybe there's nothing absurd about Israel. I wandered
out into the ordinary nighttime, down Jabotinsky Street,
named for the founder of Revisionist Zionism, Ze'ev
Jabotinsky, who wrote in 1923, "A voluntary agreement
between us and the Arabs of Palestine is inconceivable now
or in the foreseeable future." Thus Jabotinsky broke with
the father of Zionism, Theodor Herzl, who, in *Altneuland*
(1902), had a fictional future Arab character in a fictional
future Israel saying, "The Jews have made us prosperous,
why should we be angry with them?" And now the Carmel
Market was full of goods from Egypt.

From Jabotinsky Street I meandered into Weizmann
Street, named for the first president of Israel, Chaim Weizmann, who in 1919 met with Emir Faisal, the future King
of Iraq and a son of the sherif of Mecca, and concluded an
agreement that "all necessary measures shall be taken to
encourage and stimulate immigration of Jews into Palestine
on a large scale." Faisal sent a letter to the American Zionist delegates at the Versailles peace conference wishing
Jews "a most hearty welcome home."

Turning off Weizmann Street, I got lost for a while
among signpost monikers I didn't recognize but that probably commemorated people who became at least as embattled

as Jabotinsky, Herzl, Weizmann, and Faisal. I emerged on Ben-Gurion Avenue. The first prime minister of Israel was a ferocious battler. He fought the British mandate, the war of liberation, Palestinian guerrillas, and the Sinai campaign. He even won, most of the time, in the Israeli Knesset. And still he was on the lookout for peace. In the months leading up to the Suez crisis, in 1956, President Dwight Eisenhower had a secret emissary shuttling between Jerusalem and Cairo. Egypt's President, Gamal Abdel Nasser, told the emissary (in words that Yasir Arafat could use and, for all I know, does), "If the initiative [Nasser] was now taking in these talks was known in public be would be faced not only with a political problem, but—possibly—with a bullet."

A bullet was what Yitzhak Rabin got, at the end of Ben-Gurion Avenue, from a Jewish extremist, during a peace rally in the square that now bears Rabin's name. A bullet was also what Emir Faisal's brother, King Abdullah of Jordan, got, from a Muslim extremist, for advocating peace with Israel. Nasser's successor, Anwar Sadat got a bullet too.

If bullets were the going price for moderation hereabouts, then I needed another drink. I walked west along Gordon Street—named, I hope, for Judah Leib Gordon, the nineteenth-century Russian novelist who wrote in classical Hebrew, and not for Lord George Gordon, the fanatical anti-Catholic and leader of the 1780 Gordon riots, who converted to Judaism late in life and died in Newgate Prison praising the French Revolution. This brought me to a stretch of nightclubs along the beach promenade. Here, two months later, a suicide bomber would kill twenty-one people outside the Dolphi disco. Most of the victims were teenage Russian girls, no doubt very moderate about everything other than clothes, makeup, and the proper selection of dance-mix albums.

My tour guide arrived the next morning. His name was a long collection of aspirates, glottal stops, and gutturals with, like printed Hebrew, no evident vowels. "Americans can never pronounce it," he said. "Just call me T'zchv."

I called him Z. I was Z's only customer. He drove a minibus of the kind that in the United States always seems to be filled with a church group. And so was Z's, until recently. "Most of my clients," he said, "are the fundamentalists. They want to go everywhere in the Bible. But now . . . " The people who talk incessantly about Last Days have, owing to violence in the region, quit visiting the place where the world will end.

Z was seventy-five, a retired colonel in the Israeli Defense Forces, a veteran of every war from liberation to the invasion of Lebanon. "Our worst enemy is CNN," he said. His parents came from Russia in 1908 and settled on the first kibbutz in Palestine. Z was full of anger about the fighting in Israel—the fighting with the ultra-Orthodox Jews. "They don't serve in the army. They don't pay taxes. The government gives them money. I call them Pharisees."

As we walked around, Z would greet by name people of perfectly secular appearance, adding, "you Pharisee, you," or would introduce me to someone in a T-shirt and jeans who had maybe voted for Ariel Sharon in the most recent election by saying, "I want you to meet Moshe, a real Pharisee, this one."

Z said, over and over, "The problem is with the Pharisees." About Arabs I couldn't get him to say much. He seemed to regard Arabs as he did weather. Weather is important. Weather is good. We enjoy weather. We respect weather. Nobody likes to be out in weather when it gets dramatic. "My wife won't let me go to the Palestinian areas," Z said.

"Let's go to an ultra-Orthodox neighborhood," I said.

"You don't want to go there," he said. "They're dumps. You want to see where Jesus walked by the Sea of Galilee."

"No, I don't."

"And Jesus, walking by the Sea of Galilee, saw two brethren, Simon called Peter, and Andrew his brother, casting a net into the sea . . . " For a man at loggerheads with religious orthodoxy, Z recited a lot of Scripture, albeit mostly from the New Testament, where Pharisees come off looking pretty bad. When quoting he would shift to the trochaic foot—familiar to him, perhaps, from the preaching of his evangelical tourists; familiar to me from my mom's yelling through the screen door, "*You* get *in* here *right* this *mi*nute!"

As a compromise we went to Jaffa and had Saint Peter's fish from the Sea of Galilee for lunch. Jaffa is the old port city for Jerusalem, a quaint jumble of Arab architecture out of which the Arabs ran or were run (depending on who's writing history) during the war of liberation. Like most quaint jumbles adjacent to quaintness-free cities, Jaffa is full of galleries and studios. Israel is an admirably artsy place. And, as in other artsy places of the modern world, admiration had to be aimed principally at the effort. The output indicated that Israelis should have listened the first time when God said, "Thou shalt not make unto thee any graven image, or any likeness of any thing." Some of the abstract stuff was good.

I wanted to look at art. Z wanted me to look at the house of Simon the Tanner, on the Jaffa waterfront. This, according to Acts 10:10–15, is where Saint Peter went into a trance and foresaw a universal Christian Church and, also, fitted sheets. Peter had a vision of "a great sheet knit at the four corners, and let down to the earth: Wherein were all manner of four-footed beasts of the earth, and wild beasts, and creeping things." God told Peter to kill them and eat them. Peter thought this didn't look kosher— or, probably, in the case of the creeping things, appetizing. And God said that what He had cleansed should not be called unclean.

"Then is when Peter knew Christianity was for everyone, not just the Jews!" Z said, with vicarious pride in another religion's generous thought.

A little too generous. To Peter's idea we owe ideology, the notion that the wonderful visions we have involve not only ourselves but the whole world, whether the world wants to get involved or not. Until that moment of Peter's in Jaffa, the killing of heretics and infidels was a local business. Take, for example, the case of John the Baptist: with Herodias, Herod Antipas, and stepdaughter Salome running the store, it was a mom-and-pop operation. But by the middle of the first century theological persecution had gone global in the known world. Eventually the slaughter would outgrow the limited market in religious differences. During our era millions of people have been murdered on purely intellectual grounds.

"Can we go in?" I asked.

"No," Z said. "The Muslims put a mosque in there, which made the Orthodox angry. They rioted, which kept the Christians out. So the police closed the place."

For those who dislike ideology, the great thing about kibbutzim is that they're such a lousy idea. Take an Eastern European intelligentsia and make the desert bloom. One would sooner take Mormons and start a rap label. But Kibbutz Yad-Mordechai, three quarters of a mile north of the Gaza Strip, passed the test of ideology. It worked—something no fully elaborated, universally applied ideology ever does.

I'd never been to a kibbutz. I don't know what I expected—Grossinger's with guns? A bar mitzvah with tractors? Some of my friends went to kibbutzim in the 1960s and came back with tales of sex and socialism. But you could get that at Oberlin, without the circle dancing. I'm sure my poli-sci-major pals were very little help with the avocado crop. Anyway, what I wasn't expecting was a cluster of J.F.K.-era summer cottages with haphazard flower beds, sagging badminton nets, and Big Wheel tricycles on the grass — Lake Missaukee, Michigan, without Lake Missaukee.

A miniature Michigan of shrubbery and trees covered the low hills of the settlement, but with a network of drip-irrigation lines weaving among the stems and trunks. Here were the fiber-optic connections of a previous and more substantive generation of modernists, who meant to treat a troubled world with water rather than information. Scattered in the greenery were the blank metal-sided workshops and warehouses of contemporary agriculture, suggestive more of light industry than of peasanthood. And Yad-Mordechai has light industry, too, producing housewares and decorative ceramics. Plus it has the largest apiary in Israel, an educational center devoted to honey and bees, a gift shop, a kosher restaurant, and, of all things 1,300 yards from the Gaza Strip, a petting zoo.

Yad-Mordechai was founded in 1943 on an untitled, sandy patch of the Negev. The land was bought from the sheik of a neighboring village. And there, in the common little verb of the preceding sentence, is the moral genius of Zionism. Theodor Herzl, when he set down the design of Zionism in *The Jewish State* (1896), wrote, "The land . . . must, of course, be privately acquired." The Zionists intended to buy a nation rather than conquer one. This had never been tried. Albeit various colonists, such as the American ones, had foisted purchase-and-sale agreements on peoples who had no concept of fee-simple tenure or of geography as anything but a free good. But Zionists wanted an honest title search.

More than a hundred years ago the Zionists realized what nobody else has realized yet—nobody but a few cranky Austrian economists and some very rich people skimming the earth in Gulfstream jets. Nothing is zero-

sum, not even statehood. Man can make more of everything, including the very thing he sets his feet on, as the fellow getting to his feet and heading to the bar on the GV can
tell you. "If we wish to found a State to-day," Herzl wrote,
"we shall not do it in the way which would have been the
only possible one a thousand years ago.

Whether the early Zionists realized what they'd realized is another matter. Palestinian Arabs realized, very
quickly, that along with the purchased polity came politics.
In politics, as opposed to reality, everything is zero-sum.

Considering how things are going politically in Zion
these days, the foregoing quotation from Herzl should be
continued and completed.

> Supposing, for example, we were obliged to clear a
> country of wild beasts, we should not set about the
> task in the fashion of Europeans of the fifth century.
> We should not take spear and lance and go out singly
> in pursuit of bears; we should organise a large and
> lively hunting party, drive the animals together, and
> throw a melinite bomb into their midst.

On May 19, 1948, Yad-Mordechai was attacked by an
Egyptian armored column with air and artillery support.
The kibbutz was guarded by 130 men and women, some of
them teenagers, most without military training. They had
fifty-five light weapons, one machine gun, and a two-inch
mortar. Yad-Mordechai held out for six days—long enough
for the Israeli army to secure the coast road to Tel Aviv.

Twenty-six of the defenders were killed, and about 300
Egyptians.

A slit trench has been left along the Yad-Mordechai
hilltop, with the original fifty-five weapons fastened to
boards and preserved with tar. Under the viscous coatings
a nineteenth-century British rifle is discernible, and the
sink-trap plumbing of two primitive Bren guns. The rest of
the firearms look like the birds and cats that were once
mummified—by Egyptians, appropriately enough. Below
the trench is a lace negligee of barbed wire, all the barbed
wire the kibbutz had in 1948, and beyond that are Egyptian tanks, just where they stopped when they could go no
farther. Between the tanks dozens of charging Egyptian
soldiers are represented by life-size, black-painted two-
dimensional cutouts—Gumby commandos, lawn ornaments on attack.

It is the only war memorial I've seen that was frightening and silly—things all war memorials should be. Most
war memorials are sad or awful-things, come to think of it,
war memorials should also be. And this war memorial has a
price of admission-which, considering the cost of war, is
another good idea.

There was a crabby old guy at the ticket booth, whom Z
greeted with warm complaining, grouch to grouch. Then Z
took me to Yad-Mordechai's Holocaust museum, which skips
pity and goes immediately to Jewish resistance during World
War II and Jewish fighting in Palestine and Israel. Yad-
Mordechai is named for Mordechai Anielewicz, the commander of the Warsaw-ghetto uprising. The message of the

Yad-Mordechai museum is that the Holocaust memorial is in the trench at the other end of the kibbutz.

This is the second wonderful thing about Zionism: it was right. Every other "ism" of the modern world has been wrong about the nature of civilized man—Marxism, mesmerism, surrealism, pacifism, existentialism, nudism. But civilized man did want to kill Jews, and was going to do more of it. And Zionism was specific. While other systems of thought blundered around in the universal, looking for general solutions to comprehensive problems, Zionism stuck to its guns, or—in the beginning, anyway—to its hoes, mattocks, and irrigation pipes.

True, Zionism has a utopian-socialist aspect that is thoroughly nutty as far as I'm concerned. But it isn't my concern. No one knocks on my door during dinner and asks me to join a kibbutz or calls me on the weekend to persuade me to drop my current long-distance carrier and make all my phone calls by way of Israel. And given my last name, they won't.

My last name is, coincidentally, similar to the maiden name of the Holocaust-museum docent, who was Baltimore Irish and had married a young man from the kibbutz and moved there in the 1970s. "I converted," she said, "which the Orthodox make it hard to do, but I went through with it. There's a crabby old guy here who sort of took me under his wing. The first Yom Kippur after I converted, he asked me, `Did you fast?' I said yes. He said, `Stupid!' You probably saw him on the way in, behind the ticket counter. He's a veteran of the fight for Yad-Mordechai. There's a photo of him

here, when they liberated the kibbutz, in November '48."
And there was the photo of the young, heroic, crabby old
guy. And now he was behind the ticket counter at the war
memorial—not making a political career in Jerusalem or
writing a book about the young, heroic days or flogging his
story to the History Channel.

"How cool is that?" said the Baltimore Irish woman
running the Holocaust Museum.

Z and I had lunch at the kibbutz's self-serve restaurant,
where Z took his plate of meat and sat in the middle of the
dairy section. In the sky to the south we could see smoke
rising from the Gaza Strip—tires burning at an intifada
barricade, or just trash being incinerated. Public services
aren't what they might be in the Palestinian Authority at
the moment. Or maybe it was one of the Jewish settlements
in Gaza being attacked, although we hadn't heard gunfire.

These settlements aren't farms but, mostly, apartment
clusters. "Are the settlements in the West Bank and Gaza
some kind of post-agricultural, post-industrial, high-rise
Zionism?" I asked Z. "Or are they a government-funded,
mondo-condo, live-dangerously parody of nation-building?"

"Pharisees!" Z said, and he went back to eating.

After lunch we drove to Ben-Gurion's house in Tel Aviv,
a modest, foursquare, utterly unadorned structure. But the
inside was cozy with 20,000 books, in Hebrew, English,
French, German, Russian, Latin, Spanish, Turkish, and
ancient Greek. No fiction, however: a man who devoted his
life to making a profound change in society was uninterested
in the encyclopedia of society that fiction provides.

Looking at the thick walls and heavy shutters, I wondered if the house had been built to be defended. Then I twigged to the purpose of the design and gained true respect for the courage of the Zionist pioneers. Ben-Gurion came to the Middle East before air conditioning was invented-and from Plonsk, at that.

We spent the next day, at my insistence and to Z's mystification, driving around the most ordinary parts of Israel, which look so ordinary to an American that I'm rendered useless for describing them to other Americans. American highway strip-mall development hasn't quite reached Israel, however, so there's even less of the nondescript to not describe.

Z and I stood in a garden-apartment complex in Ashdod, in the garden part, a patch of trampled grass. "Here is the ugliest living in Israel;" he said. We went to a hill on the Ashdod shore, a tell actually, a mound of ancient ruins, an ash heap of history from which we had a view of—ash heaps, and the power plant that goes with them, which supplies half of Israel's electricity. Ashdod, incidentally, is a Philistine place-name, not a pun. We could also see the container port, Israel's principal deep-water harbor. "This is the place where the whale threw Jonah up," Z said.

We went to the best suburbs of Tel Aviv, which look like the second-best suburbs of San Diego. We spent a lot of time stuck in traffic. Violence in the West Bank has forced traffic into bottlenecks on Routes 2 and 4 along the coast, in a pattern familiar to anyone negotiating Washing-

ton, D.C.'s Beltway—living in a place where you're scared
to go to half of it and the other half you can't get to.

Israel is slightly smaller than New Jersey. Moses in
effect led the tribes of Israel out of the District of Columbia, parted Chesapeake Bay near Annapolis, and wandered
for forty years in Delaware. From the top of Mt. Nebo, in
the equivalent of Pennsylvania, the Lord showed Moses all
of Canaan. New Canaan is in Connecticut—but close
enough. And there is a Mt. Nebo in Pennsylvania,
although it overlooks the Susquehanna rather than the
Promised Land of, say, Paramus. Joshua blew the trumpet
and the malls of Paramus came tumbling down. Israel also
has beaches that are at least as nice as New Jersey's.

An old friend of mine, Dave Garcia, flew in from Hong
Kong to spend Easter in Jerusalem. "I like to go places
when the tourists aren't there," he said. Dave spent two
years in Vietnam before the tourists arrived, as a prisoner
of the Viet Cong. "Let's see where the Prince of Peace was
born," he said. "It's in the middle of the intifada."

Z took us from Ben-Gurion Airport to the roadblock
between Jerusalem and Bethlehem. The highway was
strewn with broken bottles, as if in the aftermath not of
war but of a very bad party. Israeli soldiers and Palestinian
Authority policemen stood around warily. Z handed us
over to an Arab tour-guide friend of his who drove a twen-
ty-five-year-old Mercedes and looked glum. Israel had lost
half its tourism, but hotels in Palestinian areas were reporting occupancy rates of 4 percent.

The Arab guide parked at random in the middle of empty Manger Square, outside the Church of the Nativity. "There is normally a three-and-a-half-hour wait," he said, as we walked straight into the Manger Grotto. The little cave has been rendered a soot hole by millennia of offertory candles. It's hung with damp-stained tapestries and tarnished lamps and festoons of grimy ornamentation elaborate enough for a Byzantine Emperor if the Byzantine Emperor lived in a basement. I imagine the Virgin Mary had the place done up more cheerfully, with little homey touches, when it was a barn.

The only other visitors were in a tour group from El Salvador, wearing bright-yellow T-shirts and acting cheerfully pious. Dave asked them in Spanish if, after all that El Salvador had been through with earthquakes and civil war, the fuss about violence and danger around here puzzled them. They shrugged and looked puzzled, but that may have been because no one in the Garcia family has been able to speak Spanish for three generations, including Dave.

According to our tour guide, all the dead babies from the Massacre of the Innocents are conveniently buried one grotto over, under the same church. Sites of Christian devotion around Jerusalem tend to be convenient. In the Church of the Holy Sepulcher the piece of ground where Jesus' cross was erected, the stone where he was laid out for burial, and the tomb in which he was resurrected—plus where Adam's skull was allegedly buried and, according to early Christian cartographers, the center of the world—are within a few arthritic steps of one another. Saint Helena, the mother of the Emperor Constantine, was over seventy—five when she traveled to the Holy Land, in 326, looking for sacred locations. Arriving with a full imperial retinue and a deep purse, Saint Helena discovered that her tour guides were able to take her to every place she wanted to go; each turned out to be nearby and, as luck would have it, for sale. The attack of real-estate agents in Palestine long pre-dates Zionism.

The Church of the Nativity is a shabby mess, the result of quarreling religious orders. Greek Orthodox, Armenian Orthodox, and Roman Catholic priests have staked out Nativity turf with the acrimonious precision of teenage brothers sharing a bedroom. A locked steel door prevents direct access from the Roman Catholic chapel to the Grotto of the Nativity, which has to be reached through the Greek Orthodox monastery, where there is a particular "Armenian beam" that Greek Orthodox monks stand on to sweep the area above the Grotto entrance, making the Armenians so angry that, according to my guidebook, "in 1984 there were violent clashes as Greek and Armenian clergy fought running battles with staves and chains that had been hidden beneath their robes." What would Jesus have thought? He might have thought, *Hand me a stave,* per Mark 11:15: "Jesus went into the temple, and began to cast out them that sold and bought in the temple, and overthrew the tables of the moneychangers."

It's left to the Muslims to keep the peace at the Church of the Nativity in Bethlehem, just as it's left to the Jews to keep a similar peace at the likewise divided Church of the Holy Sepulcher in Jerusalem. Who will be a Muslim and a

Jew to the Muslims and the Jews? Hindus, maybe. That is
more or less the idea behind putting U.N. peacekeeping
troops in Israel. This may or may not work. *The Bhagavad
Gita* opens with the hero Arjuna trying to be a pacifist:
"Woe!" Arjuna says. "We have resolved to commit a great
crime as we stand ready to kill family out of greed for king-
ship and pleasures!" But the Lord Krishna tells Arjuna to
quit whining and fight. "Either you are killed and will then
attain to heaven," Krishna says, "or you triumph and will
enjoy the earth."

Our guide took us to several large gift stores with no
other customers, aisles stacked with unsold souvenirs of
Jesus' birth. Part of the Israeli strategy in the intifada has
been to put economic pressure on the Arabs of the West
Bank and Gaza. Fear of death hasn't stopped the Arabs.
Maybe fear of Chapter 11 will do the trick. The entire
hope of peace on earth rests with badly carved olivewood
creche sets. Dave and I bought several.

Then our guide took us up a hill to the Christian Arab
village of Beit Jala, which the Israelis had been shelling
(and later would occupy). Large chunks were gone from
the tall, previously comfortable-looking limestone villas.
Shuttered housefronts were full of what looked like bullet
holes but were large enough to put a Popsicle in. "Ooh,
fifty-caliber," Dave said with professional appreciation.

"These people," our guide said, "have no part in the
violence." Dave and I made noises of condolence and agreement in that shift of sympathy to the nearest immediate victim that is the hallmark of modern morality.

"Here a man was sleeping in his bed," our guide said, showing us a three-story pile of rubble. "And they couldn't find him for days later. The Israelis shell here for no reason."

"Um," Dave said, "*why* for no reason?" And our guide, speaking in diplomatic circumlocution, allowed as how every now and then, all the time, Palestinian gunmen would occasionally, very often, use the Beit Jala hilltop to shoot with rifles at Israeli tanks guarding a highway tunnel in the valley. They did it the next night.

The owner of an upscale antiquities shop back in Bethlehem did not look as if he meant to attain any sooner than necessary, even though his stores air-conditioning unit had been knocked out by Israelis firing on nearby rioters. He arrived in a new Mercedes with three assistants to open his business especially for Dave, his first customer in a month.

The antiquities dealer was another friend of Z's. Z told us that this was the man whose grandfather was the Palestinian cobbler to whom the Dead Sea Scrolls were offered as scrap leather by the Bedouin shepherd who found them—a story too good to subject to the discourtesies of investigative journalism.

The emporium was new, built in the soon-dashed hopes of millennium traffic. The antiquities were displayed in the stark, track-lit modernity necessary to make them look like something other than the pots and pans and jars and bottles of people who had, one way or another, given up on this place long ago.

Dave collects antiques, but by profession he's an iron— and-steel commodities trader. He has also lived in Asia for years. I sat on a pile of rugs and drank little cups of coffee while Levantine bargaining met Oriental dickering and the cold-eyed brokerage of the market floor. The three great world traditions of haggle flowered into confrontation for two and a half hours. Folks from the Oslo talks and the Camp David meetings should have been there for benefit of instruction. Everyone ended up happy. No fatal zero-sum thinking was seen as bank notes and ceramics changed hands at last. Dave could make more money. And the Arabs could make more antiquities.

Why can't everybody just get along? No reasonably detached person goes to Israel without being reduced in philosophical discourse to the level of Rodney King—or, for that matter, to the level of George Santayana. "Those who cannot remember the past are condemned to repeat it," Santayana said, in one of those moments of fatuousness that come to even the most detached of philosophers. It goes double for those who can't remember anything else. And they *do* get along, after their fashion. Muslims and Christians and Jews have lived together in the Holy Land for centuries—hating one another's guts, cutting one another's throats, and touching off wars of various magnitudes.

The whole melodrama of the Middle East would be improved if amnesia were as common here as it is in melodramatic plots. I was thinking this as I looked at the Dead Sea Scrolls in the solemn underground Shrine of the Book, inside the vast precincts of the Israel Museum. Maybe all the world's hoary tracts ought to wind up as loafer soles or be auctioned at Sotheby's to a greedy high-tech billionaire for display in his otherwise bookless 4,000-square-foot cyber-den. Then I noticed that Z was reading the scrolls, muttering aloud at speed, perusing an ancient text with more ease than I can read Henry James. What's past is past, perhaps, but when it passed, this was where it went.

Z dropped us at the King David Hotel, the headquarters of the Palestinian mandate administration when the British were trying to keep the peace. In 1946 the hotel was blown up by the radical wing of the Jewish Resistance Movement, the Irgun. Some of every group were killed—forty-one Arabs, twenty-eight British, seventeen Jews, and five reasonably detached persons of miscellaneous designation. The Irgun was led by the future Prime Minister Menachem Begin, who would make peace with Egypt in the 1970s but, then again, war with Lebanon in the 1980s.

On the way to the hotel Z explained why there will always be war in the region. "Israel is strategic," he said in his most New Testamental tone. "It is the strategic land bridge between Africa and Asia. For five thousand years there has been fighting in Israel. It is the strategic land bridge." And the fighting continues, a sort of geopolitical muscle memory, as though airplanes and supertankers hadn't been invented. The English and the French might as well be fighting over the beaver-pelt trade in Quebec today, and from what I understand of Canadian politics, they are.

We were meeting Israeli friends of Dave's at the hotel, a married couple. He voted for Sharon; she voted for Ehud

Barak. Dave and I marked our lintels and doorposts with the blood of the lamb, metaphorically speaking, and drank Israeli vodka and orange juice.

"There will always be war," the husband said, "because with war Arafat is a hero and without war he's just an unimportant guy in charge of an unimportant place with a lot of political and economic problems."

"There will always be war," the wife said, "because with war Sharon is a hero and without war he's just an unimportant guy in charge of an unimportant place with. . . ."

Also, war is fun—from a distance. Late the next night Dave and I were walking back to our hotel in Arab East Jerusalem. Dave was wearing a Hawaiian shirt and I was in a blazer and chinos. We couldn't have looked less Israeli if we'd been dressed like Lawrence of Arabia (who, incidentally, was a third party to the cordial meeting between Chaim Weizmann and Emir Faisal). Fifty yards down a side street a couple of Palestinian teenagers jumped out of the shadows. Using the girly overhand throw of nations that mostly play soccer, one kid threw a bottle at us. It landed forty yards away.

On Good Friday, Dave and Z and I walked from the Garden of Gethsemane to the Lions Gate, where Israeli paratroopers fought their way into the Old City during the Six-Day War. We traveled the Via Dolorosa in an uncrowded quiet that Jesus Christ and those paratroopers were not able to enjoy. We owed our peace in Jerusalem to an enormous police presence. There have always been a lot of policemen in Jerusalem, but they did Jesus no good. Nor did the Jordanian police give Israeli soldiers helpful directions to the Ecce Homo Arch. And our Savior and the heroes of 1967 didn't have a chance to stop along the way and bargain with Arab rug merchants.

Z and the rug merchants exchanged pessimisms, Z grousing about Sharon and the Arabs complaining about Arafat. "The Israeli army tells Arafat where the strikes will come," one shopkeeper said. "They tell him, `Don't be here. Don't be there.' No one tells me."

I visited the fourteen Stations of the Cross and said my prayers—for peace, of course, although, as a Zionist friend of mine puts it, "Victory would be okay too." Jesus said, "Love your enemies.' He didn't say not to have any. In fact, he said, "I came not to send peace but a sword." Or at least staves and chains.

Then we went to the Wailing Wall, the remnant of the Second Temple, built by the same Herod the Great who killed all the babies buried near the manger in Bethlehem. Atop the Wailing Wall stands the Haram ash-Sarif, with the Dome of the Rock enclosing Mt. Moriah, where Abraham was ready to kill Isaac and where, at that moment, Muslims gathered for Friday prayers were surrounded by Israeli soldiers, some of both no doubt ready to kill too. (The Dome of the Rock also marks the center of the world for those who don't believe that the center of the world is down the street, in the Church of the Holy Sepulcher.)

In the plaza in front of the Wailing Wall religious volunteers were lending yarmulkes to Jews who had arrived bareheaded. "Well," Dave said, "my mother was Jewish, so I guess that makes me Jewish. I'd better get a rent-a-beanie and go over to the Wailing Wall and . . . wail, or something."

The yarmulkes being handed out were, unaccountably, made of silver reflective fabric. "I look like an outer-space Jew," Dave said.

"I always thought you were Catholic," I said.

"Because of *Garcia*," Dave said, "like *O'Rourke*."

"I'm not Catholic either. My mother was Presbyterian, my father was Lutheran, and I'm Methodist. I came home from Methodist confirmation class in a big huff and told my mother there were huge differences between Presbyterians and Lutherans and Methodists. And my mother said, 'We sent you to the Methodist church because all the nice people in the neighborhood go there."

"They could use that church here," Dave said. He swayed in front of the wall, like the Orthodox surrounding him, although, frankly, in a manner more aging-pop-fan than Hasidic.

What could cause more hatred and bloodshed than religion? This is the Israel question. Except it isn't rhetorical; it has an answer. We went to Yad Vashem, the Jerusalem Holocaust Memorial, and saw what the godless get up to.

There are worse things than war, if the intifada is indeed a war. As of this writing, 513 Palestinians and 124 Israelis had been killed in what is called the second intifada. About 40,000 people perished in the 1992–1996 civil war in Tajikistan that nobody's heard of. From one and a

half to two million are dead in Sudan. There are parts of
the world where the situation Dave and I were in is too
ordinary to have a name.

Late Saturday night the particular place where we
were in that situation was the American Colony Hotel, in
East Jerusalem, sometimes called the P.L.O Hotel for the
supposed connections the staff has. It is the preferred residence of intifada-covering journalists, especially those
who are indignant about Israeli behavior. The American
Colony Hotel was once the mansion of an Ottoman pasha.
Dave and I sat among palms in the peristyle courtyard, surrounded by arabesques carved in Jerusalem's golden limestone. The bedroom-temperature air was scented with
Easter lilies, and in the distance, now and then, gunfire
could be heard.

"This country is hopeless," Dave said, pouring a Palestinian Taybeh beer to complement a number of Israeli Mac-
cabee beers we'd had earlier in West Jerusalem. "And as
hopeless places go, it's not bad." We discussed another
Israel question. Why are Israeli girls so fetching in their
army uniforms, whereas the women in the U.S. military
are less so? It may have something to do with carrying guns
all the time. But Freud was a lukewarm Zionist, and let's
not think about it.

After the first Zionist Congress, in 1897, the rabbis of
Vienna sent a delegation to Palestine on a fact-finding mission. The delegation cabled Vienna saying, "The bride is
beautiful, but she is married to another man." However,
the twentieth century, with all its Freudianism, was about

to dawn, and we know what having the beautiful bride married to another man means in a modern story line. No fair using amnesia as a device for tidy plot resolution.

"Do we have to choose sides?" Dave said. But it's like dating sisters. Better make a decision or head for the Global Village limits. And speaking of sisters, I opened the *Jerusalem Post* on Easter morning and discovered that my sister's neighborhood in Cincinnati was under curfew, overrun with race riots.

THE
PEACE
PROCESS

URI SAVIR

Why Oslo
Still Matters

I F AN ISRAELI Rip van Winkle had slept from 1948 to 1998, he probably would not recognize his country today. What was once a besieged wasteland inhabited by survivors of the Holocaust and refugees from Arab lands has become a vibrant democracy and a technological and military power that has absorbed Jews from every part of the world. It has won wars of survival and has engaged in a process of peace-making with its neighbors. Israel is a revolution. Parallel to its rebirth and the building of a modern state, Israel has been engaged in a struggle to change fundamentally its relationship with the non-Jewish world, especially the Arabs. Central to this effort is the solution of the Palestinian issue.

URI SAVIR
was Israel's chief negotiator in the Oslo peace process and is currently the president of the Peres Center for Peace. *This article originally appeared in the* New York Times Magazine *and details what occurred behind the scenes during that still-important agreement.*

In 1993, Israel began secret peace negotiations in Oslo with the Palestine Liberation Organization. The Oslo peace process marked a historic attempt to bring about reconciliation between two nations fighting over the same land. For Israel, the Oslo process has produced an internal struggle as it forces the nation to answer the question that has always divided left and right: should Israel trust and cooperate with its neighbors or, as Vladimir Jabotinsky, the ideologue of right-wing revisionism, insisted, continue to live within an "iron wall"? If Oslo succeeds, the iron wall will crumble. The peace process is therefore crucial not only to Israel's struggle with the Palestinians but also to the struggle for its own identity.

For me, Oslo began on May 14, 1993, a balmy Friday afternoon, when my boss, Israel's foreign minister, Shimon Peres, asked me to his official residence in Jerusalem. Peres, dressed in a cardigan, was relaxed as I entered his living room. Avi Gil, his wise chief of staff, was already seated on one of the comfortable sofas. I sat down opposite him.

"A glass of wine?" Peres asked. I nodded and he asked dryly, "How about a weekend in Oslo?" as though he were offering cheese and crackers. "Excuse me?" I mumbled, straining to suppress my excitement. I knew that Oslo meant a first official talk with the P.L.O. Two Israeli professors, Yair Hirschfeld and Ron Pundak, had been speaking informally with the Palestinians in Oslo. On May 20, 1993, I left Israel to join the discussions.

On the way into the mountains, Terje Larsen, our Norwegian host and the head of a research institute, indoctrinated me into the "Oslo spirit." He evidently considered me a technocrat, perhaps too stiff for the mission at hand. He explained that humor was an important element, and that the interchange should be informal. For Terje, the essence of the Oslo channel was to devise solutions through free thinking, not hard-nosed bargaining.

At length, we arrived at the small Heftye Lodge, an official guesthouse. We sat for a few moments without uttering a word. Then there was a ceremonial knock on the door, and in walked Terje's wife, Mona Juul. She was followed by three Palestinians. Suddenly, there was Abu Ala standing directly in front of me.

"Meet your enemy No. 1, Ahmed Qurei, better known as Abu Ala," Terje said.

I was surprised by the man's appearance. Comfortably middle-aged, he wore thick-lensed glasses that failed to hide his penetrating glance. He, too, was dressed formally and looked more like a European businessman than the underground leader I had expected.

"Pleased to meet you," he and I muttered, aware of the significance of our unprecedented gesture as we shook hands while eyeing each other nervously. The room fell quiet for a second before Terje continued, "Now meet your enemy No. 2, Hassan Asfour."

Asfour was a political adviser to Arafat's close associate Abu Mazen (who was monitoring the talks from Tunis). As I came to know him, with his shining eyes and aloof, somewhat resentful expression, he often seemed torn between two unshakable convictions: his certainty of

Israel's abiding arrogance and his faith in the possibility of attaining peace.

"Enemy No. 3" was introduced to me as Maher al-Kurd, a tall, forthright, extremely polite man who brought to mind a German schoolmaster. Indeed, he had studied at an East German university before becoming an economic adviser to Arafat. The ice thawed a bit as Ron and Yair embraced the three Palestinians, with whom they had been partners for five months.

Terje then showed us into the wood-paneled lounge. Our initial exchange was painful.

"I left Tel Aviv at 6:30 this morning," I offered.

"We left Tunis yesterday," Abu Ala replied.

We could find nothing more to say.

Thus alone in the Norwegian night, we took our places at opposite sides of a narrow wooden table. Then, for the only time in the three years of talks that followed, I read a prepared statement. It concluded with two conditions that Rabin and Peres had insisted on. Above all, I stressed: "Jerusalem is the center of our national ethos, and if that is open to negotiation, no progress can be made. As to outside arbitration, you must decide whether we are to act as partners, and solve all our differences through dialogue, or request Security Council-like arbitration and end up with a pile of resolutions that will remain no more than numbers."

Finally, I explained that the guideline for the eventual negotiations should be to advance in stages and that it would be best that the first change should be effected in the Gaza Strip. I did not mention Jericho.

"For our part, the stress must be on security, and naturally the P.L.O. will have to cease all terror operations. There is also great potential for economic cooperation, and this we must translate into deeds. This is a historic opportunity for all of us," I concluded. "It must not be wasted."

Outside, the midnight sun still cast a dim glow as Abu Ala made his opening statement. "My colleagues and I, as well as our leadership in Tunis, are very pleased that our negotiations have finally reached an official stage. We have done important work with our friends Yair and Ron." (I noticed that they smiled as they continued taking notes.) "I would like you to convey to your leaders that our intentions, particularly those of our chairman, Yasir Arafat, are serious."

Upon hearing the name of Arafat, so long the symbol of hostility to Israel, I felt an odd sensation. As if reading my thoughts, Abu Ala continued: "There's no chance of advancing toward peace without the P.L.O. and its leaders. No one else can speak for the Palestinian people with authority and legitimacy.

"We want to live with you in peace," he said, with obvious seriousness. "We want to cooperate with you toward developing the region; encouraging the creation of a Marshall Plan for the Middle East; developing our economies, so that we can open the doors to the Arab world for you and to freedom for ourselves. The situation in the occupied territories is desperate, politically and economically. Time is running out."

Abu Ala conceded that the Washington talks were at an impasse but promised that they would go on. As to the two substantive conditions I had laid down, he explained that he would have to consult with Tunis. "But as for security," he assured us, "I have specific instructions from Arafat to accommodate you on every aspect of this matter."

He paused for a moment and then, speaking to me directly, said: "Tell me, Mr. Savir, I have heard Israel's statements that you view the P.L.O. as an existential threat. I would like to understand. Israel is a regional power and, according to the international press, a nuclear one as well. You have the finest air force in the region, a huge number of tanks, the most effective intelligence network in the world, one of the largest and most renowned armies. You call us terrorists. We call ourselves freedom fighters and have only a few Kalashnikovs, some grenades, Jeeps, and stones. Would you please explain to me how we pose an existential threat to you, and not the other way around?"

Abu Ala, having succinctly made his case—the Palestinians were David and Israel was Goliath—smiled. In time I came to understand that the Palestinians' perception of the balance of power was much as he had described it: a dwarf facing down a giant. As in so many conflicts, each side considered itself the victim.

I reflected briefly and told him: "You are a threat because you want to live in my home. In my house."

"Where are your from?" he asked.

"Jerusalem," I replied.

"So am I," he continued, somberly. "Where is your father from?"

"He was born in Germany."

"Mine was born in Jerusalem and still lives there."

"Why don't you ask about my grandfathers and their forebears?" I said, making no effort to hide my anger. "We could go back to King David. I'm sure we can debate the past for years and never agree. Let's see if we can agree about the future."

"Fine," he said, barely above a mumble.

We had arrived at our first understanding. Never again would we argue about the past. Discussing the future would mean reconciling two rights, not wrangling over ancient wrongs.

"I'd like to return to the point you raised about our security, as it stands today," I said and began drawing, as well as I could, a map of Israel, the occupied territories and then, in the proper proportion, the Arab world.

"You Palestinians have rejected our existence as a state," I continued. "From the moment of Israel's rebirth, you rallied the entire Arab world to fight us. This," I said, tapping my finger on the map, "is the true security equation." I leaned back, satisfied that I had established who the real David was in this conflict. Abu Ala was businesslike in his reply.

"I believe we've arrived at the root of the problem," he said. "We have learned that our rejection of you will not bring us freedom. You can see that your control of us will not bring you security. We must live side by side in peace, equality and cooperation. This is also the view of our leadership."

"In principle, I agree," I said, attempting to establish

common ground. "We need to progress in stages, forging a new context for relations in which peace, security and economic development can evolve together. What we need is a new road map to lead us to a state of trust."

It was about 4:00 in the morning when we all stood up, shook hands, and walked downstairs to find Terje and Mona, looking tired, yet still wide awake and patiently waiting for us.

"So?" Terje asked warily.

"There's nothing to discuss," Abu Ala said. "We're going home."

"It's all over," I added with a shrug.

For a split second Terje looked uncertain, but we reassured him with a laugh, the first instance of the humor that would serve us through the long, sometimes brutal negotiations ahead.

Mona and Terje invited me to stay with them in the center of Oslo. The unfamiliar view of the quiet city as Terje drove me to their home, the Scandinavian charm, and the warm hospitality of my hosts, all stood in sharp contrast to my turbulent emotions. I walked onto the terrace and gazed out at Oslo as it began to awaken. I wanted to reflect on the significance of the past hours while their impact was still fresh. Instead, my thoughts drifted to my late father.

An ardent Zionist and brilliant intellectual, Leo Savir was a born diplomat and a founder of Israel's foreign service. From the start, he regarded the occupation of the West Bank and Gaza as a disaster that would erode Israel's moral fiber and humanity. As far back as the late '70s, he called for a dialogue with the P.L.O. He felt that talking to the enemy was a test of Israel's maturity; that our inability even to contemplate such meetings arose from fear that led to demonization. Menachem Begin, for one, was known to compare Arafat to Hitler. A year before he died in 1986, my father published an article to this effect in the *Jerusalem Post*, and I carried it with me in my briefcase. He had been the person closest to me, and as I stood on that terrace, I suddenly felt great sadness that I couldn't tell him that I had just done the very thing that he had urged for so long. We had closed a circle, my father and I. He would have been pleased.

The next morning after breakfast, Mona and I set out to collect Ron and Yair and return to the lodge. On the way back they remarked on the "chemistry" that had developed the previous night. Terje mentioned it, too, after arriving with the Palestinians, and suggested that Abu Ala and I take a short walk in the woods. As we set out down a narrow path, Abu Ala told me that he had spent the rest of the night on the phone with Tunis, reporting his satisfaction with our meeting. Arafat and Abu Mazen had accepted our demand that East Jerusalem be excluded for now—though it would certainly be raised again in the talks on the final settlement. I was surprised by this quick and definitive reply. He said he also favored the idea of establishing autonomy in Gaza first, but noted that Arafat continued to press for the symbolic addition of Jericho. A small foothold in the West Bank was important, so that "Gaza first" would not be perceived as "Gaza last."

Then we talked about ourselves. I told Abu Ala about my family and my years with Peres. He sketched the course of his odyssey from Jerusalem through the gulf, Eastern Europe, Beirut, Cyprus, and finally Tunis. He told me of his wife and four children—one in Tunis, two in Europe, one in America—and spoke of his years with Arafat with esteem for his indomitable leader and with wry derision for his quirky work habits.

When we reached the lodge, Abu Ala suggested we turn to the draft of the declaration of principles. As we glanced over the document, I was surprised by the degree of Palestinian interest in economic ties with Israel. When I described, in general terms, the need for a quick change on the ground, Abu Ala's response was particularly positive.

"The situation in the territories is drastic, and it could explode at any moment," he said. "We must give our people hope."

"Absolutely," I concurred. "But that hope must be divorced from any violence toward us."

"The two are naturally related," Abu Ala said. "We can put a stop to the violence, provided we can promise a different future." This inverse ratio between hope and violence would remain the basic equation throughout the peace process. "The intifada must yield political gains," he continued. "You will not subdue us by force. Nor is that necessary."

"Apparently you haven't been reading the papers," I

said with muted sarcasm. "Israel has today a Government that doesn't want to rule over your people. Human rights and occupation don't go hand in hand. We know that. But only a change in your attitude, too, especially toward the political and security situation, will allow for a profound change on the ground."

It was at this point, I believe, that Abu Ala first realized he might actually be on the threshold of tough, binding negotiations. He leaned forward and looked me hard in the eye as he said: "You should know, Savir, that in the talks with Ron and Yair, we made major concessions—historic ones, from out standpoint—because we're interested in making a fresh start. But it will be very hard for Arafat to compromise beyond this."

"I thought we'd agreed not to start bargaining yet."

Abu Ala laughed, but his expression betrayed his relish for the negotiations that lay ahead. Then Yair raised an important point that the Palestinians had introduced in the exploratory talks: the need to promote reconciliation among our peoples, a "peace propaganda plan," he called it.

"You know," I warned Abu Ala, "as far as most Israelis are concerned, you're just a gang of terrorists."

"And as far as most Palestinians are concerned, you are a nation of cruel oppressors, robbing us of our lands."

In this way, we agreed, in principle, to engage our two peoples in the effort of reconciliation.

After 1,100 days of negotiations and three agreements it became clear that the peace process that began in 1993 revealed schisms in Israeli society that ran deeper than politics, as was demonstrated so horribly by the assassination of Yitzhak Rabin. What half of Israel viewed as the opening of new horizons, the other saw as leaving Israel defenseless against violence and the penetration of foreign values. The 1996 election was close (and would probably have gone the other way if not for a wave of Hamas bombings), and therefore the battle over the nature and soul of Israel was bound to continue. Now it would be under the leadership of Benjamin Netanyahu, who was determined to follow a new ideology and new policies.

"We still need you and Mr. Peres," Abu Ala told me during a private talk soon after the Netanyahu Government had been installed. "Peres is regarded by Palestinians as a world leader and a man of peace. And you must continue what we started."

"We'll fight for our beliefs through other channels," I told him. "Peres and I have decided to create a peace center dedicated to fostering cooperation between our two peoples. But the course of the diplomatic process is up to the new Government and its prime minister."

"Yes, I heard his speech," Abu Ala murmured. "We Palestinians are very worried. On the one hand he speaks about the peace process continuing while on the other he talks about expanding the settlements. The two don't go together. We don't yet know how to handle this new situation. It took us by surprise."

"I'd advise you to do your best to make peace with the new government. Remember we used to say that 'Oslo' is stronger than its opponents? Well, you have to help ensure that. Hamas had a lot to do with the outcome of the elections, but extremists can't be allowed to carry the day."

"That would be a catastrophe for the whole region," Abu Ala reflected. "People don't understand what's at stake here."

"If you make peace with a right-wing government, 80 to 90 percent of the Israeli people will support it. So you can't give up."

Abu Ala tried to smile as he shook my hand. "I'll go on trying as long as I live, and I believe you will, too," he said. Then he let out a loud laugh, adding, "I think this is our curse. . . ."

ANTHONY LEWIS

The Irrelevance of a Palestinian State

ERON BENVENISTI IS an Israeli Cassandra. Fifteen years ago, he confounded his fellow doves by the conclusion he drew in a study of the West Bank and Gaza. Israel had gone so far, he said, in settling the occupied territories and building roads and water lines and economic links that the process was irreversible. "For the foreseeable future," he said, Israel would rule all of Palestine.

Israel's election last month seemed to prove Benvenisti conclusively wrong. The voters chose Ehud Barak, who promised as prime minister to restart

ANTHONY LEWIS *is a two-time Pulitzer Prize winner and regular columnist for the* New York Times. *In this article, (which originally appeared in the* Times *in 1999), he questions the wisdom and practicality of creating a Palestinian state, given current political and geographical obstacles.*

the Oslo peace process stalled by Benjamin Netanyahu. Negotiations would be difficult, but in the end the Palestinians would surely have their state. At long last the Israeli-Palestinian conflict would be resolved. The two societies would find peace in separation.

But a visit to Israel shortly before the election convinced me that there can be no such neat resolution of the conflict. There will almost certainly be a Palestinian state; a majority of Israelis approves the idea now. But it will be a state of a peculiar kind. Its citizens will often have to go through Israeli security checks in traveling from one part of their own country to another. In entering or leaving the new Palestine, they will be subject to rigorous Israeli controls. The state will be utterly dependent on Israel economically.

In formal terms, contrary to the Benvenisti prophecy, Israel will not govern all of historic Palestine. But in the realities on the ground, I think Benvenisti was right.

Jewish settlements in the West Bank are a fundamental obstacle to the creation of a normal state for the Palestinians. They dot virtually the entire territory—except that "dot" conveys the wrong impression. Some of the settlements are urban towns, like Maale Adumim, east of Jerusalem, population 25,000. Special bypass roads to the settlements slice through the West Bank. A road from Jerusalem southwest to what is called the Gush Etzion bloc of settlements goes literally under the Palestinian village of Beit Jala, through two tunnels built at a cost of $32 million and then across a long bridge. In a last gasp, the Netanyahu government approved a plan to add four square miles to Maale Adumim, connecting it to greater Jerusalem. The status of Jerusalem itself is a formidable question for the final negotiations.

There are now between 160,000 and 190,000 Jewish settlers in the West Bank. And ideologically motivated Israelis, who believe that God gave all of the Land of Israel to the Jewish people, continue to plant new settlements. Since the Wye Agreement last October, seventeen have been established. Most consist of a few trailers, a water tank, and barbed wire on a hilltop: a bare suggestion of possession. But that is how many of the now substantial settlements began, as unauthorized seizures of Palestinian land.

The result of all this is a political map of the West Bank that looks like a collection of Rorschach blots. The Palestinian Authority has overall control, in politics and security, of widely scattered urban areas. If one adds in areas where it shares control with Israel, the P.A. has 29 percent of the West Bank. And much of that is broken up by settlements and areas of Israeli military and political control. (In overcrowded Gaza, Israeli settlements make up 27 percent of the land.)

In earlier years, the settlements had an anomalous legal status. But gradually Israeli law was extended to them so that they became extraterritorial outposts of Israel. That in turn makes it more likely that Israeli negotiators in the final peace talks due to take place will insist on making them sovereign parts of Israel. Raja Shehadeh, a noted Palestinian lawyer, told me with what I thought was wry admiration:

"Palestinians start from first principles—slogans. Israelis do things without announcing them. They meticulously made the settlements part of Israel without saying so. Now annexation is inevitable."

Again, the original view in the Israeli peace camp was that in a final negotiation with the Palestinians, Israel should enlarge its 1967 borders to include some settlements, especially along the narrow waist of the country north of Tel Aviv. Otherwise, settlers would have to leave or stay under Palestinian sovereignty. Now, even Barak favors the annexation of several large blocs of settlements.

If Israel is as forthcoming as imaginable in final-status negotiations, there will still be severe obstacles to normal life in a Palestinian state. A Palestinian professional I know gave an example. He lives in Ramallah, north of Jerusalem; he has family in Bethlehem, to the south. Unless they find alternative routes many miles out of the way, they must go through Jerusalem's expanded boundaries to visit one another. That means passing Israeli checkpoints, which is usually easy nowadays but can be a laborious, humiliating process. And there is no reason to think that would change with statehood.

"All the symbols of Oslo have not changed the fact that to drive from Bethlehem you need to go through a checkpoint," my friend said. "We'll have a state, but what kind of state? The key elements are borders and the movement of people and goods."

Israel supervises not just internal Palestinian movement but also external: people entering or leaving P.A. territory

at the borders with Jordan or Egypt, or at the new Gaza airport. A highly respected Ha'aretz reporter, Danny Rubin-
stein, wrote in April that Palestinians "are frequently
delayed for extensive investigations" by Israeli officers at
the border post. "They stand in line after line, and detailed
security searches are made of their property and bodies.
Many also complain of insults and degrading treatment."

Will that change if and when Palestinians achieve formal statehood? I doubt it. Israel will aim in negotiations to
be able to continue checking who goes in and out of the
new state.

Freedom of movement is one large question about a
Palestinian state. Economic independence is another. Economic conditions in the West Bank and Gaza have drasti-
cally worsened since Oslo. Terrorist attacks by Palestinians opposed to peace with Israel led to frequent closures of
the Israeli border. To replace Palestinian workers thus
excluded, Israeli construction and other companies
brought in guest workers from as far away as Romania.
They are still there, though Israel is trying to reduce their
number. Palestinians can again come in by the day to work,
but their ranks have declined from 150,000 before Oslo to
90,000 now.

Between 1992 and 1998 the gross national product in
Palestinian areas fell 30 percent. That disastrous figure
indicates the great dependence on employment in Israel.
Agriculture and what little industry there is are also highly
dependent. Israeli officials at the borders frequently delay
exports and imports; food rots on trucks.

All this led my Palestinian friend to a proposition that startled me. He said that if Israel treated Arabs without discrimination, he would rather be a citizen of an Israel covering all of Palestine than of "a Swiss-cheese Palestinian state."

"You see how open Israel is," he said. "People are free; products move. And there's so much intermingling of things. Look at this restaurant." We had lunch in a park on the edge of Gilo, a new Jewish suburban area of Jerusalem on formerly Arab land.

My friend was not the only Palestinian who raised the idea of being in an Israel that treated him equally rather than a Palestinian state of the kind it is likely to be. Part of that feeling reflects disappointment in Yasir Arafat's Palestinian Authority, with its corruption and disregard for human rights. But it is more than that: a sense that their state will be a strangulated and claustrophobic place.

Not that Palestinians would want to stop the drive for statehood now. "Palestinian independence must come first," my friend said. "It is a psychological necessity for us."

Nor is there any imaginable chance that Israel would agree, now, to a resolution that gave it all of historic Palestine and made the Palestinians citizens of Israel. Support for the idea of a Greater Israel has waned as Israelis have understood that it would give them a choice of treating Palestinians as second-class residents or absorbing them as citizens, thus threatening the Jewish character of the state. So there will be a Palestinian state.

When I saw Meron Benvenisti in Jerusalem in April, he asked what attributes of sovereignty the Palestinian state would have—and answered his own question:

The basic test of sovereignty is who will control the international boundaries. Will the Palestinian state have one border crossing that it alone controls? No. Or consider other aspects of sovereignty. Land? If a generous new Israeli Government gives the Palestinians half the West Bank, they will have 15 percent of historic Palestine. Water? They may control 10 percent. Beaches? Five percent. It's a great solution for the Israelis: ("Goodbye, we solved the conflict.") But, of course, it's been solved at the expense of the Palestinians, who will have a squeezed, humiliating, hemmed-in life unable to partake of most of the goods of what is one land.

All of Palestine is a binational entity, even though politics demands a different reality. It's one space.

Tsali Reshef, one of the founders of Peace Now, is a less discouraged realist. "We won the political argument against Greater Israel," he says. "But the settlers have won significantly on the ground. The result will be a worse solution for both sides, but there can be a solution."

Why worse for Israel? Hasn't it acquired territory and resources without responsibility for people of another loyalty?

It is worse for Israel because a squeezed, humiliated

Palestine might be an irredentist Palestine. It will be hard at best for Palestinians to accept an unequal division of the land they thought was theirs. It will be much harder if their state is so truncated, so cut up, that it is not viable. Henry Kissinger, who is hardly sentimental about Palestinian rights, warned recently that "Israel should agree to the greatest possible contiguity for the Palestinian state and not try to turn it into a checkerboard."

A final, more optimistic word from Meron Benvenisti: "As long as Israel controls the external borders of Israel-Palestine and decides who enters, the internal borders can be more flexible. I would call them soft borders." The Palestinians would have a state, the symbol of their nationhood, and would be able to move goods and people more freely within the space of historic Palestine. Is such a solution politically possible on either side? Would it end the conflict?

EDWARD SAID

The One-State Solution

G IVEN THE COLLAPSE of the Netanyahu Government over the Wye peace agreement, it is time to question whether the entire process begun in Oslo in 1993 is the right instrument for bringing peace between Palestinians and Israelis. It is my view that the peace process has in fact put off the real reconciliation that must occur if the hundred-year war between Zionism and the Palestinian people is to end. Oslo set the stage for separation, but real peace can come only with a binational Israeli-Palestinian state.

This is not easy to imagine. The Zionist-Israeli official narrative and the Palestinian one are irreconcilable. Israelis say they waged a war of liberation

EDWARD SAID, *head of of the Modern Language Association at Columbia University, is the author of books such as* Not Quite Right *and* Reflections on Exile. *Born in Palestine in 1935, he has long been an avid supporter of the Palestine cause and here discusses how peace can only come through unity.*

and so achieved independence; Palestinians say their society was destroyed, most of the population evicted. And, in fact, this irreconcilability was already quite obvious to several generations of early Zionist leaders and thinkers, as of course it was to all Palestinians.

"Zionism was not blind to the presence of Arabs in Palestine," writes the distinguished Israeli historian Zeev Sternhell in his recent book, *The Founding Myths of Israel*. "Even Zionist figures who had never visited the country knew that it was not devoid of inhabitants. At the same time, neither the Zionist movement abroad nor the pioneers who were beginning to settle the country could frame a policy toward the Palestinian national movement. The real reason for this was not a lack of understanding of the problem but a clear recognition of the insurmountable contradiction between the basic objectives of the two sides. If Zionist intellectuals and leaders ignored the Arab dilemma, it was chiefly because they knew that this problem had no solution within the Zionist way of thinking."

David Ben-Gurion, for instance, was always clear. "There is no example in history," he said in 1944, "of a people saying we agree to renounce our country, let another people come and settle here and outnumber us." Another Zionist leader, Berl Katznelson, likewise had no illusions that the opposition between Zionist and Palestinian aims could be surmounted. And binationalists like Martin Buber, Judah Magnes, and Hannah Arendt were fully aware of what the clash would be like, if it came to fruition, as of course it did.

Vastly outnumbering the Jews, Palestinian Arabs during the period after the 1917 Balfour Declaration and the British Mandate always refused anything that would compromise their dominance. It's unfair to berate the Palestinians retrospectively for not accepting partition in 1947. Until 1948, Jews held only about 7 percent of the land. Why, the Arabs said when the partition resolution was proposed, should we concede 55 percent of Palestine to the Jews, who were a minority in Palestine? Neither the Balfour Declaration nor the mandate ever specifically conceded that Palestinians had political, as opposed to civil and religious, rights in Palestine. The idea of inequality between Jews and Arabs was therefore built into British, and subsequently Israeli and United States, policy from the start.

The conflict appears intractable because it is a contest over the same land by two peoples who always believed they had valid title to it and who hoped that the other side would in time give up or go away. One side won the war, the other lost, but the contest is as alive as ever. We Palestinians ask why a Jew born in Warsaw or New York has the right to settle here (according to Israel's Law of Return), whereas we, the people who lived here for centuries, cannot. After 1967, the conflict between us was exacerbated. Years of military occupation have created in the weaker party anger, humiliation, and hostility.

To its discredit, Oslo did little to change the situation. Arafat and his dwindling number of supporters were turned into enforcers of Israeli security, while Palestinians were made to endure the humiliation of dreadful and noncontiguous "homelands" that make up about 10 percent of the West Bank and 60 percent of Gaza. Oslo required us to forget and renounce our history of loss, dispossessed by the very people who taught everyone the importance of not forgetting the past. Thus we are the victims of the victims, the refugees of the refugees.

Israel's raison d'etre as a state has always been that there should be a separate country, a refuge, exclusively for Jews. Oslo itself was based on the principle of separation between Jews and others, as Yitzhak Rabin tirelessly repeated. Yet over the past fifty years, especially since Israeli settlements were first implanted on the occupied territories in 1967, the lives of Jews have become more and more enmeshed with those of non-Jews.

The effort to separate has occurred simultaneously and paradoxically with the effort to take more and more land, which has in turn meant that Israel has acquired more and more Palestinians. In Israel proper, Palestinians number about one million, almost 20 percent of the population. Among Gaza, East Jerusalem, and the West Bank, which is where settlements are the thickest, there are almost 2.5 million Palestinians. Israel has built an entire system of "bypassing" roads, designed to go around Palestinian towns and villages, connecting settlements and avoiding Arabs. But so tiny is the land area of historical Palestine, so closely intertwined are Israelis and Palestinians, despite their inequality and antipathy, that clean separation simply won't, can't really, occur or work. It is estimated that by 2010 there will be demographic parity. What then?

Clearly, a system of privileging Israeli Jews will satisfy neither those who want an entirely homogenous Jewish state nor those who live there but are not Jewish. For the former, Palestinians are an obstacle to be disposed of somehow; for the latter, being Palestinian in a Jewish polity means forever chafing at inferior status. But Israeli Palestinians don't want to move; they say they are already in their country and refuse any talk of joining a separate Palestinian state, should one come into being. Meanwhile, the impoverishing conditions imposed on Arafat are making it difficult for him to subdue the highly politicized inhabitants of Gaza and the West Bank. These Palestinians have aspirations for self-determination that, contrary to Israeli calculations, show no sign of withering away. It is also evident that as an Arab people—and, given the despondently cold peace treaties between Israel and Egypt and Israel and Jordan, this fact is important—Palestinians want at all costs to preserve their Arab identity as part of the surrounding Arab and Islamic world.

For all this, the problem is that Palestinian self-determination in a separate state is unworkable, just as unworkable as the principle of separation between a demographically mixed, irreversibly connected Arab population without sovereignty and a Jewish population with it. The question, I believe, is not how to devise means for persisting in trying to separate them but to see whether it is possible for them to live together as fairly and peacefully as possible.

What exists now is a disheartening, not to say, bloody, impasse. Zionists in and outside Israel will not give up on their wish for a separate Jewish state; Palestinians want the same thing for themselves, despite having accepted much less from Oslo. Yet in both instances, the idea of a state for "ourselves" simply flies in the face of the facts: short of ethnic cleansing or "mass transfer," as in 1948, there is no way for Israel to get rid of the Palestinians or for Palestinians to wish Israelis away. Neither side has a viable military option against the other, which, I am sorry to say, is why both opted for a peace that so patently tries to accomplish what war couldn't.

The more that current patterns of Israeli settlement and Palestinian confinement and resistance persist, the less likely it is that there will be real security for either side. It was always patently absurd for Netanyahu's obsession with security to be couched only in terms of Palestinian compliance with his demands. On the one hand, he and Ariel Sharon crowded Palestinians more and more with their shrill urgings to the settlers to grab what they could. On the other hand, Netanyahu expected such methods to bludgeon Palestinians into accepting everything Israel did, with no reciprocal Israeli measures.

Arafat, backed by Washington, is daily more repressive. Improbably citing the 1936 British Emergency Defense Regulations against Palestinians, he has recently decreed, for example, that it is a crime not only to incite violence, racial and religious strife but also to criticize the peace process. There is no Palestinian constitution or basic law: Arafat simply refuses to accept limitations on his power in light of American and Israeli support for him.

Who actually thinks all this can bring Israel security and permanent Palestinian submission?

Violence, hatred, and intolerance are bred out of injustice, poverty, and a thwarted sense of political fulfillment. Last fall, hundreds of acres of Palestinian land were expropriated by the Israeli Army from the village of Umm al-Fahm, which isn't in the West Bank but inside Israel. This drove home the fact that, even as Israeli citizens, Palestinians are treated as inferior, as basically a sort of underclass existing in a condition of apartheid.

At the same time, because Israel does not have a constitution either, and because the ultra-Orthodox parties are acquiring more and more political power, there are Israeli Jewish groups and individuals who have begun to organize around the notion of a full secular democracy for all Israeli citizens. The charismatic Azmi Bishara, an Arab member of the Knesset, has also been speaking about enlarging the concept of citizenship as a way to get beyond ethnic and religious criteria that now make Israel in effect an undemocratic state for 20 percent of its population.

In the West Bank, Jerusalem, and Gaza, the situation is deeply unstable and exploitative. Protected by the army, Israeli settlers (almost 350,000 of them) live as extraterritorial, privileged people with rights that resident Palestinians do not have. (For example, West Bank Palestinians cannot go to Jerusalem and in 70 percent of the territory are still subject to Israeli military law, with their land available for confiscation.) Israel controls Palestinian water resources and security, as well as exits and entrances. Even the new Gaza airport is under Israeli security control. You don't need to be an expert to see that this is a prescription for extending, not limiting, conflict. Here the truth must be faced, not avoided or denied.

There are Israeli Jews today who speak candidly about "post-Zionism," insofar as after fifty years of Israeli history, classic Zionism has neither provided a solution to the Palestinian presence nor an exclusively Jewish presence. I see no other way than to begin now to speak about sharing the land that has thrust us together, sharing it in a truly democratic way, with equal rights for each citizen. There can be no reconciliation unless both peoples, two communities of suffering, resolve that their existence is a secular fact, and that it has to be dealt with as such.

This does not mean a diminishing of Jewish life as Jewish life or a surrendering of Palestinian Arab aspirations and political existence. On the contrary, it means self-determination for both peoples. But it does mean being willing to soften, lessen, and finally give up special status for one people at the expense of the other. The Law of Return for Jews and the right of return for Palestinian refugees have to be considered and trimmed together. Both the notions of Greater Israel as the land of the Jewish people given to them by God and of Palestine as an Arab land that cannot be alienated from the Arab homeland need to be reduced in scale and exclusivity.

Interestingly, the millennia-long history of Palestine provides at least two precedents for thinking in such secular and modest terms. First, Palestine is and has always been a land of many histories; it is a radical simplification to think of it as principally or exclusively Jewish or Arab. While the Jewish presence is longstanding, it is by no means the main one. Other tenants have included Canaanites, Moabites, Jebusites, and Philistines in ancient times, and Romans, Ottomans, Byzantines, and Crusaders in the modern ages. Palestine is multicultural, multiethnic, multireligious. There is as little historical justification for homogeneity as there is for notions of national or ethnic and religious purity today.

Second, during the interwar period, a small but important group of Jewish thinkers (Judah Magnes, Buber, Arendt and others) argued and agitated for a binational state. The logic of Zionism naturally overwhelmed their efforts, but the idea is alive today here and there among Jewish and Arab individuals frustrated with the evident insufficiencies and depredations of the present. The essence of their vision is coexistence and sharing in ways that require an innovative, daring, and theoretical willingness to get beyond the arid stalemate of assertion and rejection. Once the initial acknowledgment of the other as an equal is made, I believe the way forward becomes not only possible but also attractive.

The initial step, however, is a very difficult one to take. Israeli Jews are insulated from the Palestinian reality; most of them say that it does not really concern them. I remember the first time I drove from Ramallah into Israel, thinking it was like going straight from Bangladesh into Southern California. Yet reality is never that neat.

My generation of Palestinians, still reeling from the shock of losing everything in 1948, find it nearly impossible to accept that their homes and farms were taken over by another people. I see no way of evading the fact that in 1948 one people displaced another, thereby committing a grave injustice. Reading Palestinian and Jewish history together not only gives the tragedies of the Holocaust and of what subsequently happened to the Palestinians their full force but also reveals how in the course of interrelated Israeli and Palestinian life since 1948, one people, the Palestinians, has borne a disproportionate share of the pain and loss.

Religious and right-wing Israelis and their supporters have no problem with such a formulation. Yes, they say, we won, but that's how it should be. This land is the land of Israel, not of anyone else. I heard those words from an Israeli soldier guarding a bulldozer that was destroying a West Bank Palestinian's field (its owner helplessly watching) to expand a bypass road.

But they are not the only Israelis. For others, who want peace as a result of reconciliation, there is dissatisfaction with the religious parties' increasing hold on Israeli life and Oslo's unfairness and frustrations. Many such Israelis demonstrate against their government's Palestinian land expropriations and house demolitions. So you sense a healthy willingness to look elsewhere for peace than in land-grabbing and suicide bombs.

For some Palestinians, because they are the weaker party, the losers, giving up on a full restoration of Arab

Palestine is giving up on their own history. Most others, however, especially my children's generation, are skeptical of their elders and look more unconventionally toward the future, beyond conflict and unending loss. Obviously, the establishments in both communities are too tied to present "pragmatic" currents of thought and political formations to venture anything more risky, but a few others (Palestinian and Israeli) have begun to formulate radical alternatives to the status quo. They refuse to accept the limitations of Oslo, what one Israeli scholar has called "peace without Palestinians," while others tell me that the real struggle is over equal rights for Arabs and Jews, not a separate, necessarily dependent, and weak Palestinian entity.

The beginning is to develop something entirely missing from both Israeli and Palestinian realities today: the idea and practice of citizenship, not of ethnic or racial community, as the main vehicle for coexistence. In a modern state, all its members are citizens by virtue of their presence and the sharing of rights and responsibilities. Citizenship therefore entitles an Israeli Jew and a Palestinian Arab to the same privileges and resources. A constitution and a bill of rights thus become necessary for getting beyond Square 1 of the conflict because each group would have the same right to self-determination; that is, the right to practice communal life in its own (Jewish or Palestinian) way, perhaps in federated cantons, with a joint capital in Jerusalem, equal access to land and inalienable secular and juridical rights. Neither side should be held hostage to religious extremists.

Yet feelings of persecution, suffering, and victimhood are so ingrained that it is nearly impossible to undertake political initiatives that hold Jews and Arabs to the same general principles of civil equality while avoiding the pitfall of us-versus-them. Palestinian intellectuals need to express their case directly to Israelis, in public forums, universities, and the media. The challenge is both to and within civil society, which has long been subordinate to a nationalism that has developed into an obstacle to reconciliation. Moreover, the degradation of discourse—symbolized by Arafat and Netanyahu trading charges while Palestinian rights are compromised by exaggerated "security" concerns—impedes any wider, more generous perspective from emerging.

The alternatives are unpleasantly simple: either the war continues (along with the onerous cost of the current peace process) or a way out, based on peace and equality (as in South Africa after apartheid) is actively sought, despite the many obstacles. Once we grant that Palestinians and Israelis are there to stay, then the decent conclusion has to be the need for peaceful coexistence and genuine reconciliation. Real self-determination. Unfortunately, injustice and belligerence don't diminish by themselves: they have to be attacked by all concerned.

ROBERT STONE

Jerusalem Has No Past

T IP O'NEILL LIKED to say that all politics is local. In Jerusalem, politics is local but also moral and cosmic. Of course, politicians everywhere employ an ethical diction, however ungrammatical. And the reality of power in every city has its source in a measure of combat. But nowhere is this as true as in Jerusalem. Millions of us, raised in three major faiths, grew up believing that even apparently trivial encounters in Jerusalem's narrow streets and within the shadows of its wall determine the human condition. Its sparrows were no mere sparrows. A broken promise in the Holy City, a night of lovemaking, an act of mercy, might be studied centuries to come as a guide to the

ROBERT STONE *is the writer of such highly acclaimed novels as* A Flag for Sunrise *and* Damascus Gate. *This article, which appeared in the* New York Times Magazine *on the fiftieth anniversary of the state of Israel, examines how Jerusalem exists in constant volatile flux, continually reinventing itself.*

will of the universe. The story of a nocturnal arrest and a felon's execution there might change eternally the notion of human responsibility.

The exile of the Jews from Jerusalem became the central metaphor of the Hebrew faith. At the center of the metaphor was the city. Its stones were to be built anew in a perfected world. Or it was to be the place of ingathering and redemption.

Now, after fifty years of the Jewish state, what does the future hold for this city? Anyone walking the streets of Jerusalem today, covering the relatively short route from the American Colony Hotel, through the Damascus Gate and along the Via Dolorosa to the Jaffa Gate, across the valley of condominiums at "David's Village" and to the adjoining Hilton through Yemin Moshe, can see how intrinsically mixed are the spiritual and temporal traditions of power in the city.

The pious Hellenistic tombs from Hasmonean and Roman days and General Gordon's "Garden Tomb" both reflect the influence of world empires. The exquisite Church of St. Anne was built by warlike crusaders, converted into a mosque by Saladin, then restored to its status as a church again. The chambers of the Church of the Holy Sepulcher owe their construction to the Christian Roman emperors; the Dome of the Rock once supported a cross as the mother church of the Knights Templar. It remains unapproachable to Orthodox Jews, who fear to enter the site of the original Solomonic Temple's Holy of Holies. The Western Wall, part of the Herodian temple destroyed by the Romans, later confined to a narrow Jordanian street, now stands open before the great plaza built after 1967 where the Maghrebi Gate had stood.

All of these spiritual sites followed the fortune of earthly empires, which is to say, the fortunes of war. The glories of faith, even the most sublime, were emblems of secular triumph. The eternal question has always been settled, directly or indirectly, by force. Whose Jerusalem?

Most of the early Zionists advocated a collaborative state with the Arab inhabitants who, it was expected, would quickly recognize the benefits accruing to them from the arrival of a dynamic, idealistic, and educated new population. One who had no such expectations was Vladimir Jabotinsky. Coming of age in the years before the First World War, he partook deeply of two elements that were stirring Europe at that time.

One was nationalism, which in its normal Eastern European form was aggressive, militant, and nurtured on a well of grievances—the insults and injuries endured by small nations at the hands of neighbors or of the great empires whose Congresses had imposed the status quo. As a Jew from Russia, Jabotinsky bore grievances, personal and collective, that were not meager.

The other element was in the air, so to speak, present in art, in music like Stravinsky's *Rite of Spring,* in literature and in the work of German philosophers. It was a certain vitalism, a fusion of Eros and Thanatos, the idea of purification through struggle, of violence as life's ultimate reality and source of wisdom.

Today, walking in Jerusalem, a visitor familiar with the city can see the changes under way. The intifada is over, for the time being, and the Old City's street stalls are no longer subject to sudden strikes. Unarmed religious Jews walk to the yeshivas they've opened in the Muslim quarter of the Old City, and there seem to be more tourists, in their identical pastel baseball jackets. The street stalls outside the Damascus Gate have been cleared away. A move toward sanitation and order? A better field of operations for the police?

Centuries ago, when King David took Jerusalem, he did so by a skillful manipulation of the water supply, inspired construction, and main force. To some extent, Teddy Kollek, the city's mayor from 1965 to 1993, followed a similar policy. But there was a difference between Kollek's philosophy, that of an old socialist who knew a war when he was in one but who believed in the possibility of peace, and that of the present Likud Government. Kollek may be criticized for many things, but he loved Arab Jerusalem as a wonder of the world; it was a treasure of his city and he never wanted to destroy it.

The same could not be said for the Likud Party, which took office as a result of Benjamin Netanyahu's 1996 victory. It should be noted that under Israel's new electoral system, the victory was not a parliamentary one for Likud but a personal win for Netanyahu, who ran on the slogan "Peace with Security." There are many Israelis who interpret this result as reflecting the desire of a majority of the country's people for peace. The security aspect loomed large in the wake of the multiple bus bombings that took so many lives in Jerusalem and Tel Aviv after the Oslo accords. Recently, on April Fool's Day, students at Hebrew University carried white balloons that read "Peace With Security," a gesture reflecting less than reverence for Netanyahu and what he claims is his program. . . .

The changes in the city are there to see, some subtle, some obvious. Ehud Olmert, the Likud Mayor, has been enlarging the political boundaries of Jerusalem proper in a gerrymandering technique aimed at establishing a clear Jewish majority in the city. In some cases, this has meant driving out Arabs from their neighborhoods in order to build government housing for recent immigrants.

Since the Oslo accords and in violation of them, life has been made more and more difficult for Palestinians. A Palestinian living in one of the autonomous territories needs a permit to enter Jerusalem or, for that matter, any part of Israel. This policy is an echo of the South African pass laws, and carries about as much of a guarantee of real security. Jerusalem can be closed for days at a time even to permit holders with jobs in town. Resident Palestinians who marry nonresidents lose their residential rights. Little by little the center of Palestinian Jerusalem is being choked off. Palestinians en route through Jerusalem, from Ramallah to Bethlehem for example, can be arbitrarily refused passage.

What, then, does the future hold? Likud, secure in something very like racial superiority, seems to feel convinced that the Palestinian population, subject to pass laws, denied permission for house repairs, harassed in scores of petty ways, will somehow decide to fade away or at least to accept conditions that would have been unacceptable to African-Americans in Mississippi in the early 1950s. The religious settlers of Kiryat Arba turn to the Bible and profess to detect there texts commanding them to harry the Arabs out of the land. The hard-right Moledet Party, meanwhile, has made Arab expulsion an official party position.

Would the Arabs, given the opportunity, drive Israel into the sea? Geronimo or Crazy Horse undoubtedly would have welcomed the opportunity to burn Washington. In other words, the Palestinians can be credited with a certain comprehension of their situation. However, the overall Arab position is sometimes hard to discern.

The Palestinians of Jerusalem and the West Bank may absorb any number of insults and indignities, but no one who knows the Arab people expects them to leave their homes until they are, as proposed by Moledet, evicted by force. Nor will their increasing hopelessness and despair make them somehow more tractable. The Israeli policy of meeting Arab violence with more violence is understandable given Jewish history, but it is not necessarily the wisest solution.

This is something the Labor Party in Israel, for all its faults, understands. The Labor bloc recognizes the continuing existence of an Arab presence in Jerusalem and the West Bank. It will never agree to any formula that implies a division of the city, but it will, many Israelis believe, in some fashion accept a responsible Arab entity in exchange for peace and security. The policies of Likud and Labor are not the same, not interchangeable, not beyond the consideration of foreign observers. Their differences, and the Arab response to these differences, is the largest determinant of Israel's future.

If the walker in the city extends his perambulation to the western hills beyond Rehavia, he will encounter the perpetual lamps and massive blocks of hewn stone at Yad Vashem, the Holocaust memorial, a setting that may obviate all the rest.

An old man hands out prayers:

"O Master of the Universe, Creator of these souls, preserve them forever in the memory of Thy people."

Emerging from this great memorial to millions of innocents, the walker sees again the sweet-scented, pine-clad hills. Then he knows that nothing, nothing whatever that he has seen—St. Anne's of the Crusaders, the Dome of the Rock, the worshipers at the Western Wall and their Holy Wall itself—none of it belongs to the past. In Jerusalem there is no past, only a present, that platform between earth and heaven where history has been enacted since the beginning of time. And a future that only an all-knowing Master of the Universe, if there be One, could know.

Acknowledgments

We gratefully acknowledge all those who gave permission for written material to appear in this book. We have made every effort to trace and contact copyright holders. If an error or omission is brought to our notice we will be pleased to remedy the situation in future editions of this book. For further information, please contact the publisher.

Excerpt from *Arab and Jew: Wounded Spirits in a Promised Land*. Copyright © 1986 by David K. Shipler. Reprinted by permission of Times Books, a division of Random House, Inc.

Excerpts from *Jerusalem: One City, Three Faiths* by Karen Armstrong. Copyright © 1996 by Karen Armstrong. Used by permission of Alfred A. Knopf, a division of Random House, Inc.

Excerpt from *A History of the Jews* by Paul Johnson. Copyright © 1987 by Paul Johnson. Reprinted by permission of HarperCollins Publishers Inc.

Excerpt from *City of Stone: The Hidden History of Jerusalem* by Meron Benvenisti. Copyright © 1996 The Regents of the University of California.

"The Yellow Wind" by David Grossman. Copyright © 1988 by David Grossman. Reprinted by permission of Farrar, Straus & Giroux, LLC.

Excerpt from *A Little too Close to God* by David Horovitz. Copyright © 2000 by David Horovitz. Used by permission of Alfred A. Knopf, a division of Random House, Inc.

"The Palestinian Conversation" by Deborah Sontag. Copyright © 2002 by The New York Times Agency. Reprinted by permission of The New York Times Agency.

Excerpt from *House of Windows: Portraits from a Jerusalem Neighborhood* by Adina Hoffman. Copyright © 2000 by Adina Hoffman. Reprinted by permission of Steerforth Press, South Royalton, Vermont.

Excerpt from *To Jerusalem and Back* by Saul Bellow. Copyright © 1967 by Saul Bellow. Reprinted by permission of Viking, a division of Penguin Putnam, Inc.

"Zion's Vital Signs" by P. J. O'Rourke. Copyright © 2001 by P.J. O'Rourke. Reprinted by kind permission of the author. Originally appeared in *The Atlantic Monthly*, November 2001.

"Why Oslo Still Matters" by Uriel Savir. Copyright (c) 1998 by Uriel Savir. Reprinted by permission of International Creative Management, Inc.

"Irrelevance of a Palestinian Nation" by Anthony Lewis. Copyright © 1999 by The New York Times Agency. Reprinted by permission of The New York Times Agency.

"The One-State Solution" by Edward Said. Copyright (c) 1999 by Edward Said. Reprinted by permission of The Wylie Agency.

"Jerusalem Has No Past" by Robert Stone. Copyright © 1998 by Robert Stone. Reprinted by permission of Donadio & Olson, Inc.